THE MYTH OF
ANCIENT
EGYPT

THE MYTH OF ANCIENT EGYPT

CHARLOTTE BOOTH

AMBERLEY

First published 2011

Amberley Publishing
The Hill, Stroud
Gloucestershire, GL5 4EP

www.amberleybooks.com

British Library Cataloguing in Publication Data.
A catalogue record for this book is available from the British Library.

ISBN 978-1-4456-0274-5

Typesetting and Origination by Amberley Publishing.
Printed in Great Britain.

CONTENTS

Illustrations   7

Introduction   11

SECTION 1: THE MYTH OF EGYPT

Chapter 1   The Myth of the Nile   17

Chapter 2   Myths of the Pyramids   37

Chapter 3   The Myth of Alexandria   67

SECTION 2: THE MYTH OF EGYPTIANS

Chapter 4   The Myth of Hatshepsut   94

Chapter 5   The Myth of Akhenaten   112

Chapter 6   The Myth of Cleopatra   137

SECTION 3: THE MYTH IN THE MODERN WORLD

Chapter 7   Mummymania   160

Chapter 8   Egyptomania in the West   185

SECTION 4: REFERENCES

Notes   204

Bibliography   216

Index   221

ILLUSTRATIONS

All photographs and drawings are copyrighted to the author unless otherwise stated.

COLOUR PLATES

1. Nebamun hunting in the marshes (eighteenth dynasty). (*British Museum*)
2. Nile view at Luxor.
3. The Holy Family at church of St Sergius, Cairo.
4. Holy Family in Egypt, the Hanging Church, Cairo.
5. Red Pyramid internal burial chamber, Dahshur.
6. Sphinx of Giza.
7. Medinet Habu; some say the wings depicted frequently in Egyptian art shows a preoccupation with the sky due to extra-terrestrial origins.
8. Sarcophagus from the British Museum. Some believe the preoccupation with boats proves the early Egyptians were space-aliens.
9. Alexander the Great. (*Photograph courtesy of photos.com*)
10. Roman Amphitheatre, Kom el Dikka, Alexandria. (*Photograph courtesy of Brian Billington*)
11. Qait Bey fortress, Alexandria. (*Photograph courtesy of Brian Billington*)
12. Thutmosis III, Luxor Museum.
13. Senenmut and Neferure, British Museum.
14. Temple of Hatshepsut, Deir el Bahri.
15. Hatshepsut in male attire, Deir el Bahri, Luxor.
16. Hatshepsut as a sphinx, Egyptian Museum, Cairo.
17. Incense from the expedition to Punt, Deir el Bahri, Luxor. (*Photograph courtesy of Francesco Gasperetti from Wikimedia Commons*)
18. Akhenaten, Luxor Museum, Luxor.
19. Akhenaten in traditional pose, Open Air Museum, Karnak, Luxor.
20. Central Reading Youth Provision Black History Mural, Reading. (*Photograph courtesy of Brian Billington*)
21. Nefertiti, Ashmolean Museum, Oxford.
22. Akhenaten's sarcophagus, Egyptian Museum, Cairo.
23. Augustus Caesar plaster-cast, Ashmolean Museum, Oxford.

24. Manga Cleopatra. (*Drawing by Kasuga courtesy of Wikimedia Commons*)
25. Ptolemaic mummy, Louvre.
26. Tutankhamun's death mask, Cairo Museum. (*Photograph courtesy of Clare Banks*)
27. Mummy display, British Museum. (*Photograph courtesy of Brian Billington*)
28. Halloween display window, 101event.com, London. (*Photograph courtesy of Brian Billington*)
29. Entrance to Egyptian Avenue, Highgate Cemetery.
30. Alexander Gordon's grave, Putney Vale Cemetery. (*Photograph courtesy of Elisabeth Kerner*)
31. Cairo Museum exterior.
32. Luxor Hotel Light show, Las Vegas. (*Photograph courtesy of Paul Dunstan*)

BLACK AND WHITE IMAGES

1. Boats on the Nile. (*Photograph courtesy of Brian Billington*)
2. Hapy, the god of Nile inundation, Luxor temple.
3. Fruits of the Nile, Denderah.
4. On board a Nile Steamer. (*Courtesy of Thomas Cook Archives*)
5. Cruise boats lined up on the Nile at Luxor.
6. Church of St Sergius, Cairo.
7. The Bent Pyramid, Dahshur.
8. Great Pyramid, Giza.
9. Pyramid of Pepy, Saqqara.
10. Construction ramp, Karnak, Luxor.
11. Ramped causeway, Deir el Bahri, Luxor.
12. Various suggested ramp systems. (*Photography courtesy of David Granger*)
13. Alexander the Great, British Museum.
14. Roman city, Kom el Dikka, Alexandria. (*Photograph courtesy of Brian Billington*)
15. Byzantine village, Kom el Dikka, Alexandria.
16. Objects from the bay at Alexandria, Open Air Museum, Kom el Dikka, Alexandria.
17. Lighthouse of Alexandria from Al Gharnati (early twelfth century). (*After El Daly, 2005*)
18. Ibn Tulun mosque, Cairo. The minaret is modelled on the lighthouse of Alexandria.
19. Pompey's pillar. (*Photograph courtesy of David Newby*)
20. Senenmut, Egyptian Museum, Cairo.
21. Graffiti of Hatshepsut and Senenmut. (*After Tyldesley 1996, p. 190*)
22. Fallen obelisk of Hatshepsut. (*Photograph courtesy of Brian Billington*)
23. Hatshepsut's Obelisk, Karnak. (*Photograph courtesy of Brian Billington*)
24. Damage caused to Hatshepsut, Deir el Bahri.
25. North Palace, Amarna.
26. Paser Stela, Berlin.

27. Great Temple of Aten, Amarna.

28. Nefertiti on Akhenaten's lap, Louvre, Paris.

29. Aten symbol, Wellcome Institute, London. (*Photograph courtesy of Brian Billington*)

30. Akhenaten, Louvre, Paris.

31. Cleopatra and Caesarion, Denderah.

32. Augustus Caesar, Museo Pio Clementino. (*Photograph courtesy of Jastrow from Wikimedia Commons*)

33. Cleopatra, Louvre, Paris. (*Photograph courtesy of Jastrow from Wikimedia Commons*)

34. Cleopatra, Metropolitan Museum of Art. (*Photograph courtesy of Userpostdif from Wikimedia Commons*)

35. Woodcut from Ulm Boccaccio (1473). (*After Hamer M., 1993*)

36. KV62, Tutankhamun, Valley of the Kings.

37. Lord Canarvon's grave, Beacon Hill. (*Photograph courtesy of Brian Billington*)

38. Mummy from the Saite Period. Rositcrucian Museum. (*Photograph courtesy of Keith Schengili-Roberts from Wikimedia Commons*)

39. Upright coffins, British Museum. (*Photograph courtesy of Brian Billington*)

40. Hobby Craft display, October 2010, Swindon. (*Photograph courtesy of Brian Billington*)

41. Mummy Mural at Holborn Station. (*Photograph courtesy of Sunilo60902 from Wikimedia Commons*)

42. Sphinx as part of Cleopatra's Needle, London. (*Photograph courtesy of Brian Billington*)

43. Wilson mausoleum, Hampstead Cemetery. (*Photograph courtesy of Elisabeth Kerner*)

44. Egyptian Mausoleum, Highgate Cemetery.

45. Cairo Museum exterior detail.

46. Antinous statue, Buscot Park, Oxford. (*Photograph courtesy of Tracy Walker*)

47. Carreras Cigarette Factory, London. (*Photograph courtesy of Brian Billington*)

48. The Luxor Hotel foyer, Las Vegas. (*Photograph courtesy of Lasloravga from Wikimedia Commons*)

INTRODUCTION

In the West, Egypt is extremely popular, with almost everyone having some ideas and preconceptions about the country and its history. As an Egyptologist I am constantly asked the same series of questions over and over again; who built the pyramids, was Tutankhamun murdered, is the curse real, why were the Egyptians obsessed with death, did Cleopatra really bathe in ass's milk? It constantly surprises me that these questions immediately spring to the forefront of people's minds whenever Egyptology is mentioned, considering these theories and ideas have been debunked or answered repeatedly for decades. There appears to be a hierarchy of study in Egyptology, with the first things people learn being these age-old ideas; should their interest be piqued enough they will go through the complex act of unravelling them and arriving at the truth as we understand it today.

The myths of the pyramids, Tutankhamun and the curse are only the tip of the iceberg as far as preconceived ideas about Egypt's remarkable history go. While many of these myths are fundamentally wrong and can be disproved, it is interesting to see to what extent they are based on fact and how much on fantasy. That is what this book is about. I have taken eight of the most common myths about Egypt and investigated their origins to decipher fact from fiction. I have tried to explore where these myths originated, as well as how the myths have developed over the decades or even centuries. One thing I found particularly interesting, and a little unexpected, was that while researching each myth, I found many other myths within them – myths upon myths. It was difficult not to get caught up in these subsidiary myths and to focus on the topic in hand. For example, when investigating the myth of Alexandria I discovered there were separate myths surrounding the lighthouse, library and individuals such as Alexander the Great and Hypatia, the female scholar. When investigating the final chapter on the Egyptian legacy, I discovered intricate myths surrounding the Freemasons, pyramids and obelisks as well as sub-categories of Tutmania, all worthy of entire volumes dedicated solely to them; but I had to be brutal and limit the path of research. There were also numerous myths that cropped up throughout, such as the mysticism and magic associated with Egypt, reincarnations of famous Egyptians, ghosts and the perceived relationship with cats. Although these are not covered in this volume, I will no doubt use the research at a later stage.

The myth of Egypt as a whole is an old one, so it is not surprising that there are various strands to it. It can be viewed in the writings of the classical authors of the

Greek and Roman periods, who wrote with a sense of wonder at what the Egyptians had done and could do. They were not always writing factually, as they were fed incorrect information or based their records on myths already in place. Although there has always been an interest in Egypt through the centuries, this increased after Napoleon's expedition to Egypt and the resulting *Description L'Egypte*, something often referred to as the 'Rediscovery of Egypt.'[1] However, this is not so, as many of the myths I shall discuss in the following pages have their origins further back than the eighteenth century, indicating that Egypt had never in fact been lost in either the East or West.

Egypt has always been considered interesting, although the hook is often different for each individual. Some are simply interested in history while others feel they have a deeper connection with the ancient Egyptians. For example, in the sixteenth century Pope Alexander VI Borgia had a great interest and wanted to trace his own family tree to that of Osiris and Isis.[2]

The myth of Egypt is often one of mysticism and the occult, and the ancient texts are reputed to hold all manner of secrets, magical, technological and mystical. Egypt was considered a land of magic in the Old Testament, and all great magicians are associated in one way or another to Egypt.[3] The mysteries of the Egyptian texts were only uncovered in 1822 by Jean-Francois Champollion when he deciphered the hieroglyphics, which up until this time had seemed like mystical signs holding secrets of life and death. It was well-known from classical sources that some of the greatest minds in Greek history once studied in Egypt and it was hoped that their knowledge could be uncovered. Once they were translated, as many Egyptologists now know, many of the monuments are covered in line after line of formulaic offering formulae and most of the mysteries of the hieroglyphs are often the exact meaning of particular words. However, for the most part it is a matter of interpretation. No Egyptian text contains 'scientific' knowledge, as the Egyptians were totally unfamiliar with the concept. Mathematical papyri are often nothing more than exercises for scribes to improve their skills and medical texts can be interpreted as little more than superstition to the modern reader, albeit accompanied by sound techniques.[4] The Egyptians could be seen as an advanced society, knowledgeable and intelligent, or as a deeply spiritual society who turned to mysticism rather than science in times of need.

In *The Sphinx*, a novel by T. S. Learner, this perceived superior knowledge of the Egyptians is the key to the entire plot; the discovery and protection of the *astrarium*:

> A mechanised model of the universe that doesn't just tell mean time and sidereal time but also incorporates a calendar for movable feasts and has dials illustrating the movements of the sun, moon and the five planets known to the ancients.[5]

The actual object was considered so unusual that its age was doubted:

> It isn't bronze but some other alloy, which might explain why it's so well preserved. It seems to have some unusual magnetic properties – there's a cog-like device at the centre with what appear to be two magnets – looks as if it's meant to spin. Totally freaky. But

get this mate, the time I carbon-dated the wooden box I thought I was hallucinating, but I've checked it five times now and I'm getting the same result over and over.

The cartouches on the object were of Ramses III and Nectanebo II, some 2,000 years earlier than they were expecting.[6] This idea of technologies far advanced of the skills the Egyptians *should* possess, contrary to what we know about their tools, is a popular one, adopted not only by novelists but also by serious researchers. In the following pages you will read about ideas of alien knowledge, a superior race, sonic technologies and magical powers. Many writers often scorn these ideas, as new-age nonsense:

> Reader, do you believe in magic – in the flying carpet of the old Eastern romances? Of course you don't; but suspend your disbelief for a moment and all the magic of the printed word to transport you across thousands of miles of space and many hours of time to a scene so different from wet, cold, dismal England that it might be another planet.[7]

This is perhaps the crux of the myth: that Egypt is viewed as a magical place, and some people believe there is a spiritual reason behind this. Others, and that includes myself, believe this magic is the myth of Egypt; the preconceived ideas we hold about Egypt make it a magical place.

Many of the new-age theories and books are very aggressive towards mainstream archaeologists and Egyptologists because their ideas are not supported, sometimes reverting to personal attacks:

> Our picture of history is gradually becoming clearer, but is still only half complete and further progress is being hampered by the stubborn and often bombastic attitude of the academic community.[8]

This seems to be the argument presented whenever there is not enough supporting evidence for their theories, but this attitude in itself is, in fact, all part of the myth of Egypt, showing that everyone is susceptible to it. Archaeologists are often portrayed in films, cartoons and stories as staid and incapable of understanding the outside world and oblivious to the powers of the occult and curses;[9] they are often portrayed as fools, in fact. This has been the case since the eighteenth and nineteenth century, and even in serious archaeological programmes gimmicks are used to make the archaeologists seem more likeable or more dynamic. Take Dr Zahi Hawass (Secretary General of the Supreme Council of Antiquities of Egypt) for example, with his hat and the denim shirt, or Mick Aston from *Time Team* with his bizarre, colourful jumpers, unlikely to be worn in real life. Due to this image of oblivious academics, archaeologists are often seen to be the victims of Egyptian curses, as they simply cannot accept ideas outside of their world. In reality, this just is not the case. Their academic background and expertise mean they are able to dismiss ideas which cannot be supported by the evidence.

It is clear to see that the myths surrounding ancient Egypt are varied and have affected all aspects of Egyptian research. This book covers some of the major myths associated with Egypt, from the luxuriousness of the River Nile and why a cruise is the epitome of decadence to the myth of Alexandria as a place of learning, intelligence and culture, as well as the myths associated with who built the pyramids and various myths surrounding mummies and the dead. As well as addressing the myths themselves, I will endeavour to identify their origins and whether there any truths in them at all.

The people of ancient Egypt have also been the topic of myth-making, and three of these will be covered in this book – Hatshepsut, Akhenaten and Cleopatra, all icons of ancient Egypt for different reasons. Hatshepsut, the ultimate feminist, taking on a man's world and ruling Egypt as king instead of the inferior role of queen; Akhenaten, the peculiar-looking man who single-handedly changed the religion of Egypt from a polytheistic pantheon to a monotheistic deity; and Cleopatra, the ultimate icon of femininity and power, a queen who seduced two Roman leaders and starred in the most romantic and tragic tale of all time. All powerful myths, but how much is based on facts and evidence? The final chapter of the book examines how these myths of Egypt are an important part of Western culture, even if the myths themselves are not necessarily based on fact. The associations of Egypt with luxury, decadence, eternal building and monotheistic religion led to a number of Egyptianising elements finding their way into Western art, and domestic, industrial and funerary architecture from the early eighteenth century to the modern day, as well as being the focus of hundreds of movies, cartoons and books. This changing role of Egypt in the Western world will be discussed in detail.

It is surprising how much Egypt is a part of Western culture, even though it is based on myths and legends rather than the reality of Egypt and her history. I am sure the same could be said about other ancient cultures too, but Egypt seems to mean something different to everybody. Some focus on the decadence and luxury, others are intrigued or in awe of their engineering skills, while others see ancient Egypt as the centre of all knowledge in the ancient world. All ideas are valid. Egypt is a million different things for a million different people, making it one of the most fascinating and intriguing cultures in the world. However, it is essential that we are aware of the myths that exist. Otherwise, rather than enhancing our knowledge, they could hinder cultural development while perpetrating racist and colonialist ideals.[10] I hope this book goes some way to draw attention to the myths that exist and enable readers to acknowledge how many of them have been subconsciously adopted into our minds as fact.

SECTION 1

THE MYTH OF EGYPT

CHAPTER 1

THE MYTH OF THE NILE

One of the most intriguing myths of Egypt which has developed throughout the centuries is that concerning the backbone of Egypt, the Nile (fig. 1). The river itself is not much different from any other river in the world, in the sense that as a body of water it is essential for the provision of water, nourishment and transportation for those living on its banks. The Nile itself is a very practical river, with the ancient and modern Egyptians relying on it for water, transportation and, more specifically, the silt deposited during the annual inundation. This was the case continually from thousands of years BCE until 1971, when the High Dam at Aswan was completed, curbing the flood waters and creating a more stable environment for the Egyptian population.

Although modern reliance on the Nile is different, the modern Egyptians are dependent on these waters for the same things, albeit in a more controlled manner. The Nile, therefore, has been vital for the lives of Egyptians for thousands of years, but why is this river such a fundamental part of Western culture too? What makes this river different from the Indian Ganges or the English Thames? The simple answer is the reputation the Nile has for exoticism, decadence and luxury. Whereas the Nile for the Egyptians is their means of survival, for Westerners it is a playground, a place visited by the rich with no real consideration for the practical and necessary functions that the river fulfils.

The ancient Egyptians were aware that their very existence was dependant on the river, and as a riverine society much of their day-to-day activities were carried out here. Many working-class people made a living from the river and without them the rest of society could not function. However, the elite members of the Egyptian society did not appreciate this work and their plight is outlined in clear terms in the Middle Kingdom *Satire of the Trades*:

> The reed cutter travels to the Delta to get arrows;
> When he has done more than his arms can do,
> Mosquitoes have slain him, gnats have slaughtered him,
> He is quite worn out.

> The washer man washes on the shore, with the crocodile as neighbour;
> "Father leave the flowing water" say the son, his daughter,

1. Boats on the Nile. (*Photograph courtesy of Brian Billington*)

"It is not a job that satisfies."
The bird-catcher suffers much, as he watches out for birds;
When the swarms pass over him, he keeps saying "Had I a net!"
But the god grants it not and he's angry with his lot.

I'll speak of the fisherman also; his is the worst of all the jobs;
He labours on the river, mingling with crocodiles.
When the time of reckoning comes, he is full of lamentations;
He does not say "There's a crocodile", fear has made him blind.
Coming from the flowing water, He says "Mighty god."[1]

These descriptions make it clear river-workers were not held in high esteem. This is perhaps because the elite experienced a very different Nile to those who worked upon it, one of relaxation, hunting and fishing for pleasure (plate 1).

So how did this image of unpleasant working conditions develop over time to the myth prevalent in the eighteenth and nineteenth centuries of an exotic, magical place? During this time, rich Westerners were travelling to India for the same reasons, the weather and relaxation, although the same ideals are not associated with the Ganges, a very sacred river to the Indians. There appears to be something about the Nile that produces romantic images that other rivers do not. Where have these associations come from? What exactly is the myth of the Nile?

MYTHS OF THE NILE

This is not an easy question to answer as there is more than one myth of the Nile, which have changed and evolved over the centuries. The earliest myth is that of the ancient Egyptians themselves, which helped them to understand the world and natural phenomena. They personified the Nile, or to be more specific the Nile inundation, into the god known as Hapy (fig. 2). The inundation was the most important aspect of the Nile for the ancient Egyptians, as these floods deposited the fertile silt over the land. The silt was rumoured to be so fertile that in legends frogs spontaneously generated in the black silt and women became pregnant by simply drinking the water.[2] The importance is further emphasised by the use in the Egyptian language of the god's name, ⲓ̄⳨≋ Hapy, to simply mean inundation, invoking the god whenever the flood was discussed. The start of the inundation was referred to as 'the arrival of Hapy'[3] and due to the importance of this annual deluge, the Egyptians felt a requirement to placate him through worship and offerings.

Hapy is represented as an androgynous human male with a large stomach and pendulous breasts with Nile plants upon his head, or holding an offering tray with the produce of the Nile upon it, emphasising the fertility brought by the inundation. Hapy did not have any temples dedicated specifically to him, although there were images of him in most of the temples in Egypt (fig. 3). In general, he was worshipped in his natural form: the river itself. With no temples dedicated to Hapy, there was no dedicated priesthood, but offerings could be left at the caverns at the First Cataract,

2. Hapy, the god of Nile inundation, Luxor temple.

3. Fruits of the Nile, Denderah.

thought to be his dwelling place, or thrown directly into the river, where they would be absorbed directly by the god. The most beneficial time to leave offerings was at the beginning of the inundation itself, as described in a Middle Kingdom hymn:

> When you overflow, O Hapy, sacrifice is made for you;
> Oxen are slaughtered for you, a great oblation is made to you.
> Fowl is fattened for you, desert game snared for you,
> As one repays your bounty.[4]

The divinity of the Nile was maintained throughout the Pharaonic period, and a New Kingdom love poem describes the environment surrounding the Nile as being associated with different deities:

> I fare north in the ferry, by the oarsman's stroke.
> On my shoulder my bundle of reeds, I am going to Memphis
> To tell Ptah, Lord of Truth, give me my sister tonight!
> The river is as if of wine, its rushes are Ptah
> Sekhmet is its foliage, [the god] Iadet its buds
> Nefertum its lotus blossoms, the Golden [Hathor] is in joy
> When earth brightens in her beauty[5]

This poem could be viewed as part of the foundation of the myth of the Nile as it stands today. This poem is one of romance, love and spirituality, something many honeymooners on a Nile cruise in the twenty-first century can relate to.

The personification of the Nile has also become embedded in the Western myth of the Nile. However, whereas the ancient Egyptians believed the Nile was a god, with influence over their lives, to be worshipped and appeased, a twentieth-century author uses slightly less lofty descriptions when writing about the Nile:

> It leaves its boisterous youth behind in the gorges and canyons of the African mountains, its sulky adolescence in the swamps of the Sudan and the growling protests of its middle age in the cataracts of Nubia. By the time it passed Aswan – for man has numbered the cataracts in reverse order, so that the first is the last in the river's long journey to the sea – it has achieved the calm of old age. But if its old age is sometimes mean of mood, it can also be generous to a fault, killing with too much kindness.[6]

The personification here is of the life-cycle of a man, with various moods associated with each of the stages. Continuing in this vein, in the 1990s, at the time of great famine and drought in Ethiopia, the Nile was held responsible. An Ethiopian newspaper accused the Blue Nile, flowing into the Nile, of 'treachery, theft and robbery' due to the erosion and destruction it caused, and the theme was adopted by an Ethiopian poet who accused the river of 'arrogance, desertion and betrayal' of its homeland by allowing Ethiopians to die from drought and famine as it flowed pointlessly into the sea.[7] Both of these authors were personifying the Nile as a scapegoat rather than looking for a person more substantial to be held accountable. Unfortunately, the river was unable to defend itself against such accusations and was simply doing what it had done for thousands of years with no hidden agenda of its own.

Although, the Nile was seen as the harbinger of death by these late twentieth-century Ethiopians, it is often acknowledged as a giver of life, reflecting its dual nature. The life-giving nature was recognised from the time of the ancients themselves, and in the sixth century BCE Hectaeus addressed the river thus: 'O generous Nile, you give life,' and Herodotus a century later commented that Egypt 'was the gift of the Nile'.

The ideas of personification are clearly diverse and even appear in nineteenth-century literature. The title characters in Shaw's *Caesar and Cleopatra* (Act IV) (1898) are discussing the name they should give a city they intend to build at the source of the Nile. Cleopatra suggests they appeal to the Nile for his help:

> The Nile is my ancestor; and he is a god. Oh! I have thought of something. The Nile shall name it himself. Let us call upon him.

Before they were able to invoke the god with aid of incense and a small sphinx, they were disturbed by the cry of someone falling from the roof and the discussion ends. This idea of invoking gods in times of need was not an unusual one in the nineteenth century, but it is interesting that the Nile was chosen by Shaw over all the Egyptian gods in the pantheon who were known at that time. It suggests that at this time the Nile was considered an interesting and spiritual river, worthy of being invoked by Cleopatra.

This mythological element of the Nile in the nineteenth century was also portrayed in artwork; a particularly interesting piece is Federico Fauffini's *Sacrificing a Virgin to the God of the Nile* (1867), a ritual said to be carried out annually to appease Hapy, ensuring ample floods. However, this ritual is not pharaonic at all and first appeared in the Islamic text *Marvels of Things Created and Miraculous Aspects of Things Existing* by Zakarīyā' ibn Muhammad al-Qazwīnī (1685 CE). The ritual apparently took place in July and comprised a virgin dressed in bridal clothes being thrown into the river as a sacrifice to the goddess of the Nile. At the time, the Egyptian elders asked permission of the Muslim leader Amar bin Al-Aas to continue this ritual, but he refused as the ritual was anti-Islamic. This troubled the elders, who appealed to Al-Aas, claiming that if this sacrificial act were to be abandoned, the Nile would not flood.

Al-Aas still refused and the inundation failed. By September, when the Nile still had not risen, Al-Aas reported the incident to Hadrat Umar, who sent a card invoking the name of Allah. As instructed, Al-Aas threw the card into the river and the next morning the river rose to its full flood height, which was viewed as a sign that Allah caused the river to flood with no need for the ancient custom of sacrifice. The Egyptian elders were in awe and immediately converted to Islam.

This apparent ancient ritual displays misconceptions about the rituals of the ancient Egyptians, as images on temple walls depicted an androgynous figure with pendulous breasts, which, as the seventeenth-century Arabs could not read the hieroglypsh, were misinterpreted as representing a goddess, thereby leading to the first misinterpretation. The hymn to Hapy could be further misinterpreted; the sacrifice of desert game and oxen could develop into the body of a virgin in true Arabian Nights style. However, the text regarding this archaic ritual is clearly propaganda explaining how in Egypt the conversion to Islam was completed, displaying the contrast between the barbarism of pagan religion and Islam. As no rituals of human sacrifice are recorded during the pharaonic period to the god Hapy or any other deity, it indicates that by the seventeenth century the ancient Egyptian religion was all but forgotten and any rituals surviving into this pre-Islamic period were extremely distorted so as to be nothing like their ancient counterparts.

The myth of the river had been passed down through the centuries, making it important and influential enough to be included in political and religious propaganda. It seems more likely that the importance of the inundation rather than of the Nile deity himself, or herself, as Hapy was perceived at this time, was the key. However, it is clear these seventeenth-century scholars and religious leaders were as superstitious as the ancient Egyptians and had no real understanding of what caused the river to flood, believing their card with the name of Allah inscribed upon it was responsible in the same way that the ancient Egyptians believed their offerings of food and wine would do the same. This lack of understanding of the Nile led to another series of myths about the river.

MYTH OF THE INUNDATION

It is only in the twentieth century that the mechanisms of the inundation were fully understood, but in the preceding centuries there was still a need for explanations, and from this knowledge the ability to monitor and control it. This explanation was therefore built into the mythology of the ancient Egyptians. It was believed that the inundation began when the tears of the goddess Isis, cried over the body of her dead brother/husband Osiris, fell into the river, causing the waters to rise.[8] The rising water saw the appearance of Hapy, and this was greeted with great jubilation by the populace:

> When he floods, earth rejoices, every belly jubilates,
> Every jawbone takes on laughter, every tooth is bared ...
> Oh joy when you come! Oh joy when you come, O Hapy,
> Oh joy when you come! You who feed men and herds
> With your meadow gifts! Oh joy when you come![9]

The importance of the inundation is made abundantly clear by the connection with the most important mythology in the Egyptian pantheon, that of Isis and Osiris. This was a national myth which explained to the populace what happened to them after death, as well as explaining the most important agricultural event in the year. Combining the two myths ensured that it would be nationally known, understood and believed.

The importance of the beginning of the inundation, as well as the association with funerary rituals, was emphasised in the Old Kingdom Pyramid Text (581), which stated that the 'Meadows laugh and the riverbanks are inundated,'[10] showing the total reliance on the Nile by the living, and the inclusion in the royal funerary texts associate them with fertility and rebirth in the underworld. The coming of the inundation is compared to the arrival of the dead king as Osiris in the afterlife. The Nile was, therefore, essential for both the life and death of the Egyptians, making it fundamental to their religion.

Medieval Egyptians had no clearer understanding of the mechanisms of the inundation than the ancient Egyptians, and the thirteenth-century chronicler Jean de Joinville commented:

> Nobody knows how these inundations occur unless it be by God's will ... when morning comes, the Egyptians find in their nets cast into the river products such as ginger, rhubarb, aloes and cinnamon.[11]

The unusual list of produce suggests that Joinville had not witnessed the inundation first hand.

The Christian and Islamic religions, while not being able to explain it, celebrated the start of the inundation. The 'Night of the Drop' (17 June) was celebrated by the Coptic Christians and was built into Christian doctrine as the time when the archangel appeared in order to raise the level of the Nile.[12] The Muslims in Cairo also celebrate this day, calling it *Munadee el-Nil* or the 'Herald of the Nile', which was the day the Nile inundation was meant to start, and a messenger travelled to tell people it had risen. After the High Dam was completed in 1971, this celebration became a ritual in name only as the Nile no longer flooded.

ETHIOPIAN CONTROL

As medieval scholars did not know how the inundation began or where the source of the Nile was, various theories arose. The most interesting one, which dominated Eastern and European thought for over 500 years, was that the source of the river, and in particular the inundation itself, was controlled by Ethiopian Emperors. There is no denying that Ethiopia and Egypt were linked by the Nile, as well as with social bonds. Ethiopia controlled the source of the Nile and the silt the Egyptians relied on, but as a Christian country Ethiopia relied on the Egyptian Coptic Church for the selection of their *abun* (patriarch), viewing Egypt as a sacred land, the refuge of the Holy Family.[13]

However, various notable incidents have arisen about this theory and one of these stands out, from 1089–1090 CE, during the reign of Fatimid Sultan al-Mustansir, when the inundation in Egypt failed. It was rumoured the Ethiopian Emperor had built a mound to block the Nile. The Egyptian Sultan sent the Patriarch of Alexandria, Michael, to Ethiopia to appeal to the Emperor, who after discussion, demanded the destruction of the block. The Nile flooded 'three cubits in one night',[14] and all was well. This was a prime example of the Ethiopians knowingly trying to divert the Nile.

The earliest record of this type of event, however, was written by the Scottish explorer James Bruce (1172–1212 CE), who claimed the reason for this hostility between the two countries was because the Muslims had pushed the Christians into Ethiopia, where they were oppressed. Their revenge was to 'famish Egypt' by diverting the Nile waters. Bruce comments that the Emperor Lablibala created earthworks, which were still visible on the landscape. These attempts to divert the Nile resulted in his death. Although these earthworks are no longer evident in the archaeological record, British collector Henry Salt embraced the story. Salt, who is more famous as the man who employed Belzoni in the eighteenth century, believed that the only part of the river which Lablibala could legitimately have controlled was a tributary, the Takazze.

The hostility between Egypt and Ethiopia escalated into mythology when the Frenchman Philippe of Mezières (1330s) claimed an unnamed Ethiopian ruler diverted the river, causing a drought in Egypt and frightening the Egyptians so much that they allowed the Ethiopians to travel through their land without paying taxes. This threat continued through the centuries and in the fifteenth century one Ethiopian Emperor, Zar'a Ya'qob (1434–1468), threatened the Muslims of Egypt with making the Nile fail, with the proviso they should stop persecuting Coptic Christians:

> Are you not aware, you and your sultan, that the River Nile is flowing to you from our country and that we are capable of preventing floods that irrigate your country?[15]

He claimed the only thing stopping him was his fear of God and the suffering that it would cause.[16]

This hostility was adopted into Western literature of the sixteenth century, and the poem *Orlando Furioso* by the Renaissance poet Ludovico Ariosto (1516) has this hostility as a central theme:

> And the Egyptian Sultan, it is said,
> Pays tribute and is subject to the king,
> Who could divert into another bed
> The river Nile and thus disaster bring
> On Cairo and on all that region spread
> The plight of famine and great suffering[17]

One of the most famous operas of all time, Verdi's *Aïda* (1871), also has hostility between the two nations as its theme: an Egyptian commander falls in love with an Ethiopian princess, Aïda, who is being held captive in Egypt. A battle ensues between the Egyptians and the Ethiopians, led by the object of Aïda's love; she is torn between loyalty to her father and loyalty to the man she loves. It is a tragic love story with the hostilities between the two nations as a focal point.

In reality, the Ethiopian rulers could never have affected the Nile inundation, at least not until the modern era and the introduction of dams and dykes through the southern stretch of the Nile. This has been known since at least 1618 CE, when the Jesuit author Batazar Tellez examined the Ethiopian landscape and declared the diversion of the Nile would be impossible by the Ethiopians. By the early eighteenth century, this idea had been totally rejected in Europe with the French Cleric Abba Joachim le Grand in 1726 stating:

> We do not pretend that a canal cannot be dug from the Nile to the Red Sea, but the Abyssinians cannot do it.[18]

However, this threat was intriguing to the Western mind and the reliance by one country on another for their life-giving water makes for interesting literature, poems and artwork. Despite the dismissal of the claim of Ethiopians to be able to divert the waters of the Nile, the fear has developed and evolved in the minds of the Egyptians up until the modern era.[19] It was only in the 1960s that the Egyptian authorities finally felt free of this threat as the High Dam at Aswan was completed. It was considered a bid for freedom. After the completion of the dam, the distribution of the Nile waters now became a major issue for the Ethiopians. As the Egyptians owned the High Dam, they had control of the waters distributed to those countries south of the cataract. There was a real role reversal; now Egypt was responsible for ensuring Ethiopia got as much water as they needed. Egypt is effectively in charge of Ethiopia's water. This ownership and control was described by Rushdie Said (1993).

> A former president of Egypt offered to channel part of the water of the Nile to Jerusalem as a gesture of good will: a prominent member of Parliament once submitted a proposal to

construct a pipe line from Lake Nasser to Saudi Arabia to supply it with fresh water; and some investors presented projects to divert the "excess" waters of the Nile to the desert.[20]

However, in the same way that Ethiopian power over the water supply was considered myth, the ethical and religious issues concerning ownership were also addressed by Said:

> Among the pervasive beliefs in Egyptian culture is that water, like air, is god given and free. Any pricing system and controls on its use are totally unacceptable and almost blasphemous. The perception that water is abundant is sometimes manifested in frivolous but revealing ways.

THE ORIGINS OF THE RIVER

The ancient Egyptians would not have thought such a declaration of ownership was unreasonable, as according to their beliefs the Nile originated at the First Cataract in Aswan, giving them a *right* to the waters. They believed the waters at the First Cataract split, with half flowing to Egypt and the other half to the Sudan. Hapy was thought to reside in the caverns here, under the protection of the ram-headed god Khnum. Hapy was, therefore, primarily worshipped at the sites of Elephantine and Gebel el Silsila in this region, especially at the time of the inundation.

However, we now know that the origins of the Nile extend much further south than the First Cataract but this is a relatively new discovery, the culmination of thousands of years of exploration. The origins of the Nile have been a fascination for people since Herodotus (480–425 BCE) speculated on them. He suggested that during the winter the sun was driven off course by storms and the Nile had less water as a result, because there was no rain falling into it. He generally concluded that the source was unknown and he was told by the Egyptian priests:

> That between Syene, near Thebes and Elephantine there were two mountains of conical shape called Crophi and Mophi; and that the springs of the Nile, which were of fathomless depth, flowed out from between them. Half of the water flowed northwards toward Egypt and half towards Ethiopia.[21]

Alexander the Great was also interested in this mystery and suggested the Indian Ganges was one of the Nile tributaries. As unlikely as this seems today, until 1470 CE the Nile was reported as originating in India.

The Greek geographer Ptolemy (83–161) also speculated about the origins of the Nile and attempted to locate it in the African heartland; in his *Geography* he traced the origin to the Mountains of the Moon, the great basin and the eastern tributaries. This search for the source led to the 1436 CE myth recorded by Italian traveller Nicolo de'Conti concerning a mission organised by Prestor John, the Christian king of Abyssinia, to discover the Nile source. He believed that in order to discover the source, it was necessary to use a race of men who survived solely on fish. Therefore, he raised a group of babies with fish as their staple diet and when they grew to adulthood, they went on an expedition which led them to the Mountains of the Moon. Some men who explored saw the Nile pouring from the mountain but did not return, and the others kept what they had seen a secret, maintaining the mystery of the Nile origins.[22] The nineteenth-century explorers were slightly more successful, with English explorer John Hanning Speke (1864) proclaiming that Lake Tanganyika and Lake Victoria were the sources of the Nile.

This preoccupation with discovering the source of the Nile even found its way into nineteenth-century literature, and the title characters in Shaw's *Caesar and Cleopatra* are entertaining when the subject of the source of the Nile is raised and Apollodorus comments:

> The old men, when they are tired of life, say "We have seen everything except the source of the Nile."

Caesar imagines visiting the source of the Nile and building a great city there, 'in the great unknown'. He was particularly keen to locate the source, but was never successful.

It was only in the mid-twentieth century that the source of the Nile was traced to a number of Ugandan mountain springs and the Mfumbiro volcanoes[23] which flow into the Bahr el Jebel and eventually the White Nile before flowing into the Nile at Khartoum, where it is joined by the Blue Nile, which originates in the Ethiopian mountains; far more complex than any of the explorers could have imagined.

Even though the origin had been discovered, the excitement of the search was immortalised in the 1979 strategic board game *Source of the Nile*, which was set at the height of 'Nile Source Mania', in the nineteenth century. The object of the game was to explore Africa using a variety of transportation methods, and as areas are discovered, they are marked on a map. The players are confronted with typical exploration dangers, such as the cataracts, starvation and disease. The search for the source of the Nile had clearly gripped the imagination of the West as an exciting adventure, yet another myth associated with this enigmatic and complex river.

It is easy to see how the image of brave explorers and their exciting adventures became associated with exciting adventure-filled Nile cruises. Indeed, in many films and novels the two are closely interlinked.

THE MYTH OF DECADENCE

The discovery of the source of the Nile informed us that it is the longest river in the world, flowing for 6,695 kilometres from Uganda to the Mediterranean. Although the majority of the river flows through the Sudan, it is the Egyptian stretch of the river that comes to mind for Westerners. The early explorers, with their tales of the unusual, opened the can of worms known as tourism which is the most common element of the myth of the Nile.

The image indelibly imprinted on the mind is one of palm trees, sparkling blue water or a glorious sunset reflecting off the still water (plate 2), all viewed inevitably from a relaxing cruise boat. A Nile cruise, favoured by lovers and honeymooners, is seen as the pinnacle of holiday decadence and romance, described by one travel company as a:

> rare opportunity to enjoy the natural beauty of the river and the ancient civilisation of Egypt in an atmosphere of period elegance – almost in the style of a 'house party' from earlier times.[24]

It is these so-called house-parties of 'earlier times' that are fundamental to the myth of travelling the Nile, at least the twenty-first-century interpretation of it. It is often stated that Agatha Christie's *Death on the Nile* (1937) was the start of the decadent cruise obsession in the West, as the story concerns a number of rich individuals, along with the moustachioed Hercule Poirot, setting sail from Aswan on a paddle steamer only to find themselves in the middle of a murder mystery.

In the television productions of *Death on the Nile* the scenery is spectacular and is an important element of the story, but this is not the case in the novel itself. The novel only contains two descriptions of the landscape of Aswan – that of the rocks and that of the temple at Abu Simbel – although Christie neglects to mention the name of the temple until the following chapter. This leads to the assumption that the temple was so familiar to the intended audience of the book that she felt she did not need to name the places.

The plot of *Death on the Nile* does not really necessitate the characters being in Egypt and the setting was likely chosen for other reasons. It was essential to the plot for the main characters to be wealthy, and it was equally important they were in an enclosed space with no means of escape. In order to accommodate both of these, the Nile cruise was chosen, sending out an image to the readers of luxury, decadence and overall wealth without needing to emphasise it. In order for this to work as a literary tool, these ideas of the Nile and Egypt needed to be well-established within the minds of the Western reader. If this was the case, *Death on the Nile* cannot be the source of the Western obsession with Nile cruises, as it is clear that in 1937 the association of the Nile cruise with luxury and wealth was already fully developed and has continued to be used in literature and movies when luxury and wealth is required. In the Elizabeth Peters novels, we have Amelia Peabody travelling by dahebeeya on the Nile:

> On my first trip to Egypt I had travelled by dahebeeya. The elegance and charm of that mode of travel can only be dimly imagined by those who have not experienced it. My boat had been equipped with every comfort, including a grand piano in the salon and an outdoor sitting room on the upper deck. How many hours did I spend there, under the billowing sails, drinking tea and listening to the songs of the sailors while the magnificent panorama of Egyptian life glided by on either side.[25]

What more could a visitor want than such peaceful luxury?

4. On board a Nile Steamer. (*Courtesy of Thomas Cook Archives*)

BIRTH OF THE MODERN CRUISE

The history of cruising is an old one, with the earliest Nile cruise from Alexandria to Thebes (Luxor) dating to 47 BCE. The participants of this early cruise were none other than Cleopatra VII and Julius Caesar. This cruise was primarily a diplomatic journey to appease the population in the south after Cleopatra's brother/husband Ptolemy XIII issued a decree in their joint names stating that during a particularly low flood the produce of Upper Egypt was to be shipped to the north, leaving them to starve. When she took this trip she was twenty-three years old and pregnant with Julius Caesar's child, which sent a message of new beginnings to the people of Upper Egypt, as well as showing that Egypt was supported by the Romans. They sailed down the Nile from Alexandria, stopping at the Pyramids and Denderah along the way before reaching Thebes and visiting Karnak temple. Although used as a political tool to re-establish herself in Upper Egypt it was clearly a pleasure cruise as well, stopping at well-known sites along the way in the same manner as a modern cruise boat. Although the earliest record of a pleasure cruise, this was undoubtedly not the first cruise and it most certainly was not going to be the last.

By the mid-fifteenth century CE, with the introduction of the printing press, travel to Egypt had expanded to such an extent that the introduction of a travel guide was a necessity. A number of travel books about Egypt were translated into myriad languages, encouraging the wealthy to embark on trips there. The interest was encouraged by these guides and their elaborate claims and colourful descriptions of the sites and landscape, mainly fictitious. For the next three hundred years, the tourist trade to Egypt increased until it reached its peak in the eighteenth and nineteenth century with the growing popularity of the Grand Tour, antiquarianism and archaeological interest in all things Egyptian. At the end of the eighteenth and beginning of the nineteenth century it was popular to travel to Egypt to collect antiquities, and it was to become more intense after the decipherment of hieroglyphs in 1822, when there appeared to be a need to own antiquities bearing inscriptions.

In the days before the cruise-liner, paddle steamers were hired by the travellers, their companions and entourage (fig. 4) for their cruises down the Nile. From the 1840s onwards, the *dahebeeya* (a flat-bottomed wooden houseboat) was the favoured means of transport for the rich. Novelist and aspiring Egyptologist Amelia Edwards,[26] in her *Thousand Miles up the Nile*, produced a set of simple guidelines to choosing the correct *dahebeeya*, as she emphasises how disastrous it could be to pick a bad one. These cruises were very different to those of the modern day as they were more about being on the boat than visiting the monuments, and the vessels from Alexandria travelled to Aswan as quickly as possible with minimal stops, simply viewing the monuments as part of the passing scenery.[27] As the banks were higher in the 1840s than they are today, the views were somewhat limited.

By the 1860s tourism was at a high, and Thomas Cook & Sons had the foresight to introduce the 'package tour' to Egypt, introducing a large steam boat, holding more passengers and travelling faster than the *dahebeeya*. However, the *dahebeeya* was still commonly used until the turn of the twentieth century and the main character in *Death on the Nile*, Linnet Doyle, decided not to hire one, as she did not want to appear gauche; as in the 1930s this was seen as a wealthy and over self-indulgent way to travel.

MYTH AGAINST THE REALITY

It is these cruises of a bygone era that the modern cruises are trying to recreate as a means of keeping this romantic, decadent ideal alive. However, although they have brought back the *dahebeeya* and the paddle steamer, they are a far-cry from the experience of Cleopatra or Amelia Edwards. They are no longer the choice of the rich and famous, with a week's all-inclusive cruise costing a few hundred pounds, cheaper than a week in any European city, so although it may still be the holiday of a life-time for many, this is primarily due to the wonderful monuments than the financial implications of a Nile cruise. As many people go on a cruise as their *first* trip to Egypt in order to see as many monuments and places as possible in their week, they can no longer be considered the holiday of a lifetime.

Modern Nile cruises do not even compare to those of the nineteenth and early twentieth centuries, as the majority of the cruise companies only sail between Luxor and Aswan and many sail for approximately four hours a day, as most of the time is spent sightseeing rather than idly watching the scenery pass. Although cruises are a fantastic way of covering a large portion of Upper Egypt, they are a far cry from

5. Cruise boats lined up on the Nile at Luxor.

the relaxing tours of the 1920s and 1930s, with many tours starting at 5.30 a.m. and continuing throughout the day until mid-afternoon.

However, they are still marketed as maintaining the luxury of days gone by, with one company imploring the visitor to 'imagine relaxing comfortably on the sun deck ... whilst sipping afternoon tea or a cool gin and tonic observing the day to day life on the banks of the Nile,'[28] which once again conjures images of the early nineteenth century. However, the reality is often very different with the cruise boats docked, sometimes ten deep, so the only view from the sun-deck will be another boat (fig. 5). Other, more specialised, companies offer such packages as the 'Dahabia Nile Cruise,' and another offers a Nubian tour on a paddle steamer providing an 'atmosphere of period elegance.'[29] It is thought that 'exploring the beautiful wonders of ancient Egypt by a traditional Egyptian boat is a magical experience'.[30] It is this dream that travellers to Egypt are buying into, and most overlook the realities of a modern package Nile cruise and just see the magic and beauty of the Nile and the myth and mystery it holds.

This hold the river has over people has been an invisible force since the nineteenth century. One particularly prickly visitor was Florence Nightingale (1849–50), who described most monuments as 'ugly', but even she was overcome by the Nile's magic:

Let natural philosophers contradict me and say it is impossible when the sun is so low beneath the horizon. I say it is ... the eastern moonlight looks so supernatural ... so that seeing her above one's head and the great sail casting not a bit of a shadow on the water, one sits down resigned to the conviction that one is being carried on a phantom ship to Jinnee [ghosts or spirits] countries.[31]

WALKING IN THE FOOTSTEPS OF THE RICH AND FAMOUS

An earlier traveller in 1845, Elliot Warburton, also lost himself to the river and the views, but most of all to the immense history of Egypt:

Hark! To the jackal's cry among the moslem [*sic*] tombs! ... those plains before us have been trod by pharaohs; these waters have borne Cleopatra; yonder citadel was the home of Saladin! We need not sleep to dream.[32]

Warburton has perhaps found the key to the myth of the Nile and its attraction for centuries to hoards of travellers. The Nile has been described as the 'world's most history-laden waterway',[33] and knowing that Caesar and Cleopatra travelled the same way can add a great deal of romance to a cruise or a holiday.

When one considers the people who have travelled on the Nile, including Ramses II, Tutankhamun, Julius Caesar, Cleopatra, Moses, Jesus and the Virgin Mary, moving on to Saladin, Napoleon, numerous nineteenth- and twentieth-century authors, including Mark Twain, Agatha Christie and William Golding, as well as every well-known Egyptologist for the past two hundred years, it is hardly surprising that the Nile has developed in the Western mind as a thing to be revered and held in awe.

Perhaps this history of famous tourists has facilitated the Nile becoming an important part of Western popular culture. Even in the modern day, references to Egypt and the Nile appear regularly in art, television and film covering all genres, ranging from classics such as George Bernard Shaw's *Caesar and Cleopatra*, with Vivien Leigh portraying the queen, to the rather flippant *Queen of Denial*, immortalised by Miss Piggy in episode 409 of *The Muppet Show*. On television in the UK, various travel shows have covered Egypt, with the rather seductive Joanna Lumley hosting a four-part series called *Joanna Lumley's Nile*, where she travels from the mouth of the river to Rwanda, a more focused show perhaps than Michael Palin's *Around the World in 80 Days*, where he was also shown on the Nile in Cairo. Everyone wants to follow in their footsteps and perhaps absorb and experience a little of the magic for themselves.

What visitor to Egypt cannot fail to be impressed that they are walking in the footsteps of all of these people? Who, even the most unspiritual, can fail to be moved to think they are following the trail of the Holy Family (Jesus, Mary and Joseph) while in the streets of Cairo (plate 3) and Cleopatra at the Pyramids? The answer is very few, and this is something that modern holiday companies have also embraced: the themed tour.

The most common theme is the Ramses II tour, as this enigmatic nineteenth-dynasty king left his mark in most areas of Egypt from the Delta down to Nubia, which makes for a diverse and interesting itinerary. Other popular trips are the 'Biblical Tours,' either following the so-called route of the Exodus or the journey of the Holy Family in Egypt. All of these journeys feature the Nile as an important element.

SPIRITUAL JOURNEYS

Egypt and the Nile attract many spiritual people, whether Christian, Jewish or pagan, as it features in many texts and is essential to many religious mysteries. The Exodus story is one that attracts Christians and Jews alike as being very important for their history, but it is a controversial issue in the world of Egyptology. Biblical archaeologists want to believe the Exodus text is an historical record, whereas Egyptologists argue that with no supporting archaeological evidence this cannot be proven to be the case.[34] However, although there is no supporting evidence, no clear indication of the time period within which the Exodus occurred or any proof of the existence of Moses, this does not detract from the importance of the events. The Exodus describes how Moses freed thousands of slaves from Egyptian oppression, leading them to the Promised Land and founding the nation of Israel. Regardless of whether it is historical fact or not, the importance of the story cannot be denied. However, it is the beginning of the story which is of relevance in the mythologising of the Nile, as once the Exodus itself starts the Nile is behind them and no longer important.

The beginning of the story is the birth of the infant Moses, who was born after an unnamed Egyptian king decreed all male Hebrew children were to be drowned in the Nile. In order to save Moses, his mother Jochebed placed him in a basket and placed him on some steps leading to the Nile. Miriam, his sister, watched as the basket was picked up by the king's daughter. As the princess had no children she was unable to nurse the child, so Miriam approached her and asked whether she would accept a Hebrew nurse, which was how Jochebed came to nurse Moses, who was raised as the child of the princess.

However, the important element of the story for our purposes is the Nile itself, and here we see its duplicitous nature: a bringer of both life and death. The king was planning to drown the boys in the Nile and yet Moses was offered a new life, almost a rebirth, from the very same waters. This duality of the nature of the Nile is a very Egyptian idea, and this is a fundamental part of the story. The creative elements of the Nile are represented in this narrative, as a child was produced from the waters for the childless princess, something else that would appeal to the Egyptian populace. The Nile in this story is the bringer of life, bringing a child to the childless and enabling Jochebed to save her son and offer him a new life in the palace. This narrative is also an important part of Western culture and the 'Moses Basket' originated here in addition to ensconcing the Nile in the mind as a sacred place, and one of great significance and importance. Without the Nile the Exodus could not have occurred at all, and the nation of Israel would not exist.

Later in Biblical history, the infant Jesus was taken to Egypt by his parents to escape death at the hands of King Herod (plate 4). Although they were in Egypt for four years, there is little mention of it in the Bible other than the start of the journey:

And when they [the wise men from the East] were departed, behold the angel of the Lord appeared to Joseph in a dream, saying, Arise and take the young child and his mother and flee into Egypt and be thou there until I bring you word; for Herod will seek the young Child to destroy Him. When he arose, he took the young Child and His mother by night and departed into Egypt; and was there until the death of Herod, that it might be fulfilled which was spoken of the Lord by the prophet, saying, Out of Egypt I called My Son (Matt. 2:13-15).

The remainder of the journey of the Holy Family has survived to the modern day in a mixture of Coptic texts from Egypt and Armenia as well as oral tradition. They started their journey by travelling by donkey across the Sinai, entering Egypt at Pelusium, on the Pelusaic branch of the Nile in the Delta. They travelled through the Delta, by donkey initially, but records indicate that the Church of the Blessed Virgin at Maadi in Cairo was the point upon which they hired a boat and started their journey southwards by river, which was punctuated by stops at various sites, each marked by a church or monument commemorating miracles of Jesus or resting points. The site of Deir el Muharraq is particularly important, as the family stayed here for six months and five days of their trip. Their journey south, however, was to end at Deir Durunka, south of Assyut, where they resided in a cave before waiting for a boat to take them northwards, beginning their return to Palestine.

On the journey back to Palestine they stayed at the town of Babylon (Old Cairo), and they are thought to have stayed in a cave here which is marked by the Church of St Sergius (Abu Sargah), a site of pilgrimage for hundreds of years (fig. 6). This subterranean cave flooded during the annual inundation and was under water for two months a year. The water which flowed into this 'sacred area' was considered holy. While they were residing at Babylon, oral tradition suggests the Holy Family visited the area of the Nile where the basket of Moses was drawn out by the Egyptian princess, indicating that the exact place was known at one point in time, but now this has been lost; however, for some time it was thought the basket of Moses was stored in the Mosque of Tubah at Giza, indicating this was near the sacred spot. While they were at Giza it is likely that the Holy Family saw the pyramids at Giza, and although they had their minds on higher things one cannot help but wonder what their reaction may have been to these monuments. Were their reactions the same as ours when we glimpse them for the first time? We will never know, but it is certainly food for thought.

It is clear the myth of the Nile is a complex one which has changed and developed over the centuries, with as many different branches as the Nile itself. They can all be traced to the ancient Egyptians themselves in one way or another, as they considered the Nile, or Hapy, to be profoundly important, spiritual and essential to the lives of the Egyptian people. Something of this is present in each of the myths, as they have developed over the centuries.

The Nile was revered, and even the Egyptians held some very romantic notions about it. It was used for literary narrative, descriptions and comparisons, as presented in the *Satire of the Trades* which states:

6. Church of St Sergius, Cairo.

There's nothing better than books!
It's like a boat on water.

Comparisons between the Nile and a woman of beauty are also made regularly in New Kingdom love poetry. The Nile, however, is presented as both an obstacle and an aid to love:

My sister's love is on yonder side, the river is between our bodies;
The waters are mighty at flood time, a crocodile waits in the shallows
I enter the water and brave the waves, my heart is strong in the deep;
The crocodile seems like a mouse to me, the flood as land to my feet.
It is her love that gives me strength, it makes a water spell for me;
I gaze at my heart's desire, as she stands facing me.[35]

In ancient times, there were clearly different views regarding the Nile, in the same way as the views differ in the modern world: reality and romanticism. Rivers throughout the world are associated with the Nile in order to add something exciting to them; for example, the Mississippi is sometimes referred to as the 'Nile of America',[36] even though it does not have the same impact on America as the Nile does on Egypt. Many of the nearby settlements founded in the nineteenth century were also given

Egyptian names such as Philae, Thebes, Karnak, Luxor, Memphis, Tennessee and Cairo, Illinois.[37]

This contrast between the reality of Nile living and the beauty of it is held by the same members of society in ancient times as it is now. The workers see the reality and the wealthy (the tourists) see the beauty and exoticism. This is a fundamental part of the myth of the Nile. It is viewed by different people as different things: by the rich it is seen as a playground, for leaders and kings it is an instrument of politics and for the working-class it is the source of hard work, as one Egyptian sailor makes abundantly clear:

> He who rides the sea of the Nile must have sails woven of patience.[38]

In 1877, Amelia Edwards commented on the hard work of the *dahebeeya* captains, especially at the cataract near Aswan:

> To haul dahebeeyas up those treacherous rapids by sheer stress of rope and muscle; to steer skilfully down again through channels bristling with rocks and boiling foam, becomes now, for some five months of the year, his principal industry.[39]

This shows a juxtaposition of the romanticism of the Nile and the hard work required for those who live upon it. However, most people choose to believe the image of their own making as the 'reality' of the Nile.

So is the River Nile a god, personified by a man with pendulous breasts? A sacred waterway, featuring in the lives of Moses and the Holy Family? Is it the exotic route of thousands of cruise boats from the time of Cleopatra to the modern day? Or merely part of the daily struggle to put food in hungry mouths? It is all of these things and none of them.

It is only possible to experience one of these Niles; other realities may be seen, but as they cannot be experienced they become part of the myth and reality of the onlooker. For example, the rich Nile cruiser will witness the men fishing in the Nile but will not understand the hardship of being a fisherman; they will rather see the quaintness of the task, almost as if they are actors there for their entertainment. The fisherman may feel nothing but resentment for these idle cruisers interfering with his daily routine, not realising, especially in the modern world, that these people work hard when they are not on holiday. Everyone experiences the Nile differently and therefore will have a different idea of what the Nile is and what it means.

CHAPTER 2

MYTHS OF THE PYRAMIDS

The most famous monuments from ancient Egypt are undoubtedly the Giza pyramids, and over the centuries they have been the topic of many discussions, books and television shows. Even though there are many pyramids in Egypt, Nubia and South America, it is inevitably the Giza ones that immediately spring to mind.

The Giza pyramids have stood the test of time, have been visible for their entire 4,500-year history and have been constantly present in Western culture. Numerous questions are raised about the pyramids, the answers of which often form the myths about them. The most common questions ask who built them, how and why.

WHAT IS A PYRAMID?

Before looking at some of the myths surrounding the pyramids, we should examine what they are. Greek travellers to Egypt looked at the shape of the monuments, naming them *pyramid*, a type of cake in Greek, perhaps indicating the Greeks did not view them with the same awe and wonder as modern tourists.

Pyramids were constructed in Egypt from the Old Kingdom through to the New Kingdom, a period of almost 3,000 years, and number over 100. They were all built on the west bank of the Nile, the realm of the dead, and were the centre of wider complexes, comprising temples and subsidiary burials. Pyramids were essentially tombs, with the entrance usually on the northern side, but variations were used to try and deter the robbers, although all pyramids were entered and robbed in antiquity.

Every pyramid is mounted with a *benben* stone, or pyramidion, a small pyramid-shaped block thought to represent the mound of creation, from which all life emanated. Some *benben* stones have inscriptions and images of the solar god, showing a solar connection. An inscription found near the pyramid of Udjebten (2278–2184 BCE), a queen of Pepy II, makes reference to the gilded capstone,[1] indicating they were covered in gold, silver, electrum or copper. Some new-age theorists have suggested the original *benben* stone was made from meteoric iron, which they interpret as showing the connection with the nocturnal sky.[2]

Most pyramid complexes housed large cemeteries of nobles, officials and royal family members. The latter were sometimes buried in satellite pyramids and funerary goods have been discovered inside these, showing they were used as tombs. The closer the burial was to the main pyramid the greater their importance, and there was a distinct hierarchy based on positioning.

LEARNING BY MISTAKES

Through the long period of pyramid building, archaeologists can trace the development of pyramids, showing the ancients learned from the mistakes they made. The earliest pyramid to be built was the third-dynasty step pyramid of Djoser at Saqqara (2668–2649 BCE), which started life as a traditional mastaba tomb. Although this mastaba was impressive at 63 metres long and 8 metres high, King Djoser wanted more. The mastaba was extended lengthways before being extended upwards to make the second step of the pyramid. The extensions continued until there were six steps rising 60 metres above the ground. This pyramid was built using stone blocks, making the step pyramid the oldest stone building in the world. Each stone block was of the same dimensions as traditional mud-bricks, but designed to last for eternity. They were then covered in limestone casing blocks, giving an overall smoother appearance to the monument. Other step pyramids have been discovered in various stages of completion before evidence of trying to create a true pyramid.

The Pyramid Texts state that the step pyramid shape enabled the *ka* of the king to ascend to his ancestors in the sky:

> A staircase up to heaven is laid for him so that he may mount up to heaven nearby.[3]

This suggests step pyramids were stellar in orientation and symbolism, whereas the straight-sided pyramids were solar-based and represent a stylised image of the sun-rays.

The next stage in pyramid building was to turn the step pyramid into a true pyramid, and this was attempted by Sneferu, the first king of the fourth dynasty (2613–2589 BCE), at Meidum. The pyramid at Meidum was originally built as a step pyramid with seven steps, but before the fifth step was completed the whole structure was enlarged to eight steps, meaning the original steps needed to be extended in order to take the weight of the stone and change the angle of ascent. These steps were then filled in using stone to give smooth, straight sides. All that is visible of this pyramid now are the top three steps, as the casing stones placed over the rough core have been removed over the years and reused elsewhere. It was initially believed that this pyramid collapsed during construction, due to problems with the casing stone placement, but recent excavations have uncovered no evidence of this. This indicates it was almost completed, even though the angles were incorrect, creating a rather strange-shaped pyramid. However, the internal structure is not complete and a burial did not take place here, even though fragments of a wooden coffin were discovered within the burial chamber.

Sneferu, however, continued his pyramid building and constructed at least another two at the site of Dahshur: the Bent Pyramid and the Red or North Pyramid. The Red

7. The Bent Pyramid, Dahshur.

pyramid is second only in size to the Great Pyramid at Giza and was the first true pyramid, and even included a corbelled burial chamber similar to the Grand Gallery in the Great Pyramid (plate 5).

The Bent Pyramid (fig. 7) was built first, and was given its name due to a bend halfway up the structure caused by a change in design. This pyramid has two entrances, one in the north face and one in the south. There were also two burial chambers intended for the burial of Sneferu in his roles as King of Upper and Lower Egypt, although it was never used and was abandoned after weaknesses were discovered in the desert plateau that it was built upon.

The Red Pyramid is probably the most important of the pyramids, as it is the prototype for every true pyramid which followed. The basic core of the pyramid is built in layers, rather like a step pyramid, and limestone casing stones were then used to encase it, giving a smooth-sided true pyramid. The burial chamber is not subterranean, as in previous pyramids, but almost in the centre of the superstructure. This pyramid may have been used for the burial of Sneferu, as some human remains were discovered in the burial chamber, although whether these belong to him is unknown.

As Sneferu had perfected the true pyramid at Dahshur, all that was left in the pyramid development was to enlarge it, which is what Khufu did at Giza. The Great Pyramid (fig. 8) stands 146 metres high, and was originally encased in limestone

8. Great Pyramid, Giza.

blocks weighing 16 tonnes each. The entrance was in the north face and was entered via a descending passage which led to a subterranean chamber. A little way down this passageway was another passage that ascended to the Grand Gallery, leading to the burial chamber.

The entrance to the burial chamber was sealed by a series of portcullis blocks and plugging stones. At the base of the Grand Gallery a horizontal passage led to the so-called Queen's Chamber, although it was never intended for the burial of a queen and instead may have been a *serdab* (or statue chamber), designed to house the *ka* statue of the king.

The queens of Khufu were buried at the site, in three satellite pyramids to the east of the pyramid. The first, most northerly, pyramid was for Khufu's mother Hetepheres; the central pyramid was for his wife Meritetes; and the most southernmost belonged to Henutsen, Khufu's half-sister.[4] After the Giza pyramids were built, not many improvements could be made and the size of the Great Pyramid ensured it was one of the Seven Wonders of the Ancient World. However, pyramids were continued to be built even though the economy was weaker, resulting in smaller, poorly built pyramids. Many of the pyramids of the fifth dynasty were constructed of desert rubble or mud-brick piled up into a pyramid shaped mound and encased in stone blocks to give a smooth outward appearance. However, as the casing blocks were removed by robbers over the centuries, the pyramids themselves collapsed into the pile of rubble that they were (fig. 9).

9. Pyramid of Pepy, Saqqara.

To compensate for a rather shoddy superstructure, the internal chambers were decorated. The fifth-dynasty pyramid complex of Unas (2375–2345 BCE) at Saqqara was the first pyramid decorated with the 'Pyramid Texts' in the burial chamber and antechamber. These texts included elements of creation myths, the myth of Osiris and Isis, the myth of Horus and Seth and instruction on how to survive death in the afterlife. These texts formed the basis for the Middle Kingdom Coffin Texts and the New Kingdom Book of the Dead.

Every Middle Kingdom king had a pyramid complex, although they were now further south, in the Faiyum. It once housed the capital city at the site of Lisht and the pyramid field here boasted the pyramids of Amenemhat I (1991–1962 BCE) and Senusret I (1971–1926 BCE) of the twelfth dynasty. By the start of the New Kingdom (1540 BCE), pyramids were no longer used by the royal family as funerary monuments; they had adopted more secretive rock-cut tombs. However, the non-royal elite used the pyramid, albeit on a much smaller scale as a 'grave marker', rather like a modern tomb stone. Their function as decoration continued until the twenty-sixth dynasty (664–525 BCE). The pyramids of Abydos and Thebes at this time were mud-brick with a domed interior, similar to granaries or ovens, and were no longer part of a complex but were attached to the side a rectangular chamber leading to the shaft burial beneath. These were once again the focus of the funerary cult.

It is archaeologically evident that there was a development of pyramid building, resulting in the construction of 138 known pyramids. More are being discovered as excavations continue. This number often comes as a surprise to many people, especially those who believe the fringe theories associated with the pyramids.

THE MYTH OF THE GREAT PYRAMID

Despite the number of pyramids in Egypt, it is the Great Pyramid at Giza which people fixate on and which all myths gravitate towards. So what is the attraction? Even in the ancient world they were attractive and are the sole surviving wonder of the Ancient World, as classified by the Greek poet Antipater of Sidan in 130 BCE. The Great Pyramid also stands out from all other pyramids because of its size, and this has been a critical point for many researchers.

From the time of Charles Piazzi Smyth (1819–1900), who travelled to Giza with the intention of making careful measurements of the pyramids, people have been doing the same. Some researchers have tried estimating the number of stones used to construct the Great Pyramid, spanning from a conservative 700,000 blocks, weighing 2.5 tonnes each, to 3,947,159.[5] There are one million square metres of buttress walls and 200,000 square metres of Tura Limestone casing blocks so closely fitted together a postcard cannot be slipped between them. These figures impress many people, and are part of the fascination of this structure.

John Taylor (1781–1864), through his measurements of the pyramid, came to the conclusion the Egyptians had discovered *pi* and that the base perimeter represented the circumference of the earth at the equator.

Many new-age books use measurements and mathematics as the answer to everything, almost to the point of ignoring archaeological evidence and the human element behind the monuments. For example, Von Däniken asserts:

> Is it really a coincidence that the height of the pyramid of Cheops multiplied by a thousand million corresponds approximately to the distance between the earth and sun.[6]

Further 'fabulous' facts are presented by Collins when he informs us that the perimeter of the pyramid is equal to half a minute of latitude at the equator or 1/43,200 of the Earth's circumference, or only 120 metres short of the polar radius of the earth.[7] Such calculations could be applied to any building in the world, if it is significant that the figures have such high multiples or fall short of a significant landmark.

Such measurements are never applied to the other pyramids in Egypt, even though they were also constructed using huge amounts of masonry. In the century of Old Kingdom pyramid building, over 25 million tons of limestone were worked and moved. The Step Pyramid of Djoser was constructed with one million tonnes of masonry, the Bent Pyramid of Sneferu used 3.5 million tons of stones and the Meidum pyramid of Sneferu built with 1.5 million tonnes,[8] but it is the Great Pyramid that enthrals.

Other mysteries of the Great Pyramid include the four 'air shafts', two in the King's Chamber and two in the Queen's Chamber. The shafts are approximately 20 square centimetres and are situated in the north and south walls of the chambers. For a while they were thought to be ventilation shafts, as those in the King's Chamber reach to the outside. Some researchers claim the 'air shafts' in the King's Chamber point to Orion's Belt (Osiris) and were the destination of the *ka* of the king,[9] and the air shafts in the Queen's chamber point to the star Sirius (Isis).[10] However, the shafts in the King's Chamber do not point directly to the stars as they run horizontally for about 5 feet before ascending upwards.[11] They resemble in their structure the entrances to pyramids, supporting the idea they were designed for the *ka* of the king to leave the pyramid, ascending to the sky.

In 1992 Rudolf Gantenbrink sent a small robot, called *Upuauet 2*, up one of the shafts, showing that 65 metres along the shaft there was a stone block with two copper pins.[12] Some speculated that the end of the southern shaft may be connected in some way to the *benben* stone, with perhaps the original *benben* or the *benben* shrine behind the door,[13] while others suggest perhaps the Hall of Records is behind the door,[14] and believe it may contain a sacred library.

Ten years later, in 2002, they drilled through the door in the shaft to be confronted by another door, eight inches further along. In 2010 the SCA, University of Leeds and Dassult Systèmes in France have created a robot called *Djedi* that can alter its size to go through small holes, and a 'snake' capability so it can move around corners.

Many theories have been presented as to the purpose of the shafts. Philippe Lheureux[15] suggests they were used to channel water into the pyramid, with the conclusion that the pyramid was not a tomb. However, he fails to take into account that the openings to the shafts on the outside of the pyramid were covered with the limestone casing blocks,[16] meaning no water could enter via this route.

He claims that with water filling the burial chamber, the remaining air pressure would increase to 3.3 bars, or 33 tonnes of pressure per square metre. This compressed air would fill about a metre of space at the top of the burial chamber and push against the pressure of the weight-bearing chambers above. Such pressure would try to evacuate the water in any way possible through small cracks and fissures. He suggests the weight bearing chambers above the burial chamber acted as a type of hydraulic piston, controlling moving floors and locks. Any moving parts which came in contact with the water would have to be sealed, although Lheureux does not mention this, otherwise the water would escape through the gaps. He suggests the portcullises, generally accepted to have prevented robbers entering the tomb, were to prevent the water from escaping, but he does not make it clear what the purpose would be of building such a huge monument simply to fill it with water.

It is interesting that the air shafts in the second pyramid at Giza were never investigated or included in research of this type. These air-shafts appear to be unfinished and are situated in 'Belzoni's Chamber'.

Herodotus has always been a great source of information about the pyramids, although not all of his records are accurate and can be identified as the source of many of the myths about Egypt. One of his records concerns one of the satellite pyramids of Khufu's pyramid. However, it is more a tale of the tyrannical nature of Khufu than pyramid building *per se*:

Cheops (Khufu) moreover came, they said, to such a pitch of wickedness, that being in want of money he caused his own daughter to sit in the brothels and ordered her to obtain from those who came a certain amount of money (how much it was they did not tell me): and she not only obtained the sum appointed by her father, but also she formed a design for herself privately to leave behind her a memorial and she requested each man who came in to give her one stone upon her building: and of these stones, they told me, the pyramid was built which stands in front of the Great Pyramid in the middle of the three, each side being one hundred and fifty feet in length.

Although it seems Khufu's daughter was not buried in one of these pyramids, it is interesting to have a myth of this type surrounding the construction of one of them.

The Giza monuments have, for many centuries, led people to travel to Egypt to see them. One fourteenth-century Arabic travel guide, *The Book of Buried Pearls and of the Precious Mystery, Giving Indications Regarding the Hiding Places of Finds and Treasures*, was very popular, and when one reads the excerpt on the Great Pyramid it is easy to see why:

You will see, to right and left, many rooms and, before you, a large hall containing the body of one of the first kings of Egypt. This king is surrounded by other kings and by his sons, all of them clothed in gowns embroidered with gold thread and decorated with precious stones. Close by them you will see piles of silver, rubies, fine pearls and gold and silver statues and idols. In this great heap you must search for a recess, richly inlaid in wood and enclosing a grotto.

In this grotto you will see a large monolith which you will be able to move to one side and thereby reveal a well containing a great deal of silver deposited there by the pagans. Take as much of it as you wish.[17]

Such descriptions, while being inaccurate, were intriguing to those who had never seen the structure. Promises of treasure led many people to the pyramids as well as many people hoping for spiritual experiences.

EXPERIENCES OF THE GREAT PYRAMID

Many people claim to have had spiritual experiences while in or around the Great Pyramid, some more credible than others. The spiritual experience which most people have felt when they first see the pyramids is one of awe, and this has been described in travel writing for decades. Vivant Denon (1802), travelling to Egypt with Napoleon, described seeing the pyramids:

My soul was moved by the great spectacle of these great objects; I regretted seeing the night extend its veils over an image that dominates both eyes and imagination ... The precision of the pyramids' construction, the inalterability of their form and construction and their immense dimensions, cannot be admired sufficiently. One could say that these gigantic monuments are the last link between the colossi of art and those of nature.[18]

This is no more a spiritual experience than many of us have experienced when approaching these monuments for the first time. Most people visiting the pyramids enjoy the experience and are astonished at their size.

Not everyone, however, was impressed with them, and Florence Nightingale (1849–1850) was quite scathing in her report:

> Hardly anything can be imagined more vulgar, more uninteresting than a pyramid in itself, set up upon a tray, like a clipt yew in a public-house gardens; it represents no idea; it appeals to no feeling. It tries to call forth no part of you, but the vulgarest part – astonishment. Others however were in awe of the great monument that towered above them – at the expense. Surely size is a very vulgar element of the sublime, – duration you will say, is better, that is true; but this is the only idea it presents – a form without beauty, without ideal, devised only to resist time, to last the longest.[19]

Gustave Flaubert, a French novelist (1821–80), shared his views of disdain, albeit for a more practical reason:

> jackal's piss at the bottom and bourgeois climb to the top.[20]

He was clearly distracted away from the monument itself by the tourists and the environment, something many people can relate to today when visiting the pyramids. Rather than a peaceful trip, tourists are harassed by merchants selling tacky plastic pyramids or camel rides; only the merchandise seems to have changed. However, for everyone under-impressed with the pyramids there are hundreds who are in awe, and a handful that have had even more intense spiritual experiences. Napoleon for example, visiting in 1799, spent some time alone in the King's Chamber, in the manner of his hero Alexander the Great. He came out visibly shaken and refused to speak of the experience; when he was a prisoner on St Helena it appeared as if he was going to confess, but simply said:

> No, what's the use? You'd never believe me.[21]

Dorothy Eady, better known as Omm Sety, also claims to have had a spiritual experience at the Great Pyramid, and like Napoleon ascertains the audience will never believe it:

> I know this will sound unbelievable ... And I don't know whether it was a dream or not, but one night when I was living in Giza I found myself in a nightdress walking on the plateau beside the Great Pyramid. Suddenly I saw King Sety, who was wearing a plain white pleated robe with a wide gold collar and he came out to me and asked "What are you doing?" I replied "I'm just walking". He said "It's alright come and walk with me!"

So I went with him and all of a sudden he started to climb up the east face of the Great Pyramid. You know of course, that the proper way to climb this pyramid is from the north-east corner; but he began climbing from the middle of the east face and he looked back and said, "follow me ... and where I put my foot, you put your foot." So I started to climb up behind him ... When we got halfway up he began to walk along one of the steps and I followed and when we were exactly in the middle he pulled out a stone – not completely of course, since nobody could possibly do that – and he then said, "All right" and we went down again and walked to the edge of the plateau. "Go home and go to bed" he told me. I did.[22]

This rather pointless nocturnal journey was to spell the start of another supernatural event the following day when someone fell from the pyramid. The block they fell from was the one Sety pulled out, and on this stone was apparently a small blue flame, 'like the flame you get from kerosene lamps'. Apparently Eady was not the first visitor that day to spot it, and it was only later that evening that the accident happened. She could not work out what the connection was, but stated unequivocally:

> There wasn't anything in Sety's character that would make him kill or injure an innocent person.

This does suggest that she may have believed this was the connection, and it would not be the first time that re-animated mummies had been accused of killing the living (see chapter 7).

Others were not so modest in reporting their experiences. Aleister Crowley (1875–1947), who named himself the 'Great Beast 666' and a practitioner of magic, claims he spent one of his honeymoon nights in the King's Chamber, reading out hermitic incantations by candlelight. He claimed that gradually the walls began to glow, enabling him to read without the candle, and then later his new wife encountered an Egyptian deity.[23] However, this does need to be taken with a pinch of salt as he was known as a teller of tall tales.

Paul Brunton (1898–1981) also spent a night in the Great Pyramid in the 1930s. He was a British philosopher, mystic and traveller, who dedicated his life to all things spiritual. He claimed that in the pyramid he suffered a feeling of cold, followed by the psychic impression that the chamber was 'peopled with unseen beings', before:

> there was something abroad which I sensed as evil, dangerous. A nameless dread flickered into my heart ... monstrous elemental creations, evil horrors of the underworld, forms of grotesque, insane, uncouth and fiendish aspect gathered round me and afflicted me with unimaginable repulsion.

According to Brunton, a couple of high priests materialised, threatened him and tried to get him to leave. They placed him in the sarcophagus and he went into a trance similar to death. When he regained consciousness, he was allowed to leave and was told:

take back with thee the warning that when men forsake their creator and look on their
fellows with hate, as with the princes of Atlantis in whose time this pyramid was built,
they are destroyed by the weight of their own iniquity, even as the people of Atlantis
were destroyed.[24]

Brunton was a strange character and liked to give the impression that he was from
another planet. Such dark fantasies about the pyramid and its ethereal inhabitants
were not new and were an aspect of Arab folklore, which states that at noon and at
sunset the King's Chamber was haunted by a fanged, naked woman, like a vampire,
who seduced men, driving them mad.[25] Such tales, rather than scaring people away,
simply added to the mystery of the Giza pyramids.

WHY WERE THEY BUILT?

This mystery has led some people to reject the idea that the pyramids were built as
royal tombs. During the fourth century, some believed the pyramids of Giza were
granaries built by the Biblical Joseph, and this is depicted on the mosaic of the ceiling
of St Mark's in Venice,[26] showing the pyramids as no bigger than a man, indicating
the artist had not visited them. The size of the Giza pyramids alone should have been
enough to disprove this theory, but it was not until the fifteenth century that they
were once again viewed as tombs.[27]

Size was taken into account by Duc de Persigny (1808–1872), who tried to prove
the Giza pyramids were screens to protect against sand storms. However, this theory
would require more structures closer together to prove effective. Along the same lines,
Arab writers of the twelfth century thought they were built as a place of protection
from the flood. It was even suggested that the Sphinx (plate 6) originally stood on top
of the Great Pyramid and was dislodged during the flood.[28]

Along more scientific lines, Charles Piazzi Smyth (1819–1900) did an extensive
study on the Giza pyramids, making accurate mathematical measurements. His
colleague Robert Menzies, however, believed each block of the pyramid told the
history of the Bible from creation to the apocalypse.[29] He believed these measurements
were the key to God's plan for the universe. Despite the studies he made, he was
unable to identify this master plan, although some authors still follow this line of
research.

John Taylor (1781–1864), through his measurements of the pyramid, came to
the conclusion that the Egyptians had discovered *pi* and that the base perimeter
represented the circumference of the earth at the equator:

> [They] knew the earth was a sphere; and by observing the motion of the heavenly bodies
> over the Earth's surface, had ascertained its circumference and were desirous of leaving
> behind them a record of the circumference as correct and imperishable as it was possible
> for them to construct.[30]

He firmly believed in the Bible, and that the world was created about 4000 BCE and the Great Pyramid in 2100 BCE. As they were 'primitive', he came to the conclusion that the pyramids were divinely inspired.

A CUNNING PLAN

The idea of a master plan for the Giza Pyramids is a popular one. It has been argued that the site of the Great Pyramid indicates that it was part of a wider plan, as it is the lowest point and required major construction work to build the causeway along the eastern cliff. The best site would have been slightly north-west of the second pyramid. This unusual placement suggests to some that the three Giza pyramids were part of a master plan which included not only the pyramids but the Sphinx, temples and causeways.[31] This is proved through measurements in palms (ancient Egyptian measurement), with the comment 'although an error of one cubit (approx. 54 cms) would not be excessive'[32] to explain any discrepancies in his measurements. Such a discrepancy would be unlikely. Considering the accuracy to be found in the pyramids, one would expect this to apply to their master plan.

One of the most famous theories concerning the wider plan of the Giza Plateau is *The Orion Mystery*, which states that the pyramids are a map of the stars, with the three main pyramids forming Orion's belt:

O Horus, these departed kings are Osiris, these pyramids of theirs are Osiris, these constructions of theirs are Osiris, betake yourself to them (PT 1657).

While an interesting observation, the pyramids discussed in the Pyramid Texts are unlikely to be those at Giza, as the Pyramid Texts were first recorded in the pyramid of Unas (2375–2345 BCE), some 200 years after the Great Pyramid was built at Giza.

The researchers tried to incorporate other fourth-dynasty pyramids into the theory,[33] asserting the pyramid of Nebka at Abu Roash corresponded with the star Saiph and the pyramid of Zawyat al Aryan with Bellatrix, the left foot and right shoulder of Orion. However, Orion's belt is surrounded by stars, none of which match the satellite pyramids at Giza, which surely would have been included in the plan.[34] Even though the Dahshur pyramids did not fit the Orion constellation and there were no pyramids in the position of Betelgeuse and Rigel, the authors were not disheartened:

I could only conclude that these had never been built or that they had long since been demolished and had disappeared under the sands of the Western Desert.[35]

Bauval and Gilbert hunted the skies for a constellation that they could attribute to the Dahshur pyramids by observing they matched the Hyades constellation,[36] coming to the conclusion that the Giza pyramids represented Osiris and the Dahshur pyramids represented Seth, associated with Hyades. What is not clear is why the Dahshur pyramids were built first, as the Osiris connection was surely more important to their fumerary beliefs than Seth and Hyades? Why would the Dahshur pyramids be included and the Giza satellite pyramids omitted when they are comparable in size? Why is the fourth-dynasty pyramid at Meidum omitted from the star plan? More questions are raised than answered by this theory.

HALL OF RECORDS

A map of the skies is not the only secret the Giza plateau is said to hold. Thomas Shaw (1721) believed that there were underground passages connecting the Sphinx and Great Pyramid,[37] a theory that was adopted by Edgar Cayce (1877–1945). Between 1901 and his death in 1945, Cayce regularly went into trances, and from 1923 onwards he often told his listeners that they lived previous lives in Atlantis. He believed he had been the Atlantean spiritual leader called Ra-Ta. He claimed that in 10,500 BCE, while fleeing the flood, the Atlanteans settled in Egypt and built or at least planned the Great Pyramid, placing their Hall of Records here, which held the secrets to their vast knowledge. According to his predictions, this was to be discovered in the last 20 years of the millennium.[38] This clearly did not happen at the end of the twentieth century, but some people are still searching. The myth of Atlantis and the popularity that followed can be attributed to an American author, Ignatius Donnelly (1831–1901), who wrote *Atlantis* (1882), which sparked the imagination of many.

Cayce's Hall of Records has inspired many people to look beneath the Giza Plateau, with the first search starting in 1957 when Marjorie Hansen gained permission to bore holes in the plateau near the Sphinx, near the right paw, where Cayce claimed the Hall was located. However, as Collins states:

> Whether there is any hard evidence that it really exists has almost become superfluous to the quest to find it, since, for the New Age community.[39]

This kind of statement is quite concerning for archaeologists, as evidence is everything if one wishes to prove a theory, but with fringe theories this clearly is not the case. Petrie was even aware of this and stated:

> It is useless to state the real truth of the matter, as it has no effect on those who are subject to this type of hallucination. They can be left with the flat earth believers and other such people to whom a theory is dearer than fact.[40]

Many people have searched for the Hall of Records, including Robert Bauval, which is documented in *Secret Chamber* (1999), and Collins in *Beneath the Pyramids* (2009) bases his research on the readings of Cayce and the idea of fleeing Atlanteans. He introduces some interesting ideas based on the fifth hour of the Amduat. He suggests Giza was the site of creation, and the Amduat representations show subterranean chambers beneath the plateau and the secret chamber of Sokar. At no point does he explain the role or significance of the pyramids built before the Giza pyramids. They do not feature in his theories at all. His research, or 'quest' as the majority of new-age writers prefer to call it, led Collins to the Tomb of the Birds on the Giza Plateau, where he discovered an opening leading to a natural cave system beneath the tomb, created by flowing water thousands of years ago.

The tomb guard claimed this cave-system went to the Faiyum, some 50 miles (80 km) south of Giza.[41] Locals also told him that there was a myth of a snake called el-Hanash who guarded the caves. According to legend, once a year a secret opening allows access to the Hall of Records. The snake holds a diamond in his mouth which lights the way, but whoever comes face to face with the snake will be blinded. However, one day, someone will only be blinded in one eye. He will discover the Hall, gaining special powers.[42] When he tried to research the myth, Collins found nothing in connection to Giza, casting doubt upon its credibility.

He entered the caves via the Tomb of the Birds and although he explored for a few metres, he could not confirm how far they extend. These caves are natural, and the only human activity is sporadic parallel chiselling near the entrance. He knows that this is not the Hall of Records, but believes it is still out there somewhere. He has since made the announcement that he believes this to be the tomb of Hermes.[43] Ancient records tell us the second pyramid marked the spot where Hermes was buried in his cave tomb. He is said to be buried with an emerald tablet, which has apparently been discovered in Palestine, but does not prevent people from assuming Hermes is buried in Giza;

> It is my intuition that even before Salt and Caviglia's entry into the caves in 1817, Europeans, Italians in particular using the thriving Adriatic sea-port of Venice, came to Giza in search of the Tomb of Hermes. It is possible that they entered the caves and perhaps even removed objects that they saw as connected with Hermes in some manner, perhaps even a Green Stone fragment thought to have come from the original Emerald Tablet.

Total speculation, but enough for Collins to start the next line of research into these caves and the Tomb of the Birds.

Some years earlier, in 1999, Robert Bauval also hunted for the Secret Chamber, or Hall of Records on the Giza Plateau. His 'quest' led him to the so-called 'Tomb of Osiris' or the well under the causeway between the Sphinx and the second pyramid. The tunnel leading from the well went to a carved pillared chamber, which had two sarcophagi within, which Hawass dated to the Saite period, but Bauval confidently stated:

> My intuition told me that Hawass could be wrong. This place felt old, very old – perhaps as old as the Sphinx itself.[44]

A further tunnel ran from this chamber which Bauval guessed was running towards the south side of the Great Pyramid, but was blocked at one end. No further studies seem to have been made in the Tomb of Osiris and the Hall of Records has not been found.

WHEN DID WE FORGET?

The purpose of the pyramids was not always such a mystery, and Greek and Roman scholars refer to them as funerary monuments. At some point between 79 BCE and the fifth century CE this was doubted. Diodorus (49 BCE) mentions the pyramids, discussing the possible owners and builders:

> There is a lack of unanimity concerning these pyramids, both among the natives of the place and among historians. Some say the above-mentioned kings erected them. But some say it was certain others: for example, some claim that Armaeus made the largest one, Amosis the second and Inaros the third; and some people assert that this last is the burial place of Rhodopis the courtesan, of whom they relate that certain of the nomarchs, who were her lovers, built the structure in common out of affection for her.[45]

Diodorus here has confused the fourth dynasty and the twenty-sixth dynasty kings Amosis (Amasis) and Inaros and Armaeus (Armais). Pliny (23–79 CE) also mentions these same names. Greek travellers, on the other hand, were well acquainted with the true owners of the Giza pyramids and identified them as the tombs of Cheops (Khufu), Chephren (Khafra) and Mycerinus (Menkaura).[46] Evidence that accurate sources are vital.

Although there was some confusion regarding the names of the builders of the pyramids, there was no doubt during the Greek and Roman periods that they were tombs. While the Greeks only got the names confused, later researchers have questioned the race and even species of who built the pyramids.

WHO BUILT THE PYRAMIDS?

Any Egyptologist asked the question 'who built the pyramids?' will easily answer they were built by the Egyptians. This answer is supported by the archaeology of the pyramid sites (all of them, not just Giza), as well as the villages and tombs of those who worked on the structures.

Herodotus, writing in the fifth century BCE, states that the Great Pyramid was built in twenty years by 100,000 men. We know Khufu ruled for twenty-three years, so this timing is more or less accurate. Various studies have been carried out on the number of workers required, testing the accuracy of the report. The estimated number of blocks in the Great Pyramid is thought to be approximately 2.3–2.5 million, laid over a period of twenty to thirty years. Ancient Egyptian workmen worked an average day of ten hours, with one in every ten days off. For the pyramid to be completed in the time, thirty-four stones needed to be laid an hour, or one block every two minutes.[47]

Kurt Mendelssohn, a medical physicist, suggests 5,000–10,000 permanent stonemasons and 50,000 unskilled labourers were required to build the pyramid,[48] but Mark Lehner, of the Oriental Institute, Chicago, demonstrated that only 1,212 workers were needed. Lehner focused initially on quarrying 300 cubic metres of stone a day, and the 1,212 workers moved 8–9 stones a day. It was further estimated that it could take between one and three days for each block to be moved from the quarry to the pyramid and placed.[49] In order to manoeuvre each 2.5-ton block, a team of eight men was needed. Each team of eight could make ten trips a day from the quarry to the Giza Plateau. Therefore, to bring 340 stones to the site, thirty-four teams were required. Providing allowances for tiredness, 1,360 haulers were used for this job. Once the stones were at the pyramid site, a further ten men were needed to set a stone into place, four using levers, two for brute strength and adjustment, two stonemasons to trim the excess and two extra hands for general tasks, giving a total of 340 setters.

Lehner took into account that ancient Egyptians may be half as efficient as modern workers as they performed the tasks for longer and therefore there could be as many as 640 setters, producing a workforce of 3,452 people,[50] which was more than sufficient to build the Great Pyramid.

This workforce was split into two teams of approximately 2,000 people each, divided into five groups (called phyles), each consisting of 200 men supervised by an overseer. Within these groups there were smaller divisions of twenty to fifty men.[51] Competition between these smaller groups boosted morale, and as a motivator each team was given a name. From Menkaure's pyramid, evidence shows two teams were called 'Friends of Menkaure' and 'Drunkards of Menkaure'.[52] Such names from the Meidum pyramid included the 'Stepped Pyramid Gang', 'Boat Gang', 'Vigorous Gang', 'Enduring Gang', 'North Gang' and 'South Gang';[53] the Great Pyramid was built by the 'Craftsmen Crew' and 'How Powerful is the White Crown of Khufu'. For the ancient Egyptian foremen, these 'tags' enabled them to keep track on the volume of work produced by individual work-gangs.

In addition to these 3,452 workers who cut and manoeuvred the stone to create the Great Pyramid, it is estimated there could be an additional 20,000 auxiliary workers,[54] including carpenters, water carriers, cooks and scribes. It has also been suggested that should ramps have been used, there could be another 50,000 men who built and dismantled them. Potentially, therefore, there could have been 70,000 people involved in the construction of the Great Pyramid, although not all at one time. The on-site workers would have been less than 10,000 at one time, which raises the question: where did they all come from?

BUILT BY SLAVES?

It is widely believed that the pyramids were built by slaves, as presented by Herodotus and subsequently picked up and used in Hollywood movies, showing the Great Pyramid being built by hundreds of slaves. This idea is firmly imbedded in the modern Western mind and is often included in popular television shows. Episodes of *The Simpsons* and *Futurama* have Egyptian scenes showing the pharaoh whipping hundreds of slaves, and in the comedy show *Red Dwarf* it is stated the pyramids were built with the aid of:

whips, massive, massive whips.

This idea will clearly take a while to be removed from the minds of the populace, but the evidence is compelling enough to show slaves were not involved.

The theory of slaves building the pyramids was first mentioned by Herodotus, writing in the fifth century BCE, 2,000 years after the Great Pyramid was built. He claims 100,000 slaves were used, but should this be the case a huge security operation would be required to organise them. In such a literate society as Old Kingdom Egypt it is likely that some record of this security system would survive, but this is not the case.

On the contrary, the inscriptions in existence show they were, if not happy, then willing workers:

> His Majesty desires that no one should be compelled to the task, but that each should work to his own satisfaction.[55]

This inscription may have been carved for propaganda purposes and may not be trustworthy. However, unofficial graffiti in one of the weight-bearing chambers in the Great Pyramid at Giza states:

> We did this with pride in the name of our great king Khnum-Khufu.[56]

The workmen appear to be proud of the work they were doing, enough so that they wrote this on the wall.

So if these workers were not slaves, who were they and where did they come from? Egypt was totally reliant on the Nile for its water source and every year it flooded, depositing water and fertile silt all over the agricultural land. This meant that throughout the inundation between July and October, the fields were flooded and the farmers remained at home, repairing tools and other domestic activities. The king conscripted these farmers to work on the royal monuments. These workers were paid and housed in villages near the pyramid site. Once the flood started to abate, the farmers returned to their land. The period of conscription may have only lasted for one wet season for the unskilled labourers, whereas skilled stonemasons or administrators may have stayed year after year and were well paid for their work. Cornelius de Pauw (1773) believed Khufu built his pyramid as a job-creation scheme as a means to keep Egyptians gainfully employed,[57] and although it was probably not the only reason, this is a good description of the conscription service.

Excavations at Giza have uncovered the settlement and cemetery of the workmen who built the Giza Pyramids, with all of the pottery on the site dating to the fourth dynasty. Since 1992, a number of tombs belonging to these people have also been uncovered, many with reliefs and inscriptions indicating that their status was that of the elite. The settlement, south-east of the 'Wall of the Crow', is still being excavated and includes refectories, dormitories, bakeries and a place for preparing fish.[58] The temporarily conscripted workmen were housed in galleried structures (dormitories) with mud-brick sleeping platforms. There were sixteen of these galleries, housing up to 2,000 workmen, half the workforce needed to build the Great Pyramid.

Adjacent to the dormitories, to the east, was the dining room, a pillared hall with a series of mud-brick benches. Embedded in the mud-brick were the bones from the meat they ate, including ten types of fish, three bird species, sheep, goat, cattle and pigs, and from the distribution it is clear that those living in the galleries were on a poorer diet, consisting of the less popular fish, goats and sheep, whereas the diet of those living in the supervisory houses was far richer.[59] The men at Giza appear to have eaten a lot of meat, and the bones discovered suggest that eleven cattle and thirty-three sheep were slaughtered daily to feed the 10,000 workers,[60] including permanent and auxiliary workers. It is clear from this evidence that the workmen were well fed and were considered to be the lower elite class.[61]

Close to the settlement, south of the Wall of the Crow, the cemetery of the workmen was discovered, giving us names, titles and family connections of hundreds of workers, showing their very human and elite origins. These included an overseer called Ptah-Shepsesu, who controlled the work of a gang of 200 part-time conscripts. Another 'Overseer of the King's work', Itysen, was responsible for one side of the pyramid and supervised the transportation of the blocks for this side, showing the work was divided into manageable areas. The Overseer, Merer, was also in charge of phyle workers and supervised the work of his gang of 200 men. Each of these supervisors lived with their families in nearby houses. Not all the tombs were of overseers; the tombs of two chief bakers have been identified, Nyankh-ptah and Nefert-Heith, the latter of which had two wives: Nyankh-Hathor, with whom he had seven children, and Nefer-Hetepes, who was a 'midwife' and bore eleven children. Scenes in Nefert-Heith's tomb show the bakery in action, including a woman, Khenut, grinding grain and a servant, Kakaiankh, stoking the fire. Even the inspector of the washer men, Wahy, is buried in the cemetery,[62] a man responsible for those who washed the loincloths of the men who built the pyramids.

The human remains show that the overseers and officials lived until between fifty and sixty years old, as would be expected due to their wealthier lifestyle, whereas the male workers died between thirty-five and forty and the women between thirty-five and thirty-nine years old – average ages for all ancient Egyptians. Degenerative joint diseases in the lumbar spine and the knee were common for the workers due to excessive manual labour, and many also suffered fractures to the cranium and extremities, the most common breaks being to the ulna and radius in the arm and fibula in the leg.[63] One man survived leg amputation, indicating the workers were provided with quality healthcare.

BUILT BY ALIENS?

Although we have the human remains of the people who built the pyramids, there are still those who believe such work was beyond the skills of man. The primitive tools available at the time also add to this myth and these difficulties are emphasised when reconstructions are carried out. This has led many fringe archaeologists to believe that they were built using lost methods, techniques and tools, or even they were built by a long-lost race or extra-terrestrials.

The idea of aliens building the pyramids was introduced by Erich Von Däniken in *Chariots of the Gods*, first published in 1968. He adapted the nineteenth-century idea that the pyramids were built with divine inspiration for the modern, space-loving 1960s. Instead of the Atlanteans and God as superior intelligence, he adapted it to aliens. He believed that due to the primitive tools, it would have taken 664 years to build the Great Pyramid. Von Däniken made the connection with the stars through the artwork of the Egyptians, which he believed were overrun with images of winged creatures (plate 7) and deities travelling across the sky in boats (plate 8). He interpreted this as showing that the gods were in fact visitors from other planets:

> A Utopian archaeological year is due, during which archaeologists, physicist, chemists, geologists, metallurgists and all the corresponding branches of these sciences ought to concentrate their efforts on one single question: did our forefathers receive visits from outer space?[64]

According to Von Däniken's interpretations of the texts, these gods will return at some point and the pyramid was a freezing chamber where the significant dead could be preserved until Ra, an alien, came back from the sky to revive them. He viewed mummification as a means of preserving the body in preparation for this return. Apparently, in March 1963, a biologist from the University of Oklahoma claimed the skin cells of the Egyptian mummy, Mene, were capable of living, even though she had been dead for thousands of years. Getting a copy of this original report would be particularly interesting. Von Däniken wonders how the Egyptians learned about this method of reanimation, and speculates that the 'gods' or space travellers transmitted the information to them.

It is very difficult to take Von Däniken seriously as there are so many things about the research which is fundamentally wrong, such as stating that the galleries of the pyramids are decorated in fabulous colours and that the workmen did not use torches in the tombs as there is no sign of blackening on the walls.

Further work on the alien theory was presented in 1976 when the space probe Viking II took photographs of the surface of Mars, which to some looked like a face, whereas to others it looked like shadows on a rock. This rock formation is a mile long and 1,500 feet high, and is on a place on Mars 'where no face belongs'.[65] Some have suggested the face resembled the face of the Sphinx, and believe that Martians carved the Sphinx 12,000 years ago, before fleeing Earth to avoid an imminent comet impact. Strangely enough, the main instigator of this theory is Richard Hoagland, a former NASA consultant. He still continues these studies today with the Enterprise Mission, which investigates Mars and the Moon. He claims that they have discovered man-made structures, and near the face he claims lie crumbling, highly technological pyramids, showing they were 'left by someone who tried to make Mars home'. As the images are not conclusive, and as no one can go to Mars to investigate properly, this theory is open to interpretation. It is interesting, however, to note that the formula is the same except, instead of archaeologists and Egyptologists being attacked for disagreeing with the findings, NASA are criticised here.

HOW WERE THEY BUILT?

An even bigger question than who built the pyramids is how were they built? Even Egyptologists cannot agree on this.

Although Egyptologists have lots of ideas about construction, they all agree that it was achieved through hard work, determination and manpower. It would have been much easier if the Egyptians had left a record of how they had built them, but they did not. They clearly felt it was obvious enough that records did not need to be made. The only record we have is that of Herodotus, who was told how the pyramids were constructed:

> The method employed was to build it in steps or, as some call them tiers or terraces. When the base was complete, the blocks for the first tier above it were lifted from ground level by contrivances made of short timbers; on this first tier there was another, which raised the blocks a stage higher, then yet another which raised them yet higher. Each tier, or story had its set of levers, or it may be that they used the same one which being easy to carry they shifted up from stage to stage as soon as its load was dropped into place.[66]

This sounds perfectly plausible, and levers and rockers have been discovered in the archaeological record.

RECONSTRUCTING HERODOTUS'S MACHINE

A highway construction engineer, Lowdermilk, decided to try to recreate Herodotus's machine. He based it on a ratchet and lever system, similar to a car-jack, with the component parts created from seven hieroglyphs which he believed held symbolic meaning and a practical purpose within the construction.

The machine essentially suspended a block of stone between two external walls using looped ropes, which were raised using the ratchet mechanism which caught the loops and moved them upwards. The side walls of the machine were made using the *st* sign ⌡, (Isis), with the levers constructed from *w3s* sceptres ⌐ (divine power), which rested in notches formed the *h3st* sign ⌒⌒ (foreign lands), which acted as rockers enabling the levers to be lifted and lowered. The ropes forming the ratchet system are looped to resemble *ankhs* ☥ (eternal life), or *tyet* ⚱ (blood of Isis), while the ropes cradling the bottom of the stone block are knotted resembling the *t* ▭ and *s3* ⾖ signs. Two blocks are placed beneath the block as it is lifted so the ropes are taking the weight and with every small lift wedges are placed upon these blocks creating the *djed* pillar ⊟ (stability). He argues that as the *st*, *w3s*, *tyet* and *ankh* are often seen together in a funerary context, they must hold some significance as well as a reverence for work tools.[67]

When Lowdermilk tested his machine, it could lift a block weighing 3,160 pounds (1,436 kilos), using a team of seven men, with four men working eight *w3s* levers, two to place the wedges onto the *djed* supports and one to oversee. While this seems like a plausible means of moving the blocks, the machine is made of wood and would require importation of suitable hardwoods, as well as the employment of a team of carpenters to make enough of these machines to serve the site, as well as carpenters on standby for on site repairs. It seems a little over-thought out to be practical.

LEVITATION

Some theorists do not think such practical approaches are very exciting and suggest alternative ideas. One theory was introduced by a Californian software consultant, Maureen Clemmons, who suggested that wind power could be used to lift stone blocks through the use of kites. She carried out a number of experiments in the Californian desert, with the first successful one, in 2001, lifting a 3.5-ton obelisk into place with 15 mph winds. The tests failed when using heavier blocks, lifting 11 tonnes only a few feet off the ground. When applied to aiding the movement of blocks to build the pyramids, with the aid of rollers, the kites facilitated this transportation, as well as being capable of moving blocks up a ramp. While this method shows a possible method of moving the blocks, the absence of kites in the archaeological record should be taken into account. It is not. The seasonable element of the theory should also be taken into account, as the work rate, dependent on the wind, would be intermittent.

While her theories have a certain degree of scientific method behind it, they collapse when her inability to correctly read hieroglyphs is used as evidence. The *djed* pillar, known to be the back-bone of Osiris and to be a symbol of stability and rebirth, is interpreted by Clemmons as an anchoring method for the kites. At least this is acknowledged as being the 'weak point' in her theory.[68]

Collins, in *Gods of Eden*, also suggests levitation, but through the use of sonic technology, which he believes was widely used in early Egypt by an Elder Culture, but as the population increased and prisoners of war could be used to build large monuments, quicker ways were devised and the old sonic ways were forgotten.[69] He asserts that the Giza pyramids were built in 15,000–10,000 BCE by the Elder Culture, who then left Egypt, taking their sonic technology to other parts of the world before disappearing.[70] The pyramids were apparently built using sonic-drills cutting through granite at a speed-rate 500 times greater than modern tools, although there is no supporting evidence. He describes how they used sonic technology in the construction of the burial chamber in the Great Pyramid, using Pythagoras triangles, which he claims are best for conducting sound. This is why a voice echoes in there. He also claims the sarcophagus has acoustic properties, which were first noted by Petrie in 1881 when he removed the lid. He struck the empty box, and he said it

produced a deep bell-like sound of extraordinary, eerie beauty.

Collins thinks the internal structure of the sarcophagus was designed with this harmonic resonance in mind, whereas most people would put it down to coincidence.

Collins attempted to move large blocks of stone using this sonic theory, but all his trials in Essex were unsuccessful. He played various chords at large blocks through loudspeakers with no effect, before he decided to play the sound of a Tibetan singing bowl through the speakers. This still did not work.[71] The only evidence he has that sonic technology could move stones is tenuous. He is a great fan of the experiments of John Keeley (1827–98), who claimed he was able to move blocks and even disintegrate granite with the power of sound. However, he did not record the exact method and when he was asked by his financiers to disclose this or risk being sued, he destroyed his equipment and research. No one has ever been able to replicate these experiments. The other piece of evidence he uses are unspecific records from Tibet. A Swede recorded the travels of a man known as Jarl in the 1920s or 1930s who claims to have seen the Tibetan monks move rocks using trumpets. Neither the monks nor the temple still exist and with no real information about the witness or when it happened, this cannot be verified. As a final piece of evidence Collins presents the Biblical story of bringing down the walls of Jericho, but even he admits there is no supporting archaeological evidence for this event but:

> Of course it does not mean the event did not take place.[72]

The lack of supporting evidence for the theories presented is explained by the fact that the Elder Culture left, taking the technology with them. Collins proves the existence of the Elder Culture using the Edfu Building Texts, which refer to the time of the gods and the Hall of Records where all this lost knowledge is stored.[73]

NATURAL OUTCROPS

Another particularly entertaining theory of how the pyramid was built was introduced by Bruce Voigt in December 2006:[74]

> The Pyramids of Giza and the likes were not built by Egyptians or aliens. They simply evolved – they grew.

He believes that as a natural phenomenon they developed under water and emerged fully formed when the waters abated. When questioned about how the chambers and corridors were created, he boldly stated it was the work of squirrels and chipmunks. The Egyptians apparently laid claim to the pyramids as a reuse of natural building materials.

Another theory is that of 'creating' the large blocks in situ through the use of a mould and a concrete-type substance poured into it. However, this method, although favoured as an explanation for the manoeuvrability of such large blocks, has widely been dismissed as there are chisel marks on many of the blocks and non-uniformity in size and shape.

While the theories are interesting, they do not take into account the evidence we *do* have. There is enough archaeological evidence to put together quite plausible theories of construction, but it is important to consider all pyramids and not just the pyramids of Giza.

TOOLS

Many tools have been discovered at the pyramid sites consisting of copper chisels and hammers, and corresponding chisel marks on the limestone blocks of the pyramid show they were used at least to trim the blocks. Wooden wedges were also used in the stone quarries for the cutting of limestone, which were placed in fissures in the rock and soaked in water until they expanded and split the rock.

Tools used in the manoeuvring and placement of large blocks, in the form of rockers, have been discovered in the foundation deposit at Deir el Bahri, Luxor. Tomb scenes suggest that these rockers were used, along with wooden levers, to lift large blocks into place. These wooden rockers were semi-circular and to use them, a lever was inserted under one side of a stone block and a rocker was placed underneath. A lever was then used to raise the other side of the block. The rocker eased the movement so further wooden support blocks could be placed beneath the stone block, raising it from the floor by a few inches. This would be repeated until the blocks were raised the necessary height.

The manoeuvring of large blocks has never really been questioned by Egyptologists. One tomb at el Bersheh shows a colossal statue of the tomb owner, Djhutihotep, being transported to its final resting place. The statue is placed on wooden sledges and pulled by hundreds of men. Some men are carrying wooden levers, which were used to get the statue onto the sledge and to manoeuvre the statue at the end of its journey. These levers were 2-metre-long wooden sticks, and reconstructions indicate four of them were enough to move a block of 2.5 tons with two on each side – one lever to each man.

A New Kingdom stela from the reign of Ahmose I (1570–1546 BC), belonging to an official called Neferperet, shows large blocks transported by sledge from the Quarry of Tura pulled by oxen rather than men. Oxen could have been used for transportation on construction ramps up to a height of 20 metres (65 feet), and could do the work of many men.[75] As many of the workmen building the pyramids were farmers rendered idle due to the annual inundation, a natural assumption is that their livestock were also idle and could be used for the task of pulling large-scale blocks. In addition, during the inundation the River Nile flowed closer to the pyramid sites, so large blocks could be transported on barges to a quay near the pyramid and then transported the shorter distance across land to the structure itself.[76]

A type of 'railway' was found at the Middle Kingdom site at Lisht constructed with wooden tracks covered with alluvial mud, making the movement of large blocks easy.[77] More common, however, was a system of wooden logs placed under the sledge lubricated with the aid of Nile silt and water. As the sledge progressed, the logs were moved from the rear to the front and a large team of men were required for this task.

This method of transportation and manoeuvring enabled the first course of stones to be laid for the pyramid. Although difficult, the levers, rockers and support block method could be utilised for the next course, in addition to mud-brick elevation ramps. Herodotus mentions the use of ramps to transport blocks to the higher levels of the structure:

10. Construction ramp, Karnak, Luxor.

11. Ramped causeway, Deir el Bahri, Luxor.

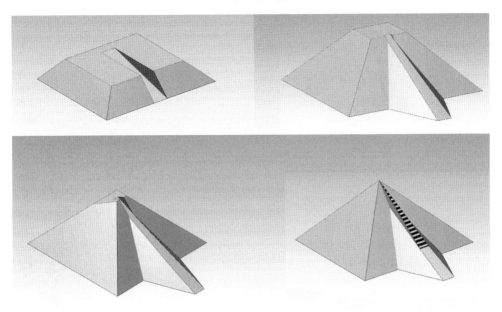

12. Various suggested ramp systems. *(Photography courtesy of David Granger)*

> It took ten years of this oppressive slave-labour to build the track along which the blocks
> were hauled – a work in my opinion, of hardly less magnitude than the pyramid itself,
> for it is five furlongs in length, sixty feet wide, forty eight feet high at its highest point
> and constructed of polished stone block decorated with carvings of animals.[78]

The best example of such a construction ramp is visible behind the first pylon at
Karnak temple in Luxor (fig. 10). It is approximately 5 metres (10 cubits) wide and
the centre was reinforced using wooden beams supporting the weight of the blocks
being transported over them, as well as the weight of the ramp itself. On either side
of the 5 metre (10 cubits) wide ramp were reinforcement walls of stone or mud-
brick and a number of these have survived, leading from quarries and stone stores
throughout Egypt (fig. 11). Large blocks were moved to the top of the monument
under construction via these ramps, and once the structure was complete the ramp
was dismantled and the material used elsewhere.

It is widely accepted that such ramps were used to build the pyramids, although
there are disagreements on the type of ramp used (fig. 12), with the main concern
being the amount of material needed to produce it. If a straight ramp was used to
construct the Great Pyramid, it would extend for over a mile and would contain as
much material as the pyramid itself. Petrie further drew attention to another problem
with this type of straight ramp. He estimated a mud-brick ramp could only sustain its
own weight up to 116 metres (380 feet), even if there were supports running through
it. As the original height of the Great Pyramid was 147 metres (485 feet), according to
Petrie's measurements it would have been unable to support its own weight and would
have collapsed. If spiral ramps were used, circling the pyramid, the height of a single

ramp would not exceed this point, but further problems occur with angles of ascent. An additional problem would be that of the entire pyramid being enclosed in mud-brick, making it impossible to notice discrepancies in angles until the ramp was removed, when it would be too late to fix any problems that had arisen. There have been many different suggestions for the placement of ramps, but none of them are faultless and not all Egyptologists agree on a single theory. However, numerous ramps have been discovered at various quarry sites, temples and pyramids, including the pyramid of Meidum, the mortuary temple of Menkaura and the pyramid of Amenemhat I at Lisht,[79] indicating that they were used frequently for the movement of large blocks for the construction of large-scale monuments. Sadly, if such a ramp was used for the construction of the Giza pyramids, all traces of the material were moved.

It is impossible to say for sure how the pyramids were built. As the internal structure of each pyramid is different, the method of construction for each pyramid was also different. This means that it is in fact impossible to ask how the pyramids were built and receive a single answer. Instead, it would be more appropriate to study each pyramid in isolation, studying the available evidence for each site, and present a methodology theory for each monument rather than a 'one size fits all' theory based on the Giza pyramids alone.

PYRAMIDOLOGY

Some authors are not so much concerned with the why and the how as with the choice of shape. The shape of the pyramid is iconic of Egypt, and in the 1960s and 1970s this shape was adopted by a group of new age individuals who believed it held power. Pyramidology became very popular and considered any pyramid regardless of size or material as powerful. However, as with anything to do with the generic term 'pyramids', it started with the Great Pyramid at Giza.

This idea originated in the 1920s with Frenchman Antoine Bovis. He visited the burial chamber of the Great Pyramid and claimed he saw dustbins in the chamber with dead cats in them. These cats were perfectly preserved, despite the humidity. However, he offers no explanation as to why there were bins of dead cats in the pyramid. He returned home and built a wooden scale model of the pyramid and placed a dead cat beneath it. He did not explain where this cat came from either, but reported that it subsequently became mummified.

In the 1960s Karel Drbal, a Czech radio engineer, continued with the experiments with pyramids and claimed a blunt razor blade could be sharpened if placed under a pyramid. He patented the Cheops Pyramid Razorblade Sharpener, which was initially made from cardboard and then from Styrofoam. Reports throughout Europe claimed yoghurt and milk kept beneath a pyramid remained fresh without refrigeration.[80] In the 1970s the mantel was grasped by Bill Schul, who wrote three books on Pyramid power: *The Secret Power of Pyramids*, *The Psychic Power of Pyramids* and *Pyramids and the Second Reality*. He conducted a series of experiments which showed that skin temperature was higher after spending an hour inside the pyramid in his garden, although the experiments were ruined by a natural drop in the outside temperature at the time of the readings.[81] They also took blood tests before and after entering the pyramids which apparently showed a drop in both red and white blood cell counts, iron and copper, but a rise in glucose for the male participants, and the exact opposite in the female participants. They cannot offer an interpretation or shed light on the possible significance. They also did not do any tests where they sat for an hour within a square or rectangular box with which to compare them to.

Such considerations were, however, taken into account by Jack Dyer in 1975 with his plant growth experiment, where he planted garden-type beans in different shaped boxes: pyramid, prisms and rectangle. After ten days' growth he measured the height and stalk diameter and for ten of the fifteen samples, those grown in the pyramid were a little bigger than the others.[82] Numerous members of the public were encouraged to carry out experiments in their own homes, all of which are used as evidence even though they were not carried out in controlled environments. We have tales of one man who put a cardboard pyramid under his fish tank and a number of the fish died as algae started to form on the tank and the water became murky. He removed the filter from the tank and placed a plastic pyramid in the water and the algae went away and his surviving fish became more active and more vibrant.[83] One woman decided to give up using cosmetic face products and instead simply used water kept in a pyramid and her skin looked better. She admits to having doubts:

> Maybe it's positive thinking, maybe it's just giving my skin a chance to breathe, but whatever, my skin hasn't looked this good in twenty years.[84]

While anecdotal experiences are hard to prove or disprove, the pyramid power phenomena eventually lost the popularity of the masses, with only the occasional book published on the subject such as Toth and Neilson's *Pyramid Power* (1985), Venugopalam's *Healing Power of the Pyramid* (2004) and Bonewitz's *Pyramid Power* (2009), which comes with its own crystal pyramid to try at home. Far more has been written about how they were built and why than the power inherent within.

PYRAMIDS IN MODERN MEDIA

No matter how the pyramids were built or who built them, they will always affect those who witness them. For this reason pyramids have been a part of Western culture for centuries, as a popular tourist destination from the pharaonic period. Burchard, visiting in 1175, could clearly only see two of the pyramids and did not appear to have got too close:

> Two mountains of square plan, built of very large stones of marble and other materials; they are admirable constructions, an arrow's distance from each other and of the same height and width ... A mile from Cairo, there was a garden of balm trees, irrigated by a sacred fountain, at which the Virgin Mary was said to have washed the infant Jesus.[85]

Some visited the site for adventure, and in 1581 French traveller Jean Palerme recorded that at the Great Pyramid:

> One gentleman eager to make the ascent did in fact reach the summit, but ... succumbed to vertigo, fell and was smashed to pieces. The crushed remains no longer looked like a human being.[86]

Not all the tourists met such a sticky end and Constance Sitwell wrote in 1927 of her visit:

> The sun beat down on that stupendous slope of stone and up on it a scattering of tiny men were crawling like sluggish flies; and I too started to climb up; we were making for the small opening that led to the King's Chamber.[87]

In addition to travel records, pyramids have been involved in fictional books, movies and cartoons reinforcing all of the myths that have built up around them. For example, in *Khai of Ancient Khem* the idea of an early superior race, with superior technology and intelligence, is embraced. A fantastic plot means historical accuracy is not necessary, as it can be passed off as their lost superior technology. The central focus of the capital of Egypt (Khem), Asorbes, is a large pyramid:

> The heart of the city was a golden pyramid, almost complete now, whose base covered twenty-three acres. Built of fifteen million tons of yellow stone, it towered to a height of almost six hundred feet.[88]

This pyramid was not just a tomb for the king, but was a complex city:

> Khasathut's pyramid was not an almost solid mountain of stone, but a multi-storied maze of shafts, corridors and chamber whose total internal capacity was perhaps as great as two per cent of the whole. That is to say for every fifty cubic feet of solid stone there was perhaps one of air or living space. There were also sophisticated air-conditioning systems, with inlets and outlets through panels of perforated stone in the pyramid's outer skin and a catchment system which provided the massive monument with its water.[89]

This pyramid was built by slaves who were treated appallingly, which distressed Khai:

> Khai, too, had found the sight of the myriad half-naked brown and verminous bodies that struggled, sweated, bled and died under the lash of Khasathut's overseers painful and offensive.[90]

King Khasathut is barbaric, insane and a tyrant who is from an alien race, which later return to their planet in the manner of Von Däniken's theory, in a giant space ship in the form of a golden pyramid.

The idea of aliens is one presented in *Dr Who* in the classic episode the *Pyramids of Mars*, where the Doctor is confronted with the extra-terrestrial Sutekh (Seth). He travels to Mars in order to locate the eye of Horus, which is situated beneath the pyramid there. He needs so solve a number of logical and philosophical problems thoroughly embracing the idea of the pyramids containing knowledge and secrets.

A reversal of the alien connection is demonstrated in the futuristic cartoon *Futurama*, *A Pharaoh to Remember* (2002). The air crew go to the planet Osiris 4, where the inhabitants are building a pyramid for the king, Hamenhotpe. The team are captured and put to work as slaves to help build the pyramid. Fry makes the association with ancient Egypt and is informed that contrary to belief, the aliens learned their skills from the ancient Egyptians. The pyramid itself has a large seated statue of the king with a door between the feet and the king was to be buried with his slaves and cats. Although somewhat futuristic in style, all the typical stereotypes are there, including a *nemes* headdress for all and slaves building the pyramids encouraged by large whips. The internal chambers of the pyramid, however, are designed to resemble a casino rather than a tomb.

In the children's book *Magnificent Mummies*, a family of mummies actually live inside the pyramid with electricity, a bedroom and everything you would expect to find in a house. In *Scooby Doo and Mummy's the Word*, beneath the pyramid is a river with a distinct upstairs and downstairs to the internal structure. When Scooby Doo and his friends leave, the mummy slams the door behind him, almost as if it is his home.

Terry Pratchett's *Pyramids* adopts the idea that the pyramids hold answers:

> The energy streaming up from their paracosmic peaks may, in chapters to come, illuminate many mysteries: why tortoises hate philosophy, why too much religion is bad for goats and what is it that handmaidens actually do.[91]

Cayce's theory of underground chambers and tunnels linking the Sphinx to the pyramid is taken up in *Beneath the Pyramid*, a tale of law and order in the time of Ramses II:

> The five conspirators stood beside the stela and consulted their map one last time, urging each other to continue despite the fear that racked them. They moved the stela aside and there before their eyes was the mud seal that marked the position of the mouth of hell, the gateway to the bowels of the earth.

The conspirators enter into the tunnel and are delighted to realise that it is:

> the long forgotten passageway ... from the Sphinx to Khufu's giant monument.[92]

The mystical side of the myth of the pyramids is not neglected in fiction and Jacq states that:

the great pyramid of Khufu, which was the mysterious energy centre on which the harmony of the entire country depended.[93]

Terry Pratchett takes this mysteriousness one step further:

> Also our special offer this aeon is various measurements of paracosmic significance built into the fabric at no extra cost.[94]

Adopting the theory of Collins, Pratchett has the pyramid built through the power of levitation, although by magic rather than sound waves. The blocks need no human interaction, other than to hold the mooring ropes keeping the blocks in check before they are put in place:

> They were flowing between the quarry and the site, drifting silently across the landscape above deep rectangular shadows.[95]

It is further asserted that the pyramids of Djelibeybi store time and needed to be 'flared off' on a daily basis to prevent rips in time occurring. He makes interesting and fun references to such theories as discussed in this chapter, claiming that pyramids do not sharpen razor blades, they simply return them to a time when they were sharp.[96]

The myths surrounding the Giza pyramids (for that is where the majority are focused) are varied, and all originate in the uncertainty surrounding these monuments and how they were built. While there is any doubt in the minds of the Egyptologists as to how they were built, there will always be theories introduced which cannot be proved or disproved. That they cannot be disproved is the key to the myths of the Giza pyramids and although the evidence is often flimsy, the main argument is that even Egyptologists are not sure. Even though we have a great deal of evidence with which to formulate plausible and provable theories, it will take a while before these fringe theories are abandoned altogether. The pyramids have been extant in Egypt for 4,500 years and have been part of our culture for centuries, and no doubt they will be an element of our culture for centuries to come. Unquestionably, more myths, theories and research will develop, enhancing our knowledge of the Egyptians and their technology.

CHAPTER 3

THE MYTH OF ALEXANDRIA

Places like Luxor or Giza in Egypt are legendary for their monuments, but they do not conjure in the mind legends about the town or the people that lived there. Alexandria, on the other hand, does. It is situated on the northern coast of Egypt, facing the Mediterranean, and for centuries was used as the main entrance into Egypt from Europe.

Alexandria was founded on the site of a small Egyptian settlement called Rhakotis by Alexander the Great (plate 9) in 331 BCE, although he died before its completion. In total there were seventeen cities bearing the name Alexandria, but only the Egyptian one has survived the test of time.

THE MYTH BEGINS

From its very foundations Alexandria has been steeped in mystery and legend and Plutarch (46–120 BCE) records the founding of Alexandria in his *Life of Alexander* (fig. 13)

> After Alexander had conquered Egypt, he was anxious to found a great and populous Greek city there, to be called after him ... As he lay asleep he dreamed that a grey-haired man of venerable appearance stood by his side and recited these lines from the Odyssey:
>
> > Out of the tossing sea where it breaks on the beaches of Egypt
> > Rises an isle from the waters: the name that men give it is Pharos
>
> Alexander rose the next morning and immediately visited Pharos ... he declared that Homer, besides his other admirable qualities, was also a very far-seeing architect and he ordered the plan of the city to be designed so that it would conform to this site.

He stopped at Mareotis and decided to build his new city here. According to legend, he planned the outline by scattering grain around the would-be perimeter, identifying where the agora, city walls and temples should be situated. In the process of doing this, a flock of birds swooped down and carried away the grain. This was seen as a good omen for Alexandria.

13. Alexander the Great, British Museum.

The plans were drawn up by Deinocrates and the initial construction was started by Cleomenes.[1] Alexander wanted the city to exceed all other cities in size and splendour. After the death of Alexander, the city grew under the reign of Ptolemy I (305–282 BCE) and was completed under Ptolemy II (285-246 BCE). Sadly, all that remains of Alexander's original city is a small section in the Shallalat Gardens near the Eastern Gate.

With such beginnings, it is hardly surprising that Alexandria became a city of myth and legend. Alexander himself was a man of myth and although he never visited the city while alive, his role in its history was not over.

ALEXANDRIA'S FIRST VIP VISITOR

When Alexander died (323 BCE), his body was apparently placed within a sarcophagus decorated with paintings of his successes. The coffin within the sarcophagus was of hammered gold and the spaces between the body and the coffin were filled with aromatic spices. The coffin was closed with a golden lid and a purple robe embroidered in gold was thrown over the lid, showing his royal status.

According to some records, Alexander wanted his body buried in the Euphrates and originally his funeral procession travelled from Babylon to Macedonia. However, it was then decided that it should be transferred to the Siwa Oasis in Egypt, where at the beginning of his reign he approached the oracle of Amun regarding his right to rule. While being transported there, Ptolemy I seized his remains, burying them at Memphis. They were then removed by Ptolemy II and placed in a royal tomb at Soma, the Greek section of Alexandria. The tomb structure was made of Greek and Egyptian marble, with a colonnaded courtyard and a flight of marble stairs leading to the subterranean chamber known as the 'Place of Lamentation'. This tomb is sadly now lost, and some think it was destroyed in the wars in the second half of the third century CE, although records indicate it was still visible during the early Islamic period. It is suggested that it may have stood on the site where the mosque of Nabi Daniel was built, at the junction of Horreya and Nabi Daniel Streets.[2]

This tomb became a site of pilgrimage throughout the Roman period, with many emperors visiting, including Julius Caesar; Marc Antony; Augustus Caesar, who adorned the body with flowers, placing a golden crown upon his head, in 30 BCE; Severus; Caracalla; Vespasian; Hadrian; and Aurelian. Other emperors simply used Alexander as a benchmark by which to measure their own deeds.

ALEXANDRIA: THE COSMOPOLITAN CITY

Alexandria was an interesting city for reasons other than being the burial place of Alexander. It was essentially a Greek city, thanks to the influence of the Ptolemies. Only three cities in Egypt were recognised as being Greek: Alexandria, Naukratis and Ptolemais Hermaion in the Thebaid, each town dominated by a Greek élite. Native Egyptians were a small proportion of the population in Alexandria as they favoured the cities further south. This segregation was encouraged by the city enclosure wall, which separated the Greek world from the Egyptian countryside. Even the coins of the early Ptolemies were based on Greek rather than Egyptian ideologies, with images of eagles and thunderbolts fully accentuating the importance of Greek/Hellenistic culture over the Egyptian. However, the burials of the Alexandrian Greeks, while initially Greek in nature, became more Egyptianised by the end of the Ptolemaic period and they had even adopted the practice of mummification.[3]

Alexandria attracted tourists during the Graeco-Roman period due to the numerous temples, large theatres, the Poseidum (a temple to the god Poseidon) and the Emporium, a shopping district with bazaars and warehouses.[4] The city was also a centre of pilgrimage for those seeking intellectual and spiritual enlightenment. Not all of Alexandria, however, was wealthy and intellectual and the Canopus region in particular had a reputation of being a seedy holiday resort, especially in Roman times – a den of iniquity full of prostitution and alcohol.[5]

The Alexandrians were very cosmopolitan in nature, with 'a tolerance for difference'. So, prostitutes and drunks were as accepted in Alexandria as everyone else. This acceptance was greatly frowned upon by Rome as it was seen as decadent and against good moral behaviour. Victorian authors using this Roman model utilised the term 'Alexandrianism' to mean 'degeneration',[6] reflecting all the negative aspects of the city.

In the Roman period, Alexandria was called *Alexandria ad Aegyptum*, meaning 'Alexandria *by* Egypt', indicating that it was not considered a legitimate part of the Eastern world and Egypt, but as an extension of Europe.

As a major cosmopolitan European city, it was a melting-pot of cultures. Archaeological evidence indicates there were Asian merchants, inhabitants from the Greek and Aegean islands, people from Syria, Cyrene, Arabia, Babylonia, Assyria, Media, Persia, Cathaginia, Italy, Gaul, Iberia and India.[7] Despite this multi-culturalism there was a distinct hierarchy in Alexandria and to be a citizen, one's father and mother should be from Alexandria. Beneath Alexandrians in the hierarchy were the Hellenes (Greeks from other cities) and the Jews, as many were Hellenised to such an extent that they no longer understood Hebrew or Aramaic.

There were a number of Jews in Alexandria living in the Jewish quarter, governed by Jewish law and council. Although they effectively lived in their own city, they accepted the Hellenistic cultural norms in both life and death and Jewish funerary stelae emulated Hellenistic forms with reference to Graeco-Roman mythology, while still retaining their Jewish identity. Clearly a case of being Alexandrian first and Jewish second, upholding the traditions of the city foremost. Many Alexandrian Jews were wealthy, working as moneylenders and merchants, although like any businessmen they were not averse to trading with other social or ethnic groups.[8]

The Jews in Alexandria were instrumental to religious history, as there is a legend that seventy rabbis were held in seventy huts on the island of Pharos by Ptolemy II and told to produce Greek versions of the Hebrew scripture, presumably to put into the library at the Mouseion. Each produced a Greek version of the Old Testament (*Septuagint*) which was identical, something viewed as a good omen. The Jews commemorated this miracle annually on the island of Pharos.[9] This is only one element helping to construct the reputation Alexandria held as a place of learning.

CHRISTIAN ALEXANDRIA

During the Christian period, Alexandria seems to have reached its peak politically and intellectually. From 325 CE the Bishop of Alexandria was not only the primate of Egypt but also of the Byzantine Church, putting Alexandria on the map in the Christian world. However, until the fifth century the Alexandrian Christians were all Greek and in 444 CE an Egyptian, Sioscorus, was elected as patriarch, much to the chagrin of the Greeks, who found this unacceptable. It was not long before he was deposed, exiled and replaced with a Hellene.[10] Excavations at Kom el Dikka (fig. 14) by the Polish/Egyptian team (1960s to present) have uncovered an elaborate fourth-century CE city, filled with theatres, bath houses, shops, roads and houses, showing at this time it was still a cosmopolitan city (fig. 15). These are the only archaeological remains preserved and boast the only surviving theatre of the four hundred that the city once had (plate 10).

The Christian history of Alexandria led to the city gaining a reputation as a spiritual place, and one worthy of increased pilgrimage. There were various pilgrimage sites

14. Roman city, Kom el Dikka, Alexandria. (*Photograph courtesy of Brian Billington*)

15. Byzantine village, Kom el Dikka, Alexandria.

in Alexandria, including the modern monastery of Abu Mina which lies on the site of the basilica dedicated to the memory of the martyr St Menas. Other martyrs include Saints Cyrus and John, who were commemorated at Menouthis. This site was not as large as Abu Mina but still very important. However, the most important martyr was St Mark, who died on the festival day of Serapis at a place called Boucalis, which means 'Oxen Pasture', to the east of town, near the modern Bibliotheca Alexandrina. He taught in Alexandria before his death and converted many people, including a number of Jews, to Christianity. The shrine was an important pilgrimage centre until 829 CE, when two Venetians acquired the body from its guardians and smuggled it out of Egypt to Venice, where the body remains today. However, this transaction was not as straightforward as it sounds and various myths have arisen surrounding the sale of this body. Some believe the guardians could not bear to part with the body of St Mark and substituted the body with that of Alexander the Great, as his popularity had waned and was replaced by St Mark.[11] If this is the case, does Alexander now lie in Venice? Or is it truly St Mark? These are questions we may never be able to answer, but are intriguing nonetheless.

However, despite this deeply Christian history, like the Jewish burials, the Christian tombs have friezes of pagan hunting and environmental scenes rather than scenes from the Bible as one would expect, showing they were Alexandrian first and Christian second. There was clearly something about the city that encouraged great patriotism. This hold was picked up by Cavafy in his *Of the Jews (AD 50)*:

> The Hedonism and Art of Alexandria
> Kept him as their dedicated son.[12]

WONDERS OF THE ANCIENT WORLD

The most famous building in Alexandria for a thousand years of its history was the Lighthouse of Pharos, which was one of the Wonders of the Ancient World, but like everything else in Alexandria there is little remaining, although fragments are being discovered in the underwater excavations taking place in the Eastern Harbour (fig. 16). Ptolemy I began the construction of the lighthouse in 290 BCE, although it was not finished until after his death, in 285 BCE, during the reign of Ptolemy II.

The lighthouse was designed by the architect Sostratos of Crudus and was built in a considerably short period of time, using large numbers of slaves for the job. It was constructed within a colonnaded courtyard and comprised four tiers; the bottom was square, the next octagonal, then cylindrical and finally the lantern at the top, projecting a beam of light which could be seen from 160 kilometres (100 miles) away (fig. 17). The tower stood a total of 135 metres high, with a statue of Poseidon standing a further 7 metres on top of the lantern. Fragments of this statue have been discovered in the waters of the Eastern Harbour. Due to the weight of this colossal structure, architectural reinforcement was required to the rock beneath it. The whole lighthouse was encased in limestone, which produced a reflective white surface,

Above: 16. Objects from the bay at Alexandria, Open Air Museum, Kom el Dikka, Alexandria.

Right: 17. Lighthouse of Alexandria from Al Gharnati (early twelfth century). (*After El Daly, 2005*)

making it more visible from the sea, and was surrounded by an enclosure wall the length of seven stadiums.

The lighthouse was not just a light, but was filled every day with hundreds of visitors, both Alexandrians and foreigners. In the first section of the lighthouse, the square section was filled with administrative offices and military barracks, including stables for over 300 horses. The octagonal section was the tourist floor, where refreshments of lamb on sticks and drinks were sold and a balcony projecting out over the sea gave beautiful views of Alexandria and the Mediterranean. The top section held the fire that burned twenty-four hours a day and was amplified using a mirror constructed from a curved sheet of polished metal or, as some suggest, finely wrought glass or transparent stone. There was a spiral ramp leading to the beacon chamber, enabling donkeys to carry the fuel for the fire. It is suggested there may have been hydraulic machinery of some type to help bring more fuel to the top of the tower.[13] The donkeys were also rented out to tourists who did not want to walk to the top of the tower, but wanted to benefit from the views. There has been some discussion as to what was used for fuel, in a country with very few trees. Herodotus discusses naphtha, a type of petroleum which forms on the surface of ponds, as a means of heat and light,[14] and some have suggested this was used. However, with the hearth being lit twenty-four hours a day, it is quite probable the stone at the top of the tower would crack under the heat.

There is a myth that the lighthouse was used as a weapon, with the mirror used to concentrate solar rays on approaching ships, setting them alight before they approached the harbour. The Arabs were apparently angered at this use of the lighthouse to scorch their ships.[15] This has been disputed, but does make an interesting myth appropriate for the builders of one of the seven Wonders of the Ancient World.

The port of Alexandria was a busy one, as this was for many centuries a major trade centre. A guide to the trade networks written in the first century CE, *Periplus of the Erythraean Sea*, claims there were ships at Alexandria from as far as the Horn of Africa, the port of Andulus and Aksumite, Empire of Ethiopian Highlands.[16] The produce shipped was varied with silk and rice imported from the Orient, ivory from Africa, and grain and corn from Egypt to be exported to Greece and Rome. It is said that Rome lived for four months of the year on grain exported from Egypt, which was nicknamed 'the breadbasket of Rome.'

There are many theories as to how the Pharos lighthouse collapsed and no one is really certain. One theory was that the lighthouse was used for over a thousand years, only to be destroyed by an earthquake in 796 CE. Another theory is that it was destroyed in 850 CE by Emperor Michael III, who was jealous of Alexandria and deceived the Arabs into destroying Alexandria's main tourist attraction. However, when Idrisi visited Alexandria in 1115 CE the lighthouse was still there and Yusuf Ibn al-Shaikh also described the lighthouse in place in 1165 CE, although the beacon had been replaced with a mosque built by Ibn Tulun (868–905 BCE). He even included the structure of the original lighthouse in his mosque in Cairo, as the minaret resembles the lighthouse tower (fig. 18). It is believed that the Alexandria lighthouse was the prototype of all lighthouses in the known world at the time.[17]

18. Ibn Tulun mosque, Cairo. The minaret is modelled on the lighthouse of Alexandria.

It is quite likely the lighthouse met its fate in the earthquake of 1365 CE. Large blocks tumbled into the sea and even in 1480 CE the foundations of the tower were still standing, although these were to be built over by the Sultan of Egypt, Qait Bey (plate 11). His fortress and castle included the marble foundation blocks in its structure.[18]

INTELLECTUAL HISTORY

After the lighthouse, the Mouseion was the second most famous building in Alexandria and one which drew thousands of people to the city, including scholars and scientists from all parts of the known world, and is the key to the myth of Alexandria. It was:

> untouched by the ravages of time, it housed everything one would ever care to know or recall, a perfect museum that one might roam with abandon, a true temple of the Muses.

The muses were goddesses of literature and the arts and this 'temple' comprised a library, palace, museum, laboratory, botanical garden and shrine. It also acted as a university, with lecture theatres, dormitories, refectory, cloisters and colonnades, and was a beacon of Greek culture, although Egyptian ideas and works were admitted once they were translated into Greek. However, the library was not open to the general public and was entered by invitation only, ensuring that only the world's greatest minds had access to the collection.

It was situated in the Beta quadrant of Alexandria, which included the royal palaces and other important administrative buildings. The Mouseion was commissioned by Ptolemy I and was completed in approximately 300 BCE. He wanted to possess every book ever written and he achieved this by any means possible. All ships entering the harbour were searched and all texts were removed in order to be copied at the Mouseion. However, rather than returning the originals to the owners, the copies were returned instead. Ptolemy was so keen to acquire as many books as possible that he was also sold many forgeries. All works were permissible as long as they were from people of note, and Oriental, Persian and Hebrew texts were translated into Greek and placed in the library. By the end of the third century BCE, a list of accepted authors had been selected and any works by them were greatly sought after in order to possess their complete works. Many great authors who were not on the list, however, were not included in the library.

Many other people over the centuries added to the collection, with their own works or those they had acquired, including the complete libraries of Aristotle, who Strabo reports was the first person to have collected a library of books. Ptolemy III (246–222 BCE) was so keen to acquire the works of Aechylus, Sophocles and Euripides that he approached the library in Athens and asked to borrow them. His reputation preceded him and they asked him to leave a large deposit of fifteen silver talents before they sent the texts. Once he had the manuscripts, he told them they could keep the silver.[19] Cleopatra VII later acquired the library of Pergamon, which had nearly a quarter of a million manuscripts, making the Alexandria library the greatest in the world. The Mouseion was reputed to hold 490,000 scrolls.

So why did Ptolemy want to collect all the books ever written in the world? One could answer that he was collecting merely to have all the ideas, histories and philosophies in one place. The library and the collection of ideas, native and foreign, was an important aspect of the multi-cultural history of Alexandria. However, how multi-cultural was the city really? The Mouseion was another element of Alexandrian culture that was preserved only for Greeks, further segregating the Egyptians from the city. Others suggest he was following the lead of the Greek tyrants Hieron of Syracuse, Polycrates of Samos and Phillip II of Macedon, who tried to soften their reputations by presenting themselves as patrons of the arts.[20] Or perhaps he agreed with the age-old premise that knowledge was power. The Ptolemies were so adamant that theirs would be the only library that they banned the export of papyrus when they heard that the Pergamon rulers wished to follow suit. This ban was only semi-successful as it simply resulted in the rulers of Pergamon introducing a new writing material, *pergamenon*, or parchment.[21]

Other libraries existed in Alexandria, including the Serapeum, which was reached by one hundred steps and held 42,800 texts. This was known as the 'Daughter Library', as it held copies of works in the main library.[22] The subterranean chambers of the Serapeum were intended for the burial of the animals from the local bull cult. At

19. Pompey's pillar. (*Photograph courtesy of David Newby*)

the site stands Pompey's Pillar, a 25-metre (70-feet) high column carved from Aswan granite with a porphyry statue on the top (fig. 19). It was said to stand on the site of the original temple. This was the most prominent temple in Alexandria, as it stood on top of the hill known as the Acropolis. The pillar has nothing to do with Pompey. It was named by the crusaders travelling to Alexandria and was probably carved during the reign of Diocletian (297 CE). The pillar itself is a thing of legend, and in 1822 twenty-two people were reputed to have held a dinner party at the top of the pillar, complete with table, chairs and a waiter.

Although the Mouseion was the largest library and seat of learning in Alexandria, there were other schools known as *didaskateia* which comprised ad hoc meetings in temples or tombs. These schools focused entirely on Greek education, culture and philosophies, excluding Egyptian traditions.[23] It was not until the Roman period that non-Greeks were educated here, with learning Greek as a foreign language being introduced. The Mouseion was open to the greatest intellectual minds of the day, and for those who were not quite up to this standard the *didaskateia* would suffice. In the Christian period these schools were used for the teaching of Christian philosophy[24] and were important for making Alexandria the centre of the Christian teaching in the second century CE. During the fifth century CE, these schools developed into organised institutions[25] where students could pay to study with well-known scholars of grammar and rhetoric. It was one of the few institutions where both Christians and pagans studied and debated together.

The Mouseion was the centre of the intellectual world from 300 CE to 642 CE, and a number of famous philosophers and intellectuals were educated in Alexandria. By the Christian period it had become one of the hotbeds of the early Christian thought, rivalling Antioch and Carthage as a centre of Christian debate.[26]

This, unfortunately, was thought by some to have led to the destruction of the library. Some have blamed Julius Caesar (100–44 BCE) for the destruction as in his *De bello alexandrine* he records setting fire to a warehouse full of papyrus, although the location of the warehouse seems too far from the library. However, after the event, Seneca (3 BCE – 65 CE) writes that 40,000 books were burned in Alexandria. This was reinforced by Plutarch, who laments:

> Caesar was forced to repel the danger by using fire, which spread from the dockyards and destroyed the 'Great Library'.[27]

The number of books burned accidently by Caesar increased over the years from 40,000 to 700,000 in the various texts discussing the Alexandrian war of Caesar. However, when Strabo visited Alexandria in 24–20 BCE he failed to mention the library, which adds credence to the theory that the library had already disappeared by this point.[28] However, the loss of the royal library was not an end to the intellectual history of Alexandria as there were other libraries which were still operational, including a small one at the Mouseion itself, the Daughter Library at the Serapeum and a collection at the Caesareion, allowing the educational traditions to continue. The Mouseion was still an active centre during the fifth century and Synesius of Cyrene, one of Hypatia's students, records seeing it and the philosophers within,[29] and Hypatia's father Theon is one of the last recorded scholars of the Mouseion.

There are, however, legends regarding Arab destruction of the Serapeum library recorded by two writers, Abdullatif of Baghdad (*c.* 1200 CE) and Ibn al Qifti (*c.* 1172 CE). They both wrote about the Arab leader Calif Omar entering Alexandria in 646 CE and destroying the library. Abdullatif, on visiting the remains of the Serapeum, commented:

> I believe ... in it was the book-store which was burnt by Amr, by order of the Caliph Omar.

Ibn al-Qifti makes it clear that a letter to Caliph Omar regarding the fate of the Daughter Library of the Serapeum was answered:

> Touching the books you mention, if what is written in them agrees with the Book of God, they are not required; if it disagrees, they are not desired. Destroy them therefore.[30]

The books were then gathered up and distributed to the various bathhouses in Alexandria to be used as fuel. Apparently, it took six months for all of the books to be destroyed. It is this element of the account which has led many scholars to doubt its authenticity. As this story had not appeared before these twelfth-century records, it is assumed to be a construction of the time and not fact. It is suggested that this was written because of the Crusaders and their desire to purchase libraries from around the world, especially of classical authors, and it is suggested that Ibn Al-Qifti was showing there were worse things than selling their books: burning them. The West adopted this theory, as it seems that we require a violent and traumatic end to this library in order to uphold the mythological status surrounding it.

Today no one knows what the Mouseion looked like or even its exact location, but it has stood as a template for libraries and scholarship the world over since then. The US Library of Congress for example, has used the Mouseion as a template and requested any information from Egypt of what the original looked like in order to place a model at the door.[31] However, there is no information at present to be given.

ALEXANDRIA AND MOB RULE

In direct contrast to the quiet cerebral practice of the Mouseion, the other legendary aspect of Alexandrian history is the violence of the mob. It is documented from the Ptolemaic period onwards that Alexandria was a volatile city, with the 'mob' taking to the streets at the slightest provocation. That is not to say that many of these altercations were not instigated by the students of the universities in Alexandria. Teachers were often very territorial and demanded loyalty from their students, which could result in confrontations between the students of rival teachers. The activities of the mob over the centuries were excessive and it would be impossible to discuss every event, but it is safe to say that the mob were present in all periods of Alexandria's history and featured in all the political, economic and religious events.

The mob affected politics; many rulers would try to avoid provoking the mob into action, as once they had begun to protest there was little or no reasoning with them. A prime example was recorded by Diodorus (first century BCE), who saw a Roman citizen accidently run over and kill a cat, which was considered a bad omen, bringing bad luck to the city. The mob chased him to his home, trapping him inside. Although Ptolemy XII sent messengers to the crowd asking them to spare the Roman's life, it was to no avail, as the next morning

> the Roman citizen's unrecognisable corpse lay battered and broken in the empty street in front of his house.[32]

The mob were not from one faction of society and at one time or another the mob would be formed from different groups. For example, during the time of Trajan, although Jews were able to integrate into the highest levels of Alexandrian society, there were various problems which resulted in conflicts between Jews and gentiles. During the tumultuous reign of Caligula in 38 CE, the Emperor and his governors used the Alexandrian mob to rise up against the Jews, resulting in many murders and the violation of the synagogues. However, in 116 CE, Jews from Libya were the instigators of riots when they attacked the city, focusing primarily on the Serapeum, resulting in a backlash and more fighting, with the pagans against the Jews.

Emperor Caracalla in 215 CE instigated rioting against the native Egyptians, as he believed they were responsible for the murder of his brother, Geta. He expelled all Egyptians from the city and, as Egyptians were already considered second-class citizens in Alexandria, this did not aid their status in the city. The true persecution of the Christians, however, began in 284 CE, the first year of Diocletian's reign and did not end until 313 CE, a period known in the Coptic calendar as the 'Era of the Martyrs'. Many martyrs were put to death, including bishops and religious leaders.

In a role reversal, in 324 CE pagan temples throughout Alexandra were being converted into churches, sparking more violence as Christian mobs rampaged across the city. The Christians were considered untouchable by the law at this time and, therefore, there were no restraints to their behaviour. Strangely enough, the monks from the monasteries were generally the most violent. However, as the pagans were generally in hiding due to their new status, the Christian mob ended up fighting among themselves.[33] Once they realised this was the case, they turned on the Jews in place of pagans.

In 385 CE, there was more violence when Bishop Theophilus had permission to restore an old basilica in Alexandria. When they were working they discovered a subterranean pagan shrine, still containing original images. These were removed and paraded through the streets, resulting in the fury of the pagans, who turned the subterranean chambers of the Serapeum into the headquarters for guerrilla warfare. They regularly prowled the streets, returning to the Serapeum with Christian prisoners. Emperor Theodosius was forced to intervene; he declared all the Christians who had died as martyrs and, as a means of eradicating the problem, he banned all pagan cults from the city and ordered the destruction of all the pagan temples in the city. The Serapeum was destroyed, and with it the Daughter Library of the Mouseion, and many people were murdered. Theophilus ordered a church to be built upon the site.

This did not stop the violence and people were still brutally murdered for their opinions and beliefs. One famous female philosopher, Hypatia, was torn to pieces in 415 CE by a hoard of monks in the streets of Alexandria, on the orders of Theophilus' successor, Bishop Cyril:

> They threw her out of her carriage and dragged her to the church called Caesarion. They stripped off her clothes and then killed her with broken bits of pottery (ostraca). When they had torn her body apart limb from limb they took it to a place called Cinaron and burned it.[34]

With no pagans left and the Jews ordered out of the city in 414 CE, there was no-one else to attack and therefore there were many inter-Christian riots, resulting in the murder of Bishop Proterius in 457 CE.[35]

In 485 CE the Alexandrian archbishop, Peter Mongus, used the passion and anger of the mob to his own political ends. The student Paralius visited the shrine of Isis and was told in a vision by the goddess that one of his classmates was a magician. When he approached the classmate, he stated that he had had the same vision but Paralius was named as the magician. Paralius returned to the shrine of Isis, but this time the goddess did not appear to him. He became enraged and started attacking the pagan gods, mocking his pagan teacher Horapollen, among others, publically, especially for their interest in the shrine of Isis at Menouthis. The students of these teachers gave Paralius a beating. The archbishop, Peter Mongus, however, became involved, using this as anti-pagan propaganda, presenting Paralius as a Christian, even though he was not. Mongus held public meetings for three days, resulting in a raid on the temple of Isis, where the priests were hauled into the streets to face the mob.[36] These riots lasted for a long weekend, with Paralius named as a martyr for the injuries he sustained for 'Christ', further enraging the Christian mob.

The violence did not wane in the seventh century CE, even when Arab leaders had boycotted Alexandria in favour of Fustat (Cairo). The Alexandrian mob did not take too kindly to being governed by anyone not of their own choosing, resulting in rioting in the streets. General Amru was sent to the city to subdue the rioters, which, as in the past, did not work, resulting in a massacre and the burning of the remaining books in the library.[37]

Even in the modern era the riots continue. There were nationalist riots in order to gain independence from the British. Riots and demonstrations became the norm and in 1922 the British declared the independence of Egypt, although they still controlled the Suez Canal, the army and the economy. However, the Suez Crisis in 1956 resulted in everyone of British, French or Jewish origin being expelled from Alexandria, some with only a small suitcase to their name. Many were born in Alexandria, living their whole life there. It was described by one as an absurd situation which was 'very painful and complex', where he was forced to 'return' to Greece, a country he had never visited.

It was very difficult for these Alexandrians and there are clubs throughout the West where they meet to discuss their beloved homeland.[38] Alexandria returned to Egypt, but there were still violent uprisings. The history of Alexandria was seen as European and was to be denied and distorted[39] to give it a distinctly non-European feel. The city was reduced to Cairo's port and today more than 70 per cent of Egypt's exports leave via Alexandria. More violence was seen under President Sadat in 1977, with the hunger riots, resulting in the Exchange, a building which to the Alexandrians represented capitalism and the venue of Nasser's speech at the start of the Suez Crisis, being burned to the ground.

More recent violence in Alexandria occurred during April 2002, nine days before the Bibliotheca Alexandrina was due to have its grand opening. The opening was postponed due to acts of aggression in Israel, which were the focus of a student protest in Alexandria. The protest, however, got out of hand and the *Middle Eastern Times* reported:

> Just metres from the steps of the Alexandria library, at the gates of Alexandria University's faculty of Commerce, an Egyptian student gasped his last breath when he died of gunshot wounds during an anti-American demonstration on April 10.[40]

In retaliation for the death of the student, the student body were potentially going to use the international event at the new library to vent their anger against Israel and American support. Although these types of demonstrations are typical in the history of the Alexandrian mob, in modern Egypt they would normally take place in Tahrir (Liberation) Square, Cairo, so it is interesting that this demonstration was carried out in Alexandria.

The demonstration resulted in students stoning the riot police and the smashing of car and shop windows, the culmination being that Mohammed Ali, the student, was shot. The opening of the Bibliotheca Alexandrina was re-scheduled for 16 October 2002, with a high security presence and a low-impact opening so as to not antagonise the mob further.

Riots have continued to take place in Alexandria, with an anti-Christian riot in 2005 taking place outside St George's church, protesting against a play they said offended Islam. The protesters threw stones at the police and the church, and the riot ended with three deaths and over a hundred people injured. Things have clearly not changed in 2,000 years – the Alexandrian mob still dictates government reactions.

ALEXANDRIA IN MODERN MEDIA

The three elements of the myth of Alexandria discussed are all prevalent in the literature, movies and artwork created about the city: the cosmopolitan city, the centre of the ancient intellectual world and the volatile nature of the mob.

The poet Theocritus (300–260 BCE) described Alexandria in his *Idylls*, focussing on the fragrant smell of the meadows, the birdsong and the background noise of goats and sheep, really bringing this early city to life.[41] Learner's description of Alexandria in the 1970s is not as idyllic, but more realistic:

> The salty tang of sea air was discernable above the exhaust fumes and the wafting scent of incense billowing from the jars placed outside the night stalls, an odour tainted by the ubiquitous but faint smell of sewage.[42]

A major element of Alexandria, past and present, was the port, the main entrance into the city for travellers and merchants alike:

> This was the largest port in the world, so sailors and traders were inevitably roistering, but they were close to the wharves and the Emporium, not so much in the broad avenues.[43]

Davis, in *Alexandria*, gives a little hint here of the liveliness of the port, while indicating they stuck to one region of the city, leaving the rest free of sailors and merchants. This is very much supported by archaeological evidence which shows the city was divided into different quadrants. Forster, in *Pharos and Pharillons*, describes the Bourse where cotton and stocks and shares were sold, which is compared to Dante's Inferno:

Divided from each other by ornamental balustrades, they increased in torment as they decreased in size, so that the inmost ring was congested beyond redemption with perspiring souls. They shouted and waved and spat at each other across the central basin which was empty but for a permanent official who sat there, fixed in ice ... the merchants hit their heads and howled.[44]

Regardless of the reason for travelling to Alexandria, the best approach was always by sea. The Greek geographer Strabo (63 BC – 24 CE) liked Alexandria so much that he stayed, recording that the best approach to the city was by sailing along the right-hand side of the Great Harbour and past the lighthouse.[45] This approach is also used in *Alexandria* by Davis, for the characters arriving from Rome:

He hitched a free ride on our ship saying he passionately wanted to study at the Alexandria Mouseion.

Many people travelled to Alexandria to study, or to be in the presence of scholars, and this is a key feature in many works of literature. However, not all approaches to this element of the myth are favourable. Sadly Aulus, in *Alexandria*, was not impressed with what he saw at the Mouseion:

Aulus was depressed and not just because the celebrated library at Alexandria was prepared to acknowledge any old tosh as long as it was written in Greek.[46]

The character Aulus was not the only visitor to the Mouseion to be disappointed with what he found there. Diodorus Siculus, writing of the visit of Scipio Aemilianun Africanus to Alexandria in 136 BCE, commented that he was disappointed that the Mouseion was 'devoid of scholars',[47] an expectation for a centre of intellectual learning.

However, these disappointments have not detracted from the general myth of Alexandria as a centre of intellectualism. The Greek poet Constantine Cavafy (1863–1933) wrote in the early twentieth century:

The teacher-city, the Panhellenic height, wisest in every discourse, every art.[48]

Even in the modern era this element of the myth was still considered important, perhaps the most important. Oscar Wilde, in *The Critic as Artist* (1891), comments on the legacy of Alexandria:

There is really not a single form that art now uses that does not come to us from the critical spirit of Alexandria, where these forms were either stereotyped or invented or made perfect.[49]

Nietzsche, in his *Birth of Tragedy* (1872), comments that 'Alexandrian man' was an inventor, calculator and scholar who led his life according to science, reason and knowledge.[50] He agrees that Western literary traditions originated in Alexandria, and we are but emulating them in the modern world.

The intellectualism of Alexandria is presented in books and poems about Hypatia of Alexandria, who apparently

taught Homer and Plato in Alexandria during the reign of Theodosius II.[51]

In 1853 Charles Kingsley, in his *Hypatia or the New Foes with an Old Face*, lamented the loss of this intellectualism:

Twenty Years after Hypatia's death, philosophy was flickering down to the very socket. Hypatia's death was its deathblow.[52]

Feminists have adopted Hypatia as an icon, focusing on her intelligence as well as the violence that ended her life:

The torture killing of the noted philosopher Hypatia by a mob of Christians in Alexandria in 415 AD marks the end of a time when women were still appreciated for the brain under their hair.[53]

A. W. Richeson adds that Hypatia's death was a blow to the world of academia in the sense that:

We have no other mathematician of importance until late in the Middle Ages.

Whereas in regard to women in academia, E. Jacobacci makes the depressing statement:

With her passing there was no other woman mathematician of importance until the eighteenth century.[54]

Intellectualism is not the only association with the term 'Alexandrian' and Cavafy uses the term primarily to mean homosexual,[55] perhaps reflecting the so-called homosexuality of Alexander and the acceptance in Alexandria of all people and life-styles.

In such an artistic, intellectual city, the people of Alexandria have become a part of the myth themselves, and in Bickerton's *The Desert and the City* he illuminates us as to what an Alexandrian should be. They should be from a

good family, Greek. Nice merchant business, shipping from India or some such. Good classical education. Am I right? ... People like you – speak three languages, read and write, sleep on goose feathers ...[56]

Many of these features are what one would expect from an inhabitant of such a cosmopolitan city. General stereotypes of Alexandrian inhabitants suggest they were pre-occupied with their appearance, extremely well-off, living in luxurious homes which exceeded that of the Romans, which Bickerton captured in his description. Davis in *Alexandria* was a lot more derogatory:

All we saw was that Alexandria was expensive, expansive and extremely Greek in style.[57]

The difference between these two authors' descriptions can be attributed to the narrator, for Bickerton's character was Egyptian and Davis' character was Roman and therefore their approaches to the city differ vastly.

A British-Alexandrian, D. J. Enright, also writes on this theme of wealth, with regard to the people and the city, which he describes as:

A rather melodramatic city and not only by British-provincial standards. Its extremes of wealth and poverty are staggering.[58]

This was not the first time the city was described as one of extremes, although the decadence and wealth is a common theme. In Shakespeare's *Antony and Cleopatra*, a drunken Pompey claims,

This is not yet an Alexandrian feast.

In the seventeenth century, it was already well-established that an Alexandrian feast was legendary and to obtain such a lofty title the feast would need to be spectacular. Alexandria was indeed famous for its wine, and both the poetry of Horace and Virgil sing its praises and popularity at Roman banquets. Cavafy clearly used Shakespeare as one of his sources and he picks up on this element of a decadent and pleasure-loving society:

If Alexandrian, you know the passion
Of our life here, the pleasure and the flame.[59]

He also added in *Myris: Alexandria AD 340* that in Alexandria there were 'wonderfully indecent night-long sessions.'[60] Even contemporary writers such as Achilles Tatius (second century) commented on the vibrancy of the people living in Alexandria:

When I contemplated the city, I thought there could never be enough inhabitants to fill it entirely; but when I looked at the inhabitants, I asked myself in amazement if there could ever be a city capable of containing them.[61]

Cavafy, in fact, totally embraced the decadent, sensual and hedonistic element of Alexandrian society and the majority of his poems were about the history of Alexandria, with this as its main theme.

This passion is also displayed through violence, as we have discussed, in the form of the Alexandrian mob. This has been a great literary tool:

He knew too, that in Alexandria, notoriously the most volatile city in the Empire, large-scale rioting could erupt on far less provocation.[62]

The mob is described throughout the historical records as being volatile and unreachable, meaning the leaders of Alexandria were always at their mercy, censoring their decisions so as not to antagonise the mob:

> You know the Alexandria Mob – taking a man into custody could blow into a public order issue in five minutes.[63]

This volatility is captured well by how Durrell's *Alexandrian Quartet* was received, a Copt complaining about a conspiracy between the Coptic Christians and the Zionists. Durrell is apparently supposed to have commented that:

> I asked an expert to read what I had written and he was concerned that the Egyptians would actually punish the Copts for this non-existent conspiracy.[64]

This does show the instability of the Alexandrian mob, where they could potentially riot over something written in fiction.

In 2010 the movie *Agora*, directed by Alejandro Amenábar, was released and portrays the story of Hypatia of Alexandria. Although there was a thread of intellectualism running through the story, it was the violence of the mob which was the main focus. Even background shots of Christians and pagans debating in the Agora resulted in Christians throwing a pagan into the fire, to prove the non-existence of their gods. This, as would be expected, led to the retaliation of the pagans against the Christians, which was fuelled by the pagan leaders themselves. Throughout the movie the ensuing violence of the Christians against the pagans is emphasised, accumulating into the crescendo of violence against Hypatia at the end of the film.

Various books have been written about Hypatia, making her a figure of legend in her own right. However, all of them focus and comment on the violence of the mob and the manner of her death. In 1720, John Toland described it as a:

> Bestial murder perpetrated by Cyril's tonsured hounds, with a fanatical gang at their heels.[65]

The crowd was presented in different ways depending on the author; Kingsley, for example, presented Hypatia's killers as fanatical Christians, whereas Mario Luzi (1978) presents them as evil, but the type of evil found in every crowd.[66]

Liddel commented on the mob during the twentieth century in a letter to George Seferis, stating that:

> All the rioting here could only touch one physically – and if one knows when it is going to happen, one can take precaution against that.[67]

He clearly felt removed from the rioting, as he felt he would not know anyone involved and therefore it would not concern him, whereas a riot in Athens would affect him. It has been suggested that this is why authors like Liddell and Durrell used Alexandria as their setting in their novels: for the simple reason that their friends were not situated here. They could write about the people they met without offending friends and peers.

The association between politics and the Alexandrian mob is one that has been clear for centuries, and is used in Learner's *Sphinx*:

> It was dangerous to voice such opinions in a country still caught up in the difficult transition from a past colonial feudalism to a more democratic socialism.[68]

This novel, set in the 1970s, refers to the revolting of the mob due to food shortages, where their ration cards were worthless and it was impossible to get the basic staple foods. This was met by rioting, leaving inhabitants of the city frightened to leave the house and politicians at a loss as to how to react.

Despite these negative aspects of Alexandria, it was still a place considered desirable to visit and Davis states:

> No Roman lives until he has scratched his name indelibly on a timeless pharaonic column, visited a Canopus brothel and caught one of the hideous diseases that have led Alexandria to produce its world famous medical practitioners.[69]

Forster comments in *Pharos and Pharillon* on Canopus, 'where the air is so thick with demons that only the most robust of Christians can breathe.'[70] This idea of being attracted to an undesirable place was a common theme in twentieth-century literature. Robert Liddell and Lawrence Durrell both hated living in Alexandria, feeling it had lost its identity and was 'a flesh-pot, sink-pot, melting pot of dullness'[71], but they both used Alexandria as the backdrop to some of their work instead of their much favoured Athens. In Liddell's *Unreal City*, he renames Alexandria as Caesarea, but claims:

> There were few places in the world more hideous that Caesarea, surely – yet he would leave it without hatred.[72]

Even Forster stated, 'The modern city calls for no enthusiastic comment'[73], and yet wrote two books about Alexandria. There is clearly something about this strange city, which was built on a classical history, with many exciting elements and eccentric inhabitants that appeal to authors and artists, even if it is to use it as a place to escape from.

BUILT ON MEMORIES

This rich history is the key to the myth of Alexandria, and it is as important today as it ever was. In the last thirty years, archaeology in Alexandria has increased as people are more and more intrigued by the ancient city, but archaeology is particularly problematic. The redevelopment of the city over the centuries, which has occurred at a remarkable pace, has damaged the archaeology and the locations of many of the ancient sites are now lost. As very few excavations had taken place before the innovations of Mohammed Ali in the 1820s, much was lost before any work had begun. All the modern high-rise buildings have deep foundations, cutting through the archaeology, and even the construction of the Bibliotheca Alexandrina was criticised for the destruction to the archaeology below. The archaeologists were able to do a quick survey which indicated a full excavation would be valuable, but it was not to be. Although the new library may be in the same region as the original library, the original has not been found and, with the modern construction here, it will never be located.

However, although the ancient remains may be fragmentary, the persistence of memory and power of tradition is important, as many of the streets and sites are named after people and events from the past. In addition, most of the great mosques and churches in Alexandria have been rebuilt and reconstructed time and time again on the same sacred sites, a continual reuse of sacred space.

During the early Islamic period, texts describe Alexandria as little more than a frontier post and an unimportant one at that, and they left the city for the busier Fustat. However, there was still an Islamic presence here, as they admired Alexandria and what it stood for. It was divided into three Islamic zones; the Manna (Pharos), al'Iskandariyyah (citadel) and Naqitah (an unknown area). Some of the most important mosques of this period were constructed around the Heptastadion causeway rather than eastwards in the centre of the Ptolemaic and Late Antique city, and indeed their new enclosure wall surrounded only a small section of the ancient city, giving some indication of the dilapidation of the city at this time. However, a twelfth-century visitor, Ibn Jubayr, claimed:

> We saw no other city where the streets are so vast or the buildings so tall, or that is more beautiful or more full of life. Its markets are very busy.[74]

Even in its dilapidated state, the city was still able to impress. A number of churches were converted into mosques, such as the Church of St Theonas, which became the Mosque of a Thousand Columns, and the Cathedral of St Athanasius, which became the Attarine Mosque.

The Ras-el-Tin Palace of the modern Egyptian royal family, who were exiled in 1953, was built on the foundations of the Roman Temple of Neptune. However, the location of the Mouseion, the original library, archive and centre of learning, is not certain and it is thought that it probably stood beneath the intersection of Sharia Nabi Daniel and Sharia Fouad/Horreya. This was not, however, to be the site of the new library, the Bibliotheca Alexandrina. The new library was situated on the coast, in the Eastern Harbour, to be visible to any boats arriving. An iconic monument known as 'the fourth pyramid', the Bibliotheca Alexandrina was designed by the Norwegian architects Snohetta in 1995 and was possibly on the original site of the Brucheion, the palace quarters of Antony and Cleopatra.

When President Nixon visited Alexandria in 1974 he was intrigued by the ancient library:

> Nixon displayed the interest that many foreigners do. He had an idealised image of Alexandria already formed in his imagination ... this became particularly obvious when Nixon asked us if could show him the site where the ancient 'universal' Library and associated Mouseion once stood.[75]

The Alexandrian memory of their Hellenistic past was key to their desire to build another library as a way to revitalise the myth that Alexandria remained a centre of intellectual knowledge. The library itself would have impressed their Hellenistic ancestors as there is space for more than four million volumes, including manuscripts, microfilm and other media held in four libraries, as well as four museums, a planetarium, four art galleries and fifteen permanent exhibitions. This is all handled by over 500 members of staff. The unusual design of the library was not greeted with reverence by all, as some thought it was insensitive to the surrounding landscape and others described it as 'alien', with the *Economist* in 2000 calling it 'a flying saucer crashed on the shores of Africa'.[76] Further controversy was reported when the maternity and childrens' hospital next door to the new library was demolished to provide adequate parking for the library facility. This, and the cost of the library, which reached over $200 million dollars, was viewed by many as negligent considering the illiteracy rates and the controversial issues of literary censorship, which is prevalent in Egypt.[77]

The opening of the Bibliotheca Alexandrina was the beginning of one of many reinventions of Alexandria, a means of recapturing their identity, although many Alexandrians felt this was drawing on the European or Greek identity of the past, in conflict with their modern Islamic one.[78] However, the decline of the city from a sprawling metropolis to a seaside town has been lamented by many and one English author, George Sandys, writing in 1610 CE states:

> Such was this Queen of Cities and Metropolis who now hath nothing left her but ruins; and those ill witnesses of her perished beauties; declaring rather that towns as well as men are vanished by the ages.[79]

When Napoleon arrived in Alexandria at the end of the eighteenth century, the city regained some of the global recognition that it had held in Antiquity, and this has been maintained until the modern day. It did not, however, maintain the interest of these explorers due to the lack of archaeology, especially when there was more of archaeological interest further south. However, by the end of the nineteenth century there had been enough accidental finds in the area to justify the opening of the Graeco-Roman Museum in 1892, which started the new archaeological discipline of archaeology in Alexandria.

Following Napoleon's arrival, Alexandria became once more a multi-cultural society, with communities of Italian, Albanian, Maltese, Armenians, Greek, French and British. The *lingua franca* was French, which was taught in the Jesuit College until the First

World War. Alexandria was still considered more European than Egyptian. Among the Greeks there was a distinction between race and nationality, and being born in Egypt did not mean one was Egyptian, almost the same as the original Alexandrian concept of citizenship. Among this newly developed population were a number of talented writers and artists, including the Alexandrian-Greek poet Constantine Cavafy (1863–1933). Perhaps because of this multi-cultural aspect of the city, it has never recaptured its identity, resulting in Alexandria being constantly reinvented. These new identities often build on the myths and legends of the past, and it has been said:

> If there is a single nation whose ancient past vindicates its current rebirth, that nation is Egypt.[80]

In the late nineteenth century, the city was reinvented as a town of sensuous delights and rich literary association. Initially, the reinvention combined contemporary Greek and Egyptian cultures, in addition to Jewish, Eastern Semitic, Roman, Christian and Islamic belief systems.

The excavations that are taking place in Alexandria today are helping to bring the city once again to the attention of the world. The discovery of antiquities helps to tie Alexandria in with Egypt and her colourful history, rather than viewing the city, as the Romans did, as part of Europe. The excavations are therefore important for the next reinvention of Alexandria, but the archaeologists face a constant battle with the modern building works, as well as the ever-encroaching coastline, which is slowly eroding the land, bringing the sea further inland and pushing many of the archaeological remains further out to sea.

It seems the modern identity of Alexandria has not been firmly established yet, but their reinvention is as one would expect, drawing from the past and melding it with the present: an important industrial city essential to the Egyptian economy, but facing the Mediterranean and Europe. The myth of Alexandria is therefore a complex one, as it is one of the few myths based on a 2,000 year old reality, but not a reality that has developed and evolved.

Since the Roman period Alexandria was not considered part of Egypt, connected more to Europe, meaning even now, it is difficult to identify the city either as an Egyptian/African city or as a European city. Forster even claimed:

> One is as far from the East here as in London.[81]

It has always been a multi-cultural city, although this is more the case in the past than today and the myth is a 'kaleidoscope of varied cultural histories'.[82] However, it has been described as the 'meeting point of East and West'[83] or even as 'the cross-roads between the West and the Middle East'.[84]

This fading identity was felt by British Alexandrians of the First and Second World Wars, and they viewed it as a 'place of exile from some paradise elsewhere'.[85] This theme is also picked up in the literature, with a character in Learner's *Sphinx* sighing:

The glory days, when Alexandria was a real metropolis. Nowadays there is such a grinding earnestness – sometimes I wonder whether I am witnessing the death of imagination itself.[86]

Many authors have made comments along these lines, including Robert Liddell, writing to a Greek poet, George Segeris, in 1941:

We don't really like Alexandria much – it is a great disappointment. It is the nearest place to Greece.[87]

E. M. Forster, who wrote two books on Alexandria, stated in a letter to his friend S. R. Masood in India:

I do not like Egypt much-or rather, I do not see it, for Alexandria is cosmopolitan. But what I have seen seems vastly inferior to India, for which I am longing in the most persistent way and I still hope to die.[88]

It is interesting that Forster, although living in Alexandria in the early twentieth century, did not feel that he was living in Egypt, something the Romans had aimed for. Despite their apparent contempt for Alexandria, Cavafy wrote numerous poems about it and E. M. Forster (1922) discusses the legend:

Her future like that of other commercial cities is dubious; and neither the Pharos of Sistratus not the Idylls of Theocritus not the Enneads of Plotinus are likely to be rivalled again. Only the climate, only the north wind and the sea remain as pure as when Menelaus, the first visitor, landed at Pharos three thousand years ago; and at night, the constellation of Berenice's hair still shines as brightly as when it caught the attention of Conon the astronomer.[89]

It is clear that he feels the myth of the past is lost in 1920s Alexandria, but it is interesting that he comments about the constants: the climate, the stars, in short the environment. Another author, Fahmy, reminds us of another continuous element in the history of Alexandria – the Egyptians.[90] Although they were the minority in Alexandria's heyday, they were present and he feels the key to finding Alexandria's identity is through the history of the Egyptian people who live and have lived there. However, even Fahmy believes:

The cosmopolitan Alexandria has indeed been lost and its loss is felt not only by the Greeks, the Italians, the French, the Armenians and the Jews who departed, but also by the Egyptians who were left behind.[91]

In *Pharos and Pharrilion*, Forster comments that:

The glories of the antique had gone, the comforts of the modern had not yet arrived.[92]

This seems to hit the nail on the head, as Alexandria is in the process of a reinvention. There is some continuity in Alexandria, something consistent for millennia, and with the opening of the Bibliotheca Alexandrina, is Alexandria once again destined to be the centre of intellectual learning? Perhaps. At least they are on the right path, and once the reinvention is complete we will see whether the myth lives on or whether it is adapted and changed, creating a new modern element to the myth of Alexandria.

SECTION 2

THE MYTH OF
THE EGYPTIANS

CHAPTER 4

THE MYTH OF HATSHEPSUT

Although so far we have discussed the landscape and cities of Egypt, the myth of Egypt can be applied to various characters from Egyptian history. The people of the past have the power to intrigue, as they are both distanced from the observer by time, but also can be related to, as their experiences, emotions and reactions are familiar and the same as those we would have in the same situation.

The myths surrounding the people of ancient Egypt develop primarily due to the gaps that exist in our knowledge of their lives. We are able to formulate an accurate biography of many people of ancient Egypt and where evidence does not exist, myths and legends go some way to complete the picture.

While many characters are known, it is the most unusual that grip the imagination and one such is Hatshepsut, a woman who took on the role of king in the eighteenth dynasty (1504–1483 BCE). Her reasons for penetrating this male environment, and her ability to do so, are interesting and intriguing to the modern mind and are interpreted in many different ways by different people.

Due to the complexity of her character and varying levels of evidence, Hatshepsut is viewed by some as a formidable, strong woman, an icon of feminism, while many have compared her to the Virgin Queen, Elizabeth I,[1] who inherited the throne in a difficult political time when there was no suitable male heir.

Due to the duality of the nature of kingship, Hatshepsut often had to make allusion to the masculinity within her. Comparisons have been made to Elizabeth I, who found herself in a similar situation; often, in her speeches she would make reference to the maleness within her. The most famous being:

> I have the body of a weak and feeble woman, but I have the heart and stomach of a king.

However, neither queen lost their femininity and both in their dowager years were represented as young and beautiful. Elizabeth was even painted as the Queen of Love and Beauty, despite her advanced age of forty-five years old.[2]

In the world of Egyptian kingship, it would have been very difficult for a woman to take over the throne, as kingship was tied so closely to religion and the gods and to change the ideology of kingship was to interfere with religion. It is obviously, therefore, a topic of great debate as to how she managed it.

Her death is also shrouded in mystery, as she seems to disappear from the records, leading to a great deal of speculation about potential murder theories, conspiracies and military coups led by Thutmosis III. So what is true? How did Hatshepsut attain the highest position in Egypt? Was she the first feminist? Was she a woman in man's clothing? A strong political icon or a woman who just wanted recognition for the job she was doing? How did she die? Was she murdered by Thutmosis III? The only way to answer these questions is to investigate the evidence we have about Hatshepsut and her reign.

WHO WAS HATSHEPSUT?

Hatshepsut was the daughter of King Thutmosis I and his wife Ahmose, born in the early years of her father's reign (1522 BCE). She had at least one full brother, Amenmose, and two half-brothers, Wadjmose and Thutmose II, the sons of a secondary wife of Thutmosis I. Amenmose died young, leaving Thutmosis II as heir to the throne.

Thutmosis I was of non-royal blood, a military man who won favour with the previous king, Amenhotep. He was allowed to marry the king's daughter, Ahmose. He died in year 12, month 9 (1512 BCE), when Hatshepsut was approximately ten years old. She was close to her father and later she moved his sarcophagus to her tomb (KV20) in the Valley of the Kings, with the intention of spending eternity with him.

It was important to have powerful support and Hatshepsut and Elizabeth I both emphasised their relationship with their much-admired fathers. Hatshepsut was a 'daddy's girl' who greatly admired the dead king. So too did Elizabeth I, who often questioned ambassadors beneath a portrait of her father, Henry VIII.[3] Hatshepsut claimed in her propaganda that her father declared her to be the heir, which was not strictly true, in the same way that Henry did not want to be succeeded on the throne by a woman.

HATSHEPSUT AND THE BIBLE

Many characters of note from ancient Egypt have their reigns tied to biblical stories by some scholars and Hatshepsut is no different. One researcher has suggested that she can be associated with the Exodus story, and in particular the story of Moses, who in the Bible is recorded as being born of Hebrew slaves in Egypt.

As mentioned previously, Moses' mother, Jochebed, in an attempt to save him from death at the hand of the unnamed pharaoh, put him in a basket and placed him 'in the flags by the river's bank' (Exodus 2:3). The basket was discovered by a daughter of pharaoh who was washing in the Nile. Moses' sister Miriam watched as the child was lifted from the basket. It is interesting to consider how Jochebed knew to leave the basket there, and how she got so close to the royal palace. The childless princess was unable to feed the child, and was approached by Miriam and asked whether she would accept a Hebrew nurse. Jochebed was then brought into the palace and paid to nurse Moses, who was raised as the child of the princess.

While many discussions have taken place regarding the identity of Moses, very few suggestions have been made regarding the identity of the princess. One scholar, Zuhdi (2003), firmly believes this princess was Hatshepsut. The evidence presented is chronological in nature, devised from the time references in the Bible, which are not in themselves reliable. Based on these dates and the subsequent assumption that Moses was born at the end of Amenhotep I's reign or the beginning of that of Thutmosis I, there are only two possible princesses, one of which died in childhood, which leaves Hatshepsut.

There are various problems with this theory, disregarding the security surrounding Hatshepsut which prevented her being approached by the sister of Moses coupled with the fact that there is no evidence of this other than the chronology that the author refers to.

As the pharaoh had declared that all new-born Hebrew children should be drowned in the Nile, surely the most dangerous place for Moses to be would be in the palace, with that very pharaoh and his daughter. Miriam then identifying the child as Hebrew and offering a Hebrew nurse surely increased the danger he was in rather than securing his safety.

If it was Hatshepsut, there is no mention anywhere of her having a son, either real or adopted, and it would be extremely unorthodox for an unmarried princess to raise a child. Especially one later married to the heir to the throne, as this could affect the succession rights.

Thutmosis I was succeeded by his thirteen-year-old son, Thutmosis II, who was married to Hatshepsut, his half-sister. Tuthmosis II died in 1504 BCE aged twenty or twenty-one, and had produced two daughters, Neferure and Neferubity. Thutmosis II also had a son by a minor wife, Isis, who became Thutmosis III (plate 12).

During the reign of Thutmosis II, Hatshepsut stood beside him as his Great Royal Wife, acting as a feminine counterpart to the masculine king, accompanying him in religious festivals and rituals. This role was generally one of support rather than any great power. Every king had numerous wives, but the Great Royal Wife was the favourite, rather like the modern first lady.

At the death of Thutmosis II, his son Thutmosis III took over the throne, although he was still an infant. Hatshepsut married the young child and ruled Egypt as his co-regent, with the assumption that as soon as Thutmosis III came of age, he would take over from her. So, from the tender age of sixteen Hatshepsut ruled Egypt. One Theban official, Ineni, describes this co-regency:

> His sister, the God's wife, Hatshepsut controlled the affairs of the Land according to her own plans. Egypt was made to labour with bowed head for her, the excellent seed of the god, who came forth from him.[4]

During this co-regency, Hatshepsut made herself prominent in the minds of the officials and the people of Egypt and she grew in popularity and power. The most

20. Senenmut, Egyptian Museum, Cairo.

powerful of these officials was her Chief Steward, Senenmut (fig. 20), who had remained loyal to the family since the reign of Thutmosis II.[5] In addition to the title of Chief Steward, he was also the Steward of the Estates of Amun, Overseer of all Royal Works and the Steward of Property of Hatshepsut Neferure.[6] He was also the personal tutor to the royal princess Neferure and is the only non-royal individual depicted with the princess in numerous statues (plate 13).

QUEEN'S LOVER?

The relationship Hatshepsut held with Senenmut has been questioned since the eighteenth dynasty. There is no doubt that he was important in the court of Hatshepsut, and it appears that he was privy to special privileges and was greatly rewarded by Hatshepsut. There are, however, graphic graffiti images from near the end of her reign showing two people in an intimate position which are often thought to represent Hatshepsut and Senenmut together (fig. 21).[7]

Senenmut was a very wealthy man and he commissioned two tombs; one in the Valley of the Nobles (TT71), appropriate for his administrative position, and the other near Deir el Bahri (plate 14), the mortuary temple of his queen (TT353), which further sparked rumours of their affair. This rumour is further fuelled by his regular appearance on shrine and temple walls at Deir el Bahri in connection with the queen,

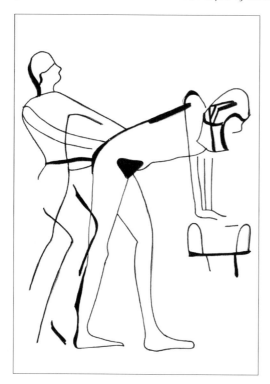

21. Graffiti of Hatshepsut and Senenmut.
(*After Tyldesley 1996, p. 190*)

and there are even images of him within some of the offering niches in the top terrace of the temple, in the act of worshipping Amun alongside Hatshepsut.[8] He stands in the position that should have been held by her husband and co-ruler, Thutmosis III. Even in Senenmut's shrine at Gebel el Silsila there is an image of the queen being embraced by the deities Sobek and Nekhbet,[9] the type of image which rarely appears in non-royal contexts, further reflecting the close relationship between Senenmut and Hatshepsut.

Despite Senenmut's wealth and status, there is no evidence that he married and no indication that he bore any children,[10] which in ancient Egypt was very unusual. Perhaps the records of his wife and family have become lost, or perhaps his intimate involvement with Hatshepsut prevented him from mentioning his wife and family, dead or alive, or indeed marrying in case he incur the wrath of the queen, jeopardising his wealth and his career.

The love affairs of Elizabeth I were also questioned, and her two favourites were the Earl of Leicester and the Earl of Essex, both of whom, like Senenmut, kept their wives carefully hidden away from the eyes of the Queen.[11] However, as with many powerful women, it was more important to present an image of chastity and purity, lest the only contribution to world history they made was their sexual activity. Cleopatra made that mistake and as history is primarily written by men, she is portrayed as a sexually active woman, bordering on a whore.

It is not unusual in texts for a powerful woman like Hatshepsut to be reduced to the 'Lover' of a powerful man. Female leaders throughout history have been the brunt of gossip such as this. Cleopatra, for example, is remembered for her sexuality rather than her politics (chapter 6) and Elizabeth I was gossiped about constantly. It is almost as if, should a woman shun the role she has been allotted in life for a more powerful one, she is viewed as unfeminine or unnatural, which inevitably leads to debauched behaviour.[12]

LOVERS' TIFF?

If Hatshepsut and Senenmut were lovers, it seems a little strange that he simply disappeared from the records between year 16 and 20 of her reign (1488–1484 BCE) and was not buried in either of his tombs. This has brought about myriad speculations, from dying abroad, drowning, or burning to death, all denying a body for burial, to the existence of a third, more impressive, tomb that has yet to be discovered. Others have suggested personal feelings or internal politics as the reason for his disappearance, suggesting perhaps that the death of Princess Neferure caused Senenmut to lose influence with the Queen, instigating a gradual decline from office. However, whether Neferure died before her mother is uncertain, although some statues of her were removed from Deir el Bahri during Hatshepsut's lifetime. Others have suggested that the images of Senenmut in the mortuary temple of Hatshepsut were created secretly. When Hatshepsut discovered this, he fell out of favour. However, if this were the case then it would be expected that she remove or re-carve the images, or at best rename them for Thutmosis III. There is, however, a statue at Deir el Bahri of Senenmut bearing the cartouche of Thutmosis III, which could have been renamed by Thutmosis after the death of the official, or Hatshepsut after his downfall.

Thutmosis III has also been accused of his death, murdering him in order to gain his throne back from Hatshepsut. He is then thought to have started a campaign of destruction against the monuments and tombs of Hatshepsut.

Although Senenmut has not been clearly identified, one of the mummies found in the Deir el Bahri cache, simply known as 'Unknown Man C', has two very distinct wrinkles on the left side of his face, by the corner of his mouth, which could be scars. These are identical to a small sketch of an official in the Metropolitan Museum of Art, New York, which bears the same marks on the left side of his mouth. This sketch may be one of the only identifiable portraits of Senenmut. As the mummies of the parents of Senenmut are in the Qasr el Einy Medical Facility in Cairo, DNA tests could be carried out to see if 'Unknown Man C' is their son.[13] If so, this could be another piece in the puzzle of the life and reign of Hatshepsut.

TRADITIONAL QUEEN

When Hatshepsut began ruling as the co-regent of Thutmosis III, she did so as a traditional queen holding titles such as Principle Wife or God's Wife, showing her loyalty to the rightful king. However, after two years of ruling Egypt she developed new titles based on kingly epithets, such as Mistress of the Two Lands. She also adopted a throne name, in the manner of a king, written in a cartouche. After five years, at twenty-three years old, she completely abandoned her queenly titles and adopted the full five-fold titulary of a king and was represented in images as a king, wearing the masculine clothes of a king, including the false beard (plate 15). These images have been interpreted by some as indicating Hatshepsut was a 'transvestite', for want of a better word – a woman who wore the male attire of a king as a means of displaying her power as king rather than the secondary role of queen. Even the ancient scribes were somewhat confused about whether to describe her as a male or female and used both masculine and feminine pronouns and grammatical terms in her inscriptions. She was sometimes named as the 'female Horus of fine gold', indicating she was a female king. If they were confused, it does not bode well for modern scholars trying to unravel this information while filling in the gaps that appear in the archaeological record.

If she was to be taken seriously in the role of king she could not be represented as a woman, as a queen holds less power than a king. However, this does not mean that the ideology itself did not lend itself to a female pharaoh. Indeed, in the creation texts the creator god has both masculine and feminine attributes, although in reality this was probably not so acceptable in the real world.[14]

A king is identified by his regalia: the false beard, the royal kilt and bull's tail, and one of his many crowns. Therefore, as Hatshepsut was ruling as a king and not queen, she needed to be recognisable as such. However, she added feminine touches and when one looks closely at the faces, they are soft and feminine with almond-shaped eyes (plate 16), unmistakably the face of a woman.[15] What is interesting, and which also negates the theory that Thutmosis III hated Hatshepsut, is his own adoption of this effeminate style in his portraiture. It is often difficult to tell images of the two apart.

The artwork, therefore, represents Hatshepsut as a traditional king, with the appropriate titles and regalia. It appears that she also performed duties normally preserved for kings, including the *hebsed* festival, traditionally carried out by the king every thirty years to prove his prowess and suitability to rule. Hatshepsut even took a 'wife' when she became king, giving her daughter Neferure the title God's Wife; she was often represented alongside Hatshepsut, in the place of the Great Royal Wife.[16] In one inscription Neferure even shares regnal years with Hatshepsut and Thutmosis III, almost as if she were a co-ruler and heir to the throne on her mother's death. Some have even suggested Hatshepsut was grooming her daughter to indeed take over the throne as king.

Changing her role from that of Great Royal Wife to king would not have been an easy task for Hatshepsut, even with the support of influential officials. She needed to prove her divine right to be king, and that she had the support of the gods. In the middle terrace of her mortuary temple, a divine birth scene is carved showing the impregnation of her mother, Ahmose, by the god Amun-Ra, disguised as her father Thutmose I. This proves she was the child of a deity and had a divine right to rule. She takes this further on the fallen obelisk at Karnak (fig 22), where she claims she is

22. Fallen obelisk of Hatshepsut. (*Photograph courtesy of Brian Billington*)

both the son and daughter of Amun.[17] Once accepted as king, she ruled with as much tradition as was possible and this is represented in her artwork.

What is unusual is that even though she proclaimed herself king and performed kingly tasks, Hatshepsut did not ignore the authority of Thutmosis III and dated her regnal years to match his. They are often depicted together in temple inscriptions as two kings rather than traditional king and queen. Many Egyptologists think they shared responsibilities, with Thutmosis III concentrating on military and foreign affairs and Hatshepsut responsible for home affairs and the economy. This has been described as the sexist interpretations of historians of the 1950s and 1960s who viewed women as peaceful creatures and men as warriors. These roles suited this preconceived idea.[18] However, such gender-based division was not the case then, as it is not the case now, and numerous powerful women have lived through the ages including Elizabeth I, Indira Ghandi and Margaret Thatcher. Hatshepsut was no weaker than these powerful women. An image on an ostraca shows a queen in a chariot, firing arrows at her enemies. This has been interpreted by some as being Hatshepsut participating in a battle, as any true king would. Whether this is the case is not clear, but it does indicate that women in ancient Egypt were not always destined for the home. It would be interesting to consider Hatshepsut in battle, as it would present the image not of a queen but of a king.

A GREAT KING

Hatshepsut's rule as king would have been considered a successful one if she had been male. As she was female, taking on the role of a man as king, her reign was seen as an aberration against the rule of Maat, or cosmic balance. The kings who ruled after her felt the need to erase her from history.

Her reign was a peaceful one, with no full-scale wars or invasions, which enabled her to concentrate on trade and the economy. Her most important activities are recorded at Deir el Bahri: the exhibition to Punt and the erection of her obelisks at Karnak.

The location of Punt has been the topic of debate for some time, and has entered the realms of myth. The images at Deir el Bahri of the flora and fauna indicate that it is in Africa somewhere, perhaps in Ethiopia, or Eritrea,[19] although many scholars place Punt somewhere in Somalia or Djibouti, or even as far south as Zanzibar,[20] as it is clear in the inscriptions that it is reached via the Red Sea.[21] Hatshepsut's expedition was not the only one to Punt, although it is the best recorded and therefore something that is always associated with her. This expedition was for the acquisition of numerous exotic goods, including animals, ivory, wood, gold, apes, exotic animals, frankincense and myrrh trees (plate 17). These trees were brought to Egypt, roots included, and planted alongside the causeway which led to her temple, and the tree pits can still be seen today. Incense was an important part of temple ritual and was used on a daily basis as perfume, to fumigate houses and for medical prescriptions. As myrrh was not native to Egypt it was necessary to trade for it, and if Hatshepsut had been successful in growing these trees in Egypt, it may have been possible to turn them into a natural resource. However, as her temple was destroyed near the end of Thutmosis III's fifty-four-year rule, some twenty years after Hatshepsut's death, the trees were uprooted and the plan never came to fruition. This influx of luxury goods into Egypt would have raised the profile of Hatshepsut in the minds of the elite, as her success demonstrated that the gods supported her. It has, however, been suggested that this expedition to Punt may have been a ploy to keep the army occupied during such peaceful times,[22] as the expedition was accompanied by at least five shiploads of soldiers.[23] Keeping them busy may have prevented them from revolting against this female king.

The second important event recorded at Deir el Bahri was in year 16 (1488 BCE), the transportation of two great obelisks from the quarries at Aswan. They were transported to Thebes on low rafts of 100 metres in length by 30 metres in width. The obelisks themselves have long since disappeared, so the exact heights are unknown, but they were erected at Karnak amid a public festival of celebration. It took seven months from start to finish before the obelisks were completed,[24] and they were two of the four obelisks she commissioned at Karnak temple, two of them totally covered in gold and the other two covered to approximately half way down the shaft. One of these obelisks is still standing, and is the tallest in Egypt at 29.5 metres (96 feet 9 inches) (fig. 23).[25]

23. Hatshepsut's Obelisk, Karnak. (*Photograph courtesy of Brian Billington*)

TOMBS OF HATSHEPSUT

Hatshepsut had two tombs, as would be expected of a queen turned king. While she was queen of Thutmosis II, she built a tomb west of the Valley of the Kings at Wadi Sikket Taqa el Zeide[26] suited to her queenly status, and although she was not buried there it holds her intended quartzite sarcophagus.

Once king, Hatshepsut took over the tomb of her father Thutmosis I (KV20). She enlarged it and placed the body of her father in a new burial chamber, where she intended to be buried alongside him. A sarcophagus intended for her burial was also discovered there. However, the body of Thutmosis I was removed from this tomb and placed in another tomb (KV38) by Thutmosis III, who clearly did not want his grandfather buried alongside her. Where she was buried we do not know, although she started building her own tomb in the Valley of the Kings (KV42) and excavations have clearly identified the tomb as hers.

WHERE DID SHE GO?

However, she does not appear to have been buried in KV42. The last record of Hatshepsut was dated to day 10, month 6 of her 22nd year – early February 1476 BCE.

24. Damage caused to Hatshepsut,
Deir el Bahri.

Thutmosis III reigned alone after this date. Mystery surrounds this disappearance
and the reasons for it are uncertain, amounting to various theories including a natural
death of old age,[27] as Hatshepsut she was nearly forty at this time, assassination, or
forcible removal by Thutmosis III and his henchmen.

Thutmosis is often held responsible because of the destruction of Hatshepsut's
monuments, although this does not happen until twenty years after Hatshepsut's
disappearance. Temple images of her were replaced by images of Thutmosis I or III, or
they were completely removed, leaving an outline where she originally stood (fig. 24).
Her obelisks at Karnak were enclosed within high walls, so although still present,
they were not visible. Some believe such destruction could only have been carried out
through hatred, although others question the time lapse between her disappearance
and the destruction. Was Thutmosis perhaps forced to carry out the destruction as
political expediency? As Hatshepsut flouted the laws of Maat and anyone supporting
her would be erased from history by later kings, was Thutmosis III protecting his own
legacy? In the twenty years of ruling alone he had built an empire, the like of which
was unknown before his reign. Though loyal to Hatshepsut, was he prepared to lose
credit for his achievements?

Thutmosis III may have been reluctant to destroy her monuments because,
although she was his rival politically, she was his step-mother and raised him through
childhood, in addition to acting as his co-regent and mentor. He probably held this
woman in some affection.

Other theories suggest that Hatshepsut retired from public life in year 22 and it was a further twenty years until she died, at approximately sixty years old. After her death and burial, Thutmosis III may have acted upon his hatred or political acumen and instigated the destruction of her monuments and her name.

REDISCOVERY OF HATSHEPSUT

This erasure of Hatshepsut was successful and by the time of Cleopatra she was all but forgotten, only to be reborn after the decipherment of hieroglyphs in the nineteenth century. The rediscovery itself was interesting, as it tells us a great deal about the politics of the time. Champollion was able to read the cartouche of Thutmosis III and could identify that this cartouche had been carved over another, which he read as Amenenthe. Although this name was accompanied by feminine titles, he was certain that Amenenthe was a man and even commented on the conundrum of titles such as Daughter of the Sun, and yet the figure had cartouches of a king. He produced a most elaborate tale as to who Amenenthe was. Apparently there was an heiress, Queen Amense, a sister of Thutmosis II, who married Thutmosis II, and then married Amenenthe after Thutmosis II's death. Both ruled Egypt in her name, although why was never specified. When Queen Amense died, Amenenthe took the co-regency with Thutmosis III, who then proceeded to erase Amenenthe from history.

It came to Karl Richard Lepsius in 1942–45 to introduce the radical idea that the masculine appearance was misleading and the inscriptions should be noted instead:

> She never appears on her monuments as a woman, but in male attire; we only find out her sex by the inscriptions. No doubt at that period it was illegal for a woman to govern.[28]

Although he was on the nail here and had her name tantalisingly close with Hat—u Numt Amun, he placed her in the seventeenth rather than eighteenth dynasty.

THE HUNT FOR THE MUMMY

As the tombs of Hatshepsut were unused, the mummy of Hatshepsut has been unavailable for study, meaning all theories are unproven. However, this all changed in 2007 when the body of Hatshepsut was 'discovered'. It had always been clear that Hatshepsut was buried according to tradition, with high class mummification and a collection of funerary goods, as some of this funerary equipment was discovered, consisting of a shabti figure, a signet ring engraved in turquoise and set in gold, a lion-headed red jasper gaming piece with her cartouche engraved on it,[29] a linen winding-sheet inscribed with her name and a box bearing her name which contained some mummified viscera and a loose tooth, which may or may not belong to her.

In 2006, Zahi Hawass decided to re-investigate two mummies discovered in the tomb of the Hatshepsut's wet-nurse, In-Sitre. The tomb itself was re-discovered in

1989 and consisted of a pit with a flight of steps leading to a doorway blocked with large stones. The debris in the entrance included a variety of small objects, mummy wrappings, faience beads and a copper adze blade, indicating a burial had definitely taken place here.[30] There was also the face from a coffin, originally gilded although stripped by robbers, and on close examination it showed a notch on the chin where a divine beard could be attached. Both mummies were female, and it was thought an indication that Hatshepsut could be buried here.[31]

The tomb was originally discovered by Howard Carter in 1903 and re-opened by Ayrton in 1908. Carter discovered the bodies of two elderly women, one in a lidless coffin with the name and title of the Great Royal Wet Nurse, In-Sitre, and the other lying on the floor without a coffin. He removed a number of mummified geese, which were left as food offerings for the deceased, and closed up the tomb. When Ayrton entered the tomb, he removed the coffin chest and the mummy which resided in it to Cairo in 1908. The other body was left inside the tomb until 1989, when Donald Ryan entered.[32] Neither of the bodies were identified, although the body with no coffin had her left arm crossed over her chest, with a clenched fist as if she was holding something, in the manner of eighteenth-dynasty royalty. The body in the coffin was approximately 5 feet tall, bald in front, but with long hair at the back and Hawass commented in 2006:

> She has long wavy white hair remaining on her head. I think the face is quite royal and believe that anyone who sees it will have the same reaction.[33]

The coffin was bigger than the body within it, standing at 7 feet in length, and was interpreted as proof that it did not originally belong to the body. The mummy lying on the floor was an elderly obese woman, who may have fit the coffin. She had curly reddish-blonde hair, some of which was shedding onto the floor of the tomb.[34] She was clearly wealthy and her mummification was of a high standard, although due to her obesity she had been eviscerated through the pelvic floor[35] rather than a cut in the left side of the torso.

Donald Ryan and Elizabeth Thomas believed the obese mummy to be Hatshepsut, whereas Zahi Hawass disagreed at the time:

> I personally do not believe that this could be Hatshepsut. This woman was elderly at death and had been very fat in life, with huge pendulous breasts: and the position of her arm is not convincing evidence of royalty.[36]

Why a queen could not be fat and old is never fully explained, but this is clearly evidence of the mythologising of Hatshepsut. The images of her on statues and inscriptions show a young, slender woman, and although we know that these were artistic conventions we formulate an image in our head. Very few of the statues of the kings resemble the actual mummies that are found and we do not like anything Egyptian to be less than glamorous. However, the obesity of Hatshepsut is not so difficult to comprehend, as she led a good (and long) life with lots of rich and exotic food, with high meat content in her diet. The majority of Egyptians could not afford to eat so well and therefore did not gain weight easily. As her images at Deir el Bahri show, Hatshepsut had Punt in her pocket and all that went with it.

In 2007, Hawass changed his mind about which was the royal mummy, and it was announced in July that Hatshepsut had been identified. He discussed the obese lady in an article on his website: 'When I saw her, I believed at once that she was royal, but had no real opinion as to who she might be,' and that when he had a second look at the coffined mummy, 'to me her face and features did not look particularly royal.'[37]

Even an experienced man like Hawass is not able to differentiate a royal mummy from a non-royal mummy without proper scientific research methods being introduced, and it is evident that everyone is subject to the myth.

The two mummies were examined and it was noticed that the obese mummy from the floor of the tomb had a tooth missing that matched the tooth in the box marked with Hatshepsut's name. Further examination of the mummy in KV60 showed she was a fifty-year-old lady who suffered heavily from tooth decay and probably died of cancer, or complications from diabetes.[38]

In order to prove this mummy was that of Hatshepsut DNA tests were carried out, financed by the Discovery Channel, on the two mummies from KV60, Hatshepsut's grandmother Ahmose Nefertari and her father, Thutmosis I. Although usable DNA was extracted from the KV60 mummies and Ahmose-Nefertari, there was none available from Thutmosis I.

Dr Corthals from Manchester's KNH Centre for Biomedical Egyptology, after overseeing the DNA tests:

> When the DNA of the mystery mummy was compared with that of Hatshepsut's ancestors, we were able to scientifically confirm that the remains were those of the 18th dynasty queen.[39]

Egyptologists must now be kicking themselves that she was neglected in the tomb since 1903, simply because she was lying on the floor and the wet-nurse In-Sitre was in the coffin. This makes you wonder what other secrets are hidden within the stores of the Valley of the Kings or the Cairo Museum. If these results are accurate and this mummy is that of Hatshepsut, then it indicates she died of natural causes, refuting all theories of assassination by Thutmosis III.

HATSHEPSUT IN WESTERN CULTURE

Although not as popular in Hollywood as Cleopatra, in 2010 Hatshepsut caught the attention of American television producers and they announced there was to be a twelve-part television drama series, *Pharaohs*, of epic proportions, telling the story of Hatshepsut and Thutmosis III.[40]

It will be a big-budget series, financed by European, Middle Eastern and American partners, and although at the time of writing this has not been aired, it is an exciting prospect.

Thirteen years previously, a couple known only as Rick and Carol decided to write a screenplay about the life of Hatshepsut called the *Daughter of Ra*. The research they did led them to a conclusion:

> What we really came away with was a genuine appreciation for the woman and her deeds. It is obvious she was a very intelligent and strong leader. Not only did she become the only female king in ancient Egypt, but she did it with the support of Egypt's extensive government bureaucracy. We feel her assumption of kingship was more than a desperate attempt to hold onto power. With her royal lineage, she still would have held great power and influence. After all, she was daughter of a king, sister of a king, wife of a king and daughter of the Great Royal Wife. If you add that up along with her obvious intelligence and political savvy, she would have been a force to reckon with for the rest of her life. Something drastic had to happen for her to become Pharaoh and for the male-dominated government to permit it.[41]

While the play does not appear to have been produced yet on the stage or screen, the writers are so enamoured with the subject that they have a selection of suggested stars for the title role, including Rachel Weisz, Halle Berry and Catherine Zeta Jones. It is surprising that no movies have been made about Hatshepsut, as according to the authors of the screenplay:

> In contemporary terms, Hatshepsut not only broke the glass ceiling ... she shattered it! She truly is the first great woman of history! Her story needs to be told!

Hatshepsut is one of those characters that, while not necessarily consciously known by everyone, is lurking in the background, as is made clear by Terry Pratchett in *Pyramids*, who makes an obscure reference to her in a discussion about the royal family of Djelibeybi (a very loosely disguised Egypt):

> "Yes Sire," he said patiently "Of course. And she is also your uncle, your cousin and your father."
>
> "Hold on. My Father ..."
>
> The Priest raised his hand soothingly. "A technicality," he said. "Your great-great-Grandmother once declared she is king as a matter of political expediency and I don't believe the edict was rescinded."[42]

Hatshepsut does, however, touch people's lives, women in particular, and one poet, Ruth Whitman, turned to Hatshepsut in the 1940s, when there was a conflict between her own femininity and her ambition:

> Hatshepsut, speak to me.
> I'm a woman like you,
> Ambitious, passionate like you.[43]

She wrote a series of poems which alternate between the poet and Hatshepsut narrating as they tell the details of their lives, as if they were old friends, talking of their families and inspirations. She really emphasises the woman that was Hatshepsut, while off-setting this against a modern woman for context.

Caldecott, however, in her *Hatshepsut; Daughter of Amun*, focused on the political prowess of Hatshepsut, with the opening scene being the moment Hatshepsut presented herself as king for the first time to a court of nobles and foreign dignitaries. The calculation and planning is evident in every orchestrated event:

> Hatshepsut mounted the steps to the throne regally, but did not sit down. She turned and stood facing the crowd. The barque of Amun was brought to rest before her, but not lowered to the floor.
>
> She did not give the signal for the crowd to rise, but there was scarcely a person in the hall that did not raise his or her head enough to stare, fascinated. Hatshepsut gazed straight ahead at the curtained shrine.
>
> Suddenly three huge golden falcons appeared, apparently from nowhere and began to circle the hall. Round and round they went, seven times, their wings raising such a wind that every garment and wig and lock of hair began to flutter. The curtain in front of the shrine was blown aside and from within a beam of light blazed out directly onto the body of Hatshepsut. It was as though she were transformed into gold, her slight figure expanded to tower over them. The three falcons one by one alighted on the back of her throne, also illuminated by the brilliant and eerie light. A voice boomed out. It did not seem to come from anyone in the hall, not even from the shrine. It was in the air above them, vibrating like a mighty drum-roll in their hearts.
>
> "This is my chosen one. This is the King who will return the Two Lands to my feet. Worship him, you princes, you noblemen, you farmers, servants and slaves. Write his name and his mighty deeds on everlasting stone, you scribes. Cover him with my breath of incense, you priests. Hatshepsut. Maat-ka-Ra. Horus of Pure Gold. Sovereign of the Two Lands. King of North and South. Son of the Sun. Beloved Daughter of Amun. Living in Splendour Forever."

Hatshepsut's showmanship and political acumen is clear in this scene and Caldecott emphasises this ever-present intelligence. As a small child she made the vow that:

> When she grew up she would make it her business to know everything!

This sentiment was carried on into her years as pharaoh, as she told her daughter Neferure that it was important to be aware of everything that is going on around her:

> and should be able to read anything and everything that was written and hear everything that was said.

Pita's Hatshepsut was also presented as an inquisitive child, who wanted nothing more than to sit upon her mother's lap and listen to her talk:

> I am very proud of you Hatshepsut. The intelligence of your heart is as sharp as Thoth's beak. There will be time for more questions later ...[44]

Both Pita and Caldecott use the apparent closeness between Hatshepsut and her father as a means of showing her character as a child: one of a young girl craving the attention of a very busy and powerful man who is then devastated by his death. In the funeral scene in *Hatshepsut; Daughter of Amun*, Hatshepsut is seething with jealousy at the grief displayed by the other women, as her father was hers and not theirs.

Caldecott has embraced the propaganda created by Hatshepsut regarding her relationship with her father and has Thutmosis I taking her to Karnak temple dressed as a male heir, fully supporting her in what would be her future quest to take over the throne as king. Even though she took on a masculine role, dressing in male attire as the role dictated, she never loses her femininity:

> She was the sort of person who walked into a room full of people and from that moment no one in the room was aware of anyone else. Beautiful women faded into the background. Men became shadows. It was not that she was so beautiful, but she gave the impression of beauty, the impression that beauty was actively being created before their eyes. Every movement of hers seemed to draw the world with it. He couldn't explain it. He had tried to resist staring at her, resenting her effect on him, but time and again he had found himself tongue-tied and awkward in her presence.

Her female nature is also apparent when she is shown the treasure of the temple of Montu and desperately wants to lift a necklace from it and put it on because:

> It was so beautiful. More beautiful than anything she had ever seen.

What woman has not uttered these words whether looking at shoes, jewellery or clothes?

Not all novels about Hatshepsut present her as a straightforward woman doing a man's job. The children's story *Mara, Daughter of the Nile*[45] adopts Hatshepsut as a wicked stepmother who imprisons Thutmosis III in the palace. Hatshepsut, while portrayed as beautiful, is haughty and cruel, enjoying the misery of Thutmosis III. Her unpopularity due to her vainglorious overspending and the usurpation of the throne from the true king leads to a plot to overthrow her and place Thutmosis III on the throne instead.

The Amulet of Amon Ra[46] also has at the centre of the story a plot to assassinate Hatshepsut; it is essentially a story of time travel, where sand within an amulet transports young Jennifer into the time of Hatshepsut and the body of an ancient Egyptian girl, Dje-Nefer. When she finally meets Hatshepsut, she finds a kind, gentle woman who is being defamed by followers of Thutmosis III, who want the populace of Egypt to believe the gods have abandoned Egypt due to her unorthodox rule.

It appears that there is more freedom of expression in the books for young readers, who are in fact telling someone else's story, than the adult novels which concentrate more on the biography than the characterisations. Hatshepsut was a great king and would no doubt have been revered as such if she were male. She increased the wealth of Egypt, she maintained peace and although there were a few small uprisings, it was nothing that was not dealt with quickly. She was pious and dedicated to her god Amun, and the gods also seemed to favour her.

It must, therefore, have been very frustrating for her to know she was doing a good job, as good as her father in fact, and yet she would have known she would receive no credit and in traditional fashion she would have known her name, reign and monuments were destined to be erased. Despite this, she carried on regardless; truly a pioneer of feminists, a multi-dimensional character in a sea of pharaohs following tradition. She broke the mould and has inspired many women in the modern world, and will continue to do so for decades to come.

CHAPTER 5

THE MYTH OF AKHENATEN

A character that really needs no introduction is Akhenaten, who has captured the imagination of Egyptologists and lay people for over a century. Even people with no specific interest in Egypt and Egyptology will have some knowledge of Akhenaten, or at least his wife Nefertiti. Many political and religious groups have adopted Akhenaten almost as a patron and he has, over the years, been compared to Moses, Martin Luther, Oliver Cromwell, Adolf Hitler, Stalin and Christ.[1] However, the adoption of Akhenaten into Western culture is a relatively modern construct. He is not mentioned in classical texts due to the eradication of his name by the ancient Egyptians and prior to 1836 CE there were no artefacts from the Amarna period in any collection in the world.[2] Despite this, there are more books written about him than any other king in Egyptian history, with the exception of Tutankhamun, his son.

Akhenaten has grasped the imagination of many, primarily because of his religious revolution, often interpreted as the first monotheistic religion. Christians have, therefore, embraced him and Biblical archaeologists hope to prove his understanding of one god, which has led to theories identifying him with Moses and the spiritual predecessor of Mohammed of the Islamic faith. The artistic style adopted during this period is also a key element of the myths surrounding Akhenaten and regardless of whether one likes the art or not, it is impossible to ignore the gaunt, elongated features of Akhenaten, mirrored in images of his wife, children and courtiers. Many theories have been introduced regarding Akhenaten and this imagery, some more bizarre than others, and Margaret Murray commented in 1949:

> The Tell el Amarna period has had more nonsense written about it than any other period in Egyptian history ... in the case of Akhenaten the facts do not bear the construction often put on them.[3]

Myths have arisen about this king, about practically every aspect of his life, and, although not supported by evidence, have been accepted by many as 'fact'. In order to ascertain the truth about Akhenaten and where the myths have originated, we need to examine them side by side.

25. North Palace, Amarna.

WHO IS AKHENATEN?

What made Akhenaten prone to such myth-making are the archaeological gaps in the knowledge that Egyptologists have, meaning other theories cannot be proved or disproved. Despite this excessive interest, in the wider context of Egyptian history, Akhenaten was not a particularly important king. He ruled for less than two decades, only seventeen years (1350–1334 BCE), and although he caused major upheaval during these seventeen years, his deeds were quickly undone and Egypt returned to normality.

HIS PARENTS

Some scholars have set up Akhenaten and his parents as the ultimate Oedipal outfit, with a domineering mother and a distant father. Akhenaten was the second son of Amenhotep III and Queen Tiye and was born under the name Amenhotep, which he later changed to Akhenaten to honour his newly revered deity. As a second son, Akhenaten was never meant to inherit the throne but between year 16 and 27 of Amenhotep III's reign (1370–1359 BCE), his older brother Thutmosis died, leaving him as heir to the throne.

Akhenaten has often been described as a sickly youth, based on the epithet he chose in later life, Great in his Duration, meaning the Long-Lived, which has been interpreted as an expression of hope on behalf of the king. However, this is the first element of the myth surrounding Akhenaten, as without a clear identification of the mummy of the king it is impossible to ascertain his state of health. This apparent poor health is often used to explain why Akhenaten is not depicted riding into battle and dispensing of enemies, as well as going someway to explain the unusual artwork of the period.

SICKLY KING

The unusual proportions displayed by Akhenaten and the royal family have intrigued scholars and have led to some interesting ideas explaining why Akhenaten displayed himself, his wife and his children in such an unorthodox fashion. The explanation for this artistic style has often been sought in medicine, although no two researchers agree on a single theory. Some authors have put together some elaborate explanations of the illnesses:

> The little Prince Amenhotep was already developing constitutional weaknesses which rendered his life very precarious. His skull was misshapen and he must have been subject to occasional epileptic fits.[4]

Ghalioungui suggested that in the early years of his reign, Akhenaten had acquired a disease affecting both his body and mind, which led to the religious and artistic changes.[5] Some have suggested this was a condition called lipodystrophy, a disturbance of the fat metabolism, where subcutaneous fat disappears from some areas of body while other areas are unaffected, although in advanced cases it normally affects the top half of the body. Although general health is maintained there can be psychological issues, which could lead to the religious zealousness. It has also been suggested that it was not Akhenaten who suffered from this, but rather Nefertiti. Akhenaten therefore represented himself in this manner out of sympathy for his once-beautiful wife.[6] As Nefertiti was only one of Akhenaten's wives, this seems unlikely and is generally supported by those who view him as a monogamous family man. If his Chief Wife became mentally unstable and her appearance changed so drastically, it is more likely he would have sent her to the harem (fig. 25), replacing her with one of his secondary wives.

Others have postulated that Akhenaten was not suffering from lipodystrophy but hyperpituitarism, a condition of the pituitary gland. This condition can cause excessive growth spurts, with the lower jaw, cheekbones, hands and feet growing at an accelerated rate. The large, distorted images from Karnak temple (plate 18) of Akhenaten are said to display these symptoms. However, as one of the symptoms is a 'diminished activity of the sex-glands',[7] one would think it could be instantly dismissed as we have the evidence he fathered at least six daughters.

Grafton Elliott Smith diagnosed Akhenaten with Frölich's Syndrome or Dystrophia Adiposogenitalis, a condition of the pituitary gland that can lead to obesity and is used to explain Akhenaten's large hips and pendulous breasts. If contracted before adolescence, the genitalia remain infantile, the voice high and body hair limited. In later stages it can cause hydrocephalus, resulting in bulging of the parietal bones of the skull,[8] which some have claimed is evident in the artwork. However, he failed to take note of two major symptoms: mental retardation and impotence.

Klinefelter's Syndrome has also been attributed to Akhenaten, which causes the male sufferer to develop breasts, small testes and very long legs. In later life the sufferer develops a high pitched voice and limited facial hair growth.[9] A further possibility is suggested by Burridge: Marfan's Syndrome. This is a rare hereditary disorder affecting one in 10,000 people, but the chances of contracting it are increased with intra-family marriages. The sufferer grows very tall and thin, has elongated extremities, a wide pelvic girdle, abnormally elongated skull and a localised distribution of subcutaneous fat. Burridge believes all of these symptoms (and others) are represented by the statues of Akhenaten. He believes the statues of Akhenaten are realistic representations, as are other elements of the Amarna art.[10]

If he was a sufferer of Marfan's, both he and his children would have a weak cardiovascular system and, due to cone-shaped corneas, would probably be blind for most of their adult lives, with a greater sensitivity to cold. Marfan's Syndrome, unlike some of the other disorders, does not affect the brain and often sufferers are bright and intelligent. These symptoms have been used to explain some of the oddities of Amarna art. In the artwork, the royal family are very tactile, with open displays of affection. Akhenaten's obsession with the Aten, the only deity whose rays he could physically feel on his skin, for some, hint towards blindness.

As this condition is hereditary, the initial carrier is questioned. A spoof in the *National Enquirer* claimed the mummy of Yuya, the grandfather of Akhenaten, bears remarkable similarities to a Marfan's sufferer. Akhenaten has been adopted as a kind of patron to Marfan's sufferers. Examination in 2010 of Yuya, Tutankhamun and KV55, which DNA has proved to be his father, show that none suffered from Marfan's Syndrome or any other of the suggested diseases,[11] debunking these theories entirely, meaning the artwork must have some other significance. Examination of KV55 also shows us that he stood just under 5 feet 7 inches and was approximately twenty-five years of age. Should this be Akhenaten, it indicates that he had a long co-regency with his father to account for a seventeen-year reign. The only unusual aspect of his body is evidence of minimal hypogonadism, which means the development of the body is towards the feminine, with a slight, slender figure.[12] The evidence is so minimal that it would have no other symptoms and certainly would not make Akhenaten resemble the statues.

ARTISTIC STYLISATION

All of these disease theories are based on artistic representations rather than examination of the remains of Akhenaten. This assumes the statues are portraits and not a medium of representing religious ideals.[13]

Colossal statues from the temple of Akhenaten at Karnak show him naked, displaying no genitalia. The disease theories would have us believe, an indication of his impotence and infertility. In order to explain how an impotent and infertile man could father six daughters, it is suggested he contracted a disease after he fathered his daughters, or even that Nefertiti cuckolded him with a variety of partners. Mariette even suggested he had been castrated as a prisoner in the Sudan, although where this idea originated is unknown as there is no evidence to support this.[14]

Tom Holland's novel *Sleeper in the Sands* suggests the appearance of Akhenaten is evidence of his 'other worldliness', and he is in fact from another planet. The sexless imagery, however, could represent not Akhenaten but Nefertiti,[15] which calls into question how realistic these images can be if Akhenaten and his wife are indiscernible from each other. Early discoverers of much of the Amarna art believed the images of Nefertiti and Akhenaten were in fact two queens as the characteristics of both were so similar. This led to French scholar Lefébure (1838–1934) deducing that Akhenaten was a woman who chose to dress like a man. Although this theory is totally dismissed by modern scholars, at the time this reflected the attitude of historians, which was to determine what was 'wrong' with Akhenaten to explain the effeminate and androgynous imagery.[16] Some authors have suggested that such androgynous characteristics represent 'a hidden aversion to masculinity, or at least no inclination to, or pride in its exhibition',[17] which is a bold statement when faced with imagery which no one truly understands.

This led to the myth that Akhenaten was homosexual, which has been published by both Egyptologists and fiction writers. The main evidence for Akhenaten being homosexual is the Paser Stela (fig. 26) housed in the Berlin museum. The Stela was designed for a military office, Paser, and depicts two kings, identified by their royal crowns, with the foremost figure wearing the double crown of Upper and Lower Egypt and the other king wearing the blue crown. The king seated on the right wearing the blue crown, and identified by many as King Smenkhkare, has his arm around the shoulders of Akhenaten. These identifications were made even though the cartouches, while carved, have not been completed and are all blank. This led many Egyptologists to surmise in the 1920s that Akhenaten must be homosexual and this seemed to be supported by other intimate scenes from the Amarna period. This idea was adopted by Thomas Mann, who portrayed Akhenaten in his novel as wearing makeup, henna on his nails and dressing like a decadent aristocrat.[18] The novel *On a Balcony* (1958) describes Akhenaten's sexual attraction to Horemheb, as well as his rather strange predilection to wearing gloves made from human skin to prevent mortals from touching him.

In 1973, John Harris suggested that this was not Smenkhkare as originally thought, as there were not enough cartouches for two kings. There were seven cartouches in total, two for the Aten, two for Akhenaten and one for the remaining figure, who was said to be not a king but a queen – Nefertiti. However, this was not the first time this theory has been suggested. Norman Davis, in the 1920s, suggested Smenkhkare was none other than Nefertiti, based on the study of throne and birth names of both Smenkhkare and Nefertiti. Unfortunately this theory was ignored[19] until fairly

26. Paser Stela, Berlin.

recently, in the last fifteen years or so, when numerous Egyptologists now agree with this idea. The theory that Nefertiti ruled as Akhenaten's co-regent is supported by another small stela from the Berlin museum, also unfinished, which shows Akhenaten and Nefertiti under the sun-disc. Although the cartouches are also blank, there are three full-sized ones and a fourth squashed into the available space as an afterthought. It would appear the role of Nefertiti changed while it was being commissioned.[20]

Surely this shows an artistic style attempting to display certain characteristics or ideals. As Akhenaten's ideals changed, so did the art-work. At the beginning of his reign, Akhenaten is displayed in traditional form (plate 19), but as his dedication to the cult of the Aten increased he is shown in a more androgynous fashion, with male and female characteristics displaying his divine nature,[21] his ability to create in the manner of a god. It is suggested they are representations of the king and queen as Shu and Tefnut.[22] These images are not intended to show a portrait of the king, but rather reflect his divine nature and display his differences from the rest of the human race.[23]

AFROCENTRIC APPROACH

Afrocentrism was introduced in the mid-nineteenth century, when black scholars emphasised the difference between African Egypt and White Europe in ancient times. A great pioneer of this was Edward Wilmot Blydon (1832–1912), who carved the word Liberia on one of the pyramids as a means of advocating Africa (including Egypt) as a safe place for freed slaves. He wrote an interesting article called *The Negro in Ancient History*, which influenced an African American journalist and author, Pauline Hopkins (1859–1930), in her novel *Of One Blood. Or, the Hidden Face*. In the novel, the ancient Egyptian civilisation has survived in secret, awaiting a black king who will enable them to come out of hiding. She makes allusions to Moses being black and there are indirect references to the reign of Akhenaten.[24] One of the best known advocators of the Afrocentric approach was the Senegalese scholar Cheikh (Sheikh) Anta Diop (1923–1986), who studied, among other things, Egyptology in the Sorbonne but twice failed his PhD on the subject of Egypt as the first African high culture. Not only did he assert that black Africans were the perpetrators of Egyptian culture, but as Egyptian culture influenced Greek culture, black Africans were the origin of the West's Graeco-Roman heritage. Some Afrocentrists go as far as claiming Stonehenge was also built by black Africans, as Pliny describes the ancient Britons in a manner which could be interpreted as suggesting they were black.[25]

As early as 1911 and Weigall's *Akhnaton; Pharaoh of Egypt*, the ethnic origin has been questioned by scholars. Weigall suggested that Yuya, the grandfather of Akhenaten, was not Egyptian, as his name was not Egyptian and was not rendered easily in the language.[26] This has since been adopted by Afrocentrists who feel black history has been stolen by whites. They have also adopted Tiye, Nefertiti and Akhenaten as black, despite any evidence to the contrary.

Again the artwork is instrumental in this theory of black origins for Akhenaten, as the Karnak statues are viewed as stereotypically African, with thick lips and broad nostrils. Egyptologists often refer to the Amarna artistic style as grotesque, which Afrocentrists take as proof that the white historians are racist. The small head of Tiye, made of ebony, showing an older woman, is also taken as proof that Akhenaten was black, and the apparent importance of the matriarchal figure in the Amarna period is viewed as an African cultural element. The idea of a matriarchal society, however, has been widely disputed by most Egyptologists for decades.

Anna Melissa Graves also insists on using the artwork as proof of black origin for the Amarna family, and comments that Akhenaten was:

> less negroid than his mother ... and the portrait busts of his daughters show them all to be beautiful quadroons, though perhaps octoroons.

It seems counterproductive in an argument to prove the family's black origins that she states the daughters were mixed-race and could pass as white.[27]

Maulana Karenga, a promoter of black history in the 1960s, uses not simply art, but also the concept of Maat as proof of black origin. He interprets Maat as being righteousness, cosmic harmony and respect for ancestors, which he asserts is an African concept. As Akhenaten was constantly associated with Maat, being called 'The King who Lives on Maat' and 'Beloved of Maat', this emphasises that Akhenaten was black. He clearly does not take into account all the other cultures and religions which also have the same concept; for example the concept of *rta* in India, representative of all the same things and more.

The Central Reading Youth Provision Black History Mural in Reading, Berkshire, was painted as a lineage of heroes of black history (plate 20). It is separated into five sections, with the black face of 'Blackenaten' and Nefertiti with the Giza pyramids in the background. There are hieroglyphs above these Egyptian figures which read, 'Rage is what god loves to hearken to: and you should love up to yourself in his name.' Black Mohammed, the prophet of Islam, is on the other side of Akhenaten,[28] indicating the Afrocentrists associate Akhenaten with the beginnings of Islam, no doubt instigated by the belief he was a monotheist. Akhenaten is the first in a king list of black heroes, with Toussaint l'Ouverture, Malcolm X, Martin Luther King, Emperor Haile Selassie and Bob Marley following. The mural was commissioned by Reading Council and therefore almost gives this history the same legitimacy as a war memorial.

This mural was designed to show the black historical legacy as introduced by W. D. Fard in 1930s Detroit. He emphasised the importance of black history and used the Akhenaten portrayed in Breasted's *The Conquest of Civilisation* (1926), while bizarrely ignoring Breasted's colonial assertions that the white race was the carrier of civilisation. Akhenaten was presented as fearless, a man full of vision and the founder of a new era, and this appealed to the African American community living through the depression. Fard was the influence for Elijah Mohammed, a leader of radical Black Muslim groups, who have adopted Akhenaten as the first monotheist, connecting the foundation of Islam in Egypt while bypassing Jewish and Christian traditions.

A simple answer is available to this question of Afrocentrism and lies in the human remains surviving from Egypt. White supremacists of the nineteenth century used the mummies and skeletons of the ancient Egyptians, as well as studies of artwork and hair samples, to prove the Egyptians were Caucasian.[29] While these studies are no longer accepted, Afrocentric supporters should perhaps turn to the human remains themselves. According to the Afrocentrists, Tiye was definitely black based on the ebony statue, but surely it would be more appropriate to study her body and that of her parents. The hair of the Elder Lady from KV35 has been positively matched to hair in Tutankhamun's tomb labelled as belonging to Queen Tiye, suggesting this mummy is probably hers. Studies of the body may indicate whether black African features are present; however, the mummies of her parents, Yuya and Tuya, would also need to be studied, although on appearance alone they do not appear to be black African. The bodies of Tutankhamun and his two daughters are clearly identified, as is their mother, the KV21A mummy, and the body of Akhenaten was recently identified as probably being the body in KV55.[30] KV21A may be the sister of Tutankahmun as well as his wife, meaning she would be the daughter of KV55 (Akhenaten) and would also be black. Should any of these mummies display black African characteristics then this would be better evidence to use than the stylistic artwork.

FAMILY

Shortly before coming to the throne Akhenaten married an unknown noble woman named Nefertiti, who is sometimes believed to be the daughter of Ay, the brother of

Queen Tiye and the king who followed Tutankhamun onto the throne. This assertion is based on a title held by his wife Tiy, that of 'wet nurse' of Nefertiti, indicating that although probably not her mother, she could be her step mother.[31] However, as her parents' names are not mentioned in any inscriptions, the debate regarding her origins will continue. This marriage produced six known daughters, Meritaten, Meketaten, Ankhesenepaten (the future wife of Tutankhamun), Neferneferuaten, Neferneferure and Setepenre. There is no record of Akhenaten and Nefertiti having any sons, although Tutankhamun is called 'Son of the King' on a block from Amarna.

In 2010, the body of Tutankhamun and that of KV55 were studied, and it was ascertained that as they had a number of unique anthropological features in common, as well as an identical blood group, KV55 was probably the father of Tutankhamun.[32] The study revealed that Yuya and Tuya, the parents of Tiye, were definitely his great-grandparents, Elder Lady and Amenhotep III were his grandparents and KV55 and the Younger Lady were his parents. Does this mean KV55 is Akhenaten? Possibly, but we are really none the wiser unless we can prove that Tiye was the mother of KV55. Is the Younger Lady Nefertiti, as suggested by Joanne Fletcher?[33] This is inconclusive, so although the names are not confirmed, science has confirmed the genealogy.

Akhenaten's harem of wives is often overlooked by many researchers who wish to present him as a good 'Pseudo-Christian' king, with great love for his wife Nefertiti. Perhaps he did love her, but evidence shows he had at least four wives: Nefertiti, Kiya and Tadukhipa, a Babylonian princess,[34] as well as his daughter Ankhesenepaten, who was later married to Smenkhkare and Tutankhamun. It is even possible they had a child together called Ankhesenepaten Tasherit (The Younger).

AKHENATEN AND THE ATEN

Akhenaten's notoriety, and indeed the myths that have arisen, are primarily due to his religious revolution and his apparent determination to obliterate all gods other than the Aten (or sun-disc).

The Aten, however, was not introduced by Akhenaten and was mentioned in the Coffin Texts as early as the twelfth dynasty (1991–1878 BCE). At this time, Aten was shown as a man with the head of a falcon surmounted by a sun disc, similar to the iconography of Re-Horakhty, and was an important element of the solar cycle. Akhenaten altered the imagery to that of a sun-disc with rays ending in hands holding an ankh. Although this imagery is synonymous with the Amarna period, it was introduced earlier and is seen on Amenhotep II's stela at the Giza sphinx. The ankh signs offered by the Aten are only ever offered to members of the royal family.

The rise of the Aten started during the reign of Amenhotep III, as it was pushed up the hierarchy of the pantheon in an attempt to limit the power of the Priesthood of Amun, whose power almost equalled his own. At the start of Amenhotep III's reign, the office of High Priest of Amun and that of Chief Minster were held by one man, Ptahmose, but by the end of his reign the two posts had been separated, diminishing

27. Great Temple of Aten, Amarna.

the power held by one man. Akhenaten's destruction of other gods was about more than the power of the priesthood.

In the first couple of years of Akhenaten's reign the changes to the religion were subtle, beginning with enclosing Aten's name within two cartouches, as if part of a royal titulary, the first time systemisation of the royalty of the god had occurred.[35] The Aten was treated as a king and given regnal years corresponding with Akhenaten's, indicating the king and the god were equal.[36] At this point, other deities of the Egyptian pantheon co-existed alongside the Aten. It was only in year 9 (1341 BCE) that Akhenaten closed the temples dedicated to other deities, re-directing their revenue to the Aten temples at Amarna (fig. 27).

In the later years of his reign, Akhenaten's campaign against other deities focussed on Amun and Akhenaten's men destroyed his temples throughout Egypt, damaging statues and images, including the name of Amun, which was chiselled out of inscriptions, including from the cartouche of his own father Amunhotep. In some instances, wherever the word 'gods' in plural appeared, it was also hastily chiselled away.[37] To many people, this behaviour gives the impression of monotheism, but when one delves further into Akhenaten's religious beliefs this is clearly not the case.

WORSHIPPING THE ATEN

The cult of the Aten and the religious practices associated with the cult were unlike anything that had gone previously in Egyptian history, although there were numerous elements which were still in existence.

The temples to the Aten hold the key to the religious practices. All the Aten temples were open-roofed and therefore bright and airy, whereas traditional temples were shadowy and dark. With an open-roofed temple there was no need for a cult statue, and the processional way through the centre of the temple ended with an elevated altar rather than a dark, enclosed sanctuary. Aten could therefore be viewed in every corner of the temple, eliminating the reliance on images, although the temples were far from bare, with dedicatory stelae and rows of offering tables constantly piled with food offerings. These offerings were left in the rays of the sun, so Aten could absorb nourishment from them before they were distributed to the priests of the Aten.

The nature of the Aten was also different to other gods as he had no human or animal form,[38] and did not speak, meaning there was no 'Holy Book' or mythology about the deity. The Aten was androgynous and represented the light emanating from the sun. Without any form of doctrine surrounding this god, Akhenaten claimed to receive his information and teachings directly from the Aten,[39] not as a prophet, but rather as an element of the god himself. Akhenaten then placed this 'teaching' or 'instruction' into the heart of his subjects through an oral tradition, perhaps standing at the Window of Appearances giving sermons. The Hymn to the Aten, found in the tomb of Ay at Amarna, explains the concept:

> There is none who know you (Aten) except your son Neferkheperure-waenra (Akhenaten).
> For you make him aware of your plans and strength.[40]

Many people have even attributed this hymn to Akhenaten himself, marking him as a poet and spiritual leader. The only person capable of communicating with Aten was Akhenaten, who, as discussed, raised himself to the same status as the god by placing the insignia of kingship upon the god. When the artistic representations are studied closely, Akhenaten and the royal family worshipped Aten directly, standing outside with their arms raised in adoration on behalf of themselves and the people. However, all non-royals are shown as worshipping Akhenaten, as if he were a god.[41] Akhenaten had clearly set himself up as an equal to the god, giving him the divine right to be worshipped.

AKHENATEN OF THE UNDERWORLD

Akhenaten was a replacement god for the ordinary people, and this concept is taken further regarding the funerary beliefs of the Egyptians. In the tombs of the officials from Amarna, the traditional images of the gods of the underworld are replaced with Akhenaten and the royal family. They worship Aten as the tomb owner worships the royal family, demonstrating the only way to obtain an afterlife was through worshipping Akhenaten.[42] It has been suggested that Akhenaten replaced Osiris and the Hall of Judgement, and everyone needed to address him before they could be reborn.[43] Akhenaten even invaded the personal worship of the ordinary people, with images of the royal family in their household shrines.

HENOTHEISM OR MONOTHEISM?

It is apparent that rather than replacing the vast pantheon of Egyptian gods with Aten, for the majority of the people of Egypt the replacement was Akhenaten himself. This throws doubt on the theory of monotheism. Monotheism by definition means the worship of one god, whereas in Egypt at this time there were at least two gods: Aten and Akhenaten.

It is even indicated that there were three deities worshipped at this time, as would be traditional, as most Egyptian gods are part of a divine triad comprising god, consort and child. As Aten does not have any mythology, at first glance Aten appears not to be part of such a triad. However, on closer inspection, he was part of a triad consisting of Aten, Akhenaten and Nefertiti, who were all worshipped in their own right. Aten represented the solar creator god, Akhenaten Aten's offspring, Shu, and Nefertiti Aten's consort, Tefnut.[44] It appeared that while Akhenaten favoured Aten over all other deities and endeavoured to decrease their power through ignoring them, there were a number of traditional gods present within his new religious revolution.

Akhenaten and Nefertiti were often represented as Shu and Tefnut, the deities of air and moisture respectively, and the children of the sun-god, clearly demonstrating their divine nature. The sacred bull of Heliopolis, an oracle of the sun-god Ra, was kept at Amarna,[45] although it has been suggested that this was in order to antagonise the priests of Heliopolis. Even the royal insignia of the *uraeus* seen adorning the crown of Akhenaten and the sun disc itself represents a traditional deity, the cobra goddess, Wadjet, who had adorned the crowns of pharaohs since the Old Kingdom. Even in the Hymn to the Aten, the so-called masterpiece written by Akhenaten, the introduction invokes more than the Aten:

> Praise of Re Horakhty, Rejoicing on the Horizon, in His Name as Shu Who Is in the Aten disc, living forever and ever.[46]

A deity who is consistently invoked throughout his reign was the goddess Maat, the goddess of justice and cosmic balance. From the start of his reign Akhenaten is given the epithet 'Living on Truth', (*ankh em maat*), which became almost the mantra for his reign: living according to what is right and true. However, his interpretation of what Maat meant differed from the traditional view, hence he felt justified in eliminating the gods of the afterlife. He seemed to believe that Egypt had strayed from the righteous path in everything, and therefore he became involved not only in the larger aspects of life and culture but also the smaller aspects[47] such as building materials, changing the large cumbersome stone blocks for the smaller *talatat* blocks reminiscent of those used to build the step pyramid of Djoser. He was 'Beloved of Maat' because in his own mind he had restored Egypt to the right and just way.

This indicates that Akhenaten carefully selected which gods were 'banned' and which were useful to the Aten, and indeed the Akhenaten cult. It demonstrates specifically that he *believed* in the pantheon of Egyptian gods and therefore was not a monotheist, but rather chose to revere one god who is not the only god, which is henotheistic.[48]

CHRISTIANITY IN ITS INFANCY

However, these other deities and Akhenaten's elevation to deity is often overlooked and certain scholars focus on the so-called monotheism of the period. One of the greatest advocates of Akhenaten as a monotheist, at least in print, was Arthur Weigall, who was present at but not part of the excavation of Tutankhamun's tomb. Weigall's Akhenaten was a monotheist, a monogamist, a family man and a great teacher of religion:

> The first apostle of the Simple Life.[49]

Akhenaten's most famous teaching is that of the Great Hymn to the Aten, from Ay's tomb. There are distinct similarities between the Hymn and Psalm 104 from the Book of Psalms in the Bible. There are eight points of comparison between them and this is often quoted as proof of monotheistic and 'Christian' doctrine.

The Hymn to Aten states:

> The land is in darkness, in the manner of death.
> They sleep in a room, with heads wrapped up,
> Nor sees one eye the other.
> All their goods which are under their heads might be stolen,
> (But) they would not perceive (it).
> Every lion is come forth from his den;
> All creeping things, they sting.
> Darkness is a shroud and the earth is in stillness,
> For he who made them rests in his horizon.

This is compared with verse 20 from Psalm 104:

> Thou makest darkness and it is night: wherein all the beasts of the forest do creep forth.
> The young lions roar after their prey and seek their meat from God.

This verse from the Hymn to the Aten:

> At daybreak, when thou arisest on the horizon,
> When thou shinest as the Aten by day,
> Thou drivest away the darkness and givest thy rays.
> The Two Lands are in festivity every day,
> Awake and standing upon (their) feet,
> For thou hast raised them up.
> Washing their bodies, taking (their) clothing,
> Their arms are (raised) in praise at thy appearance.
> All the world, they do their work.

This is compared to verse 23 from Psalm 104:

> The sun ariseth, they gather themselves together and lay them down in their dens. Man goeth forth unto his work and to his labour until the evening.

This verse from the Hymn to the Aten:

> The birds which fly from their nests,
> Their wings are (stretched out) in praise to thy ka.
> All beasts spring upon (their) feet.
> Whatever flies and alights,
> They live when thou hast risen (for) them.

This is often compared with verse 12 of the Psalm:

> By them shall the fowls of the heaven have their habitation, which sing among the branches

The Hymn to the Aten:

> The ships are sailing north and south as well,
> For every way is open at thy appearance.
> The fish in the river dart before thy face;
> Thy rays are in the midst of the great green sea.
> Creator of seed in women,
> Thou who makest fluid into man,
> Who maintainest the son in the womb of his mother,
> Who soothest him with that which stills his weeping,
> Thou nurse (even) in the womb.

Similarities are seen between this and verse 25 of Psalm 104:

> So is this great and wide sea, wherein are things creeping innumerable, both small and great beasts.
> There go the ships: there is that leviathan, whom thou hast made to play therein.

The verse from the Hymn to the Aten:

> Who givest breath to sustain all that he has made!
> When he descends from the womb to breathe
> On the day when he is born,
> Thou openest his mouth completely.

This is compared to verse 29 of the Psalm:

Thou hidest thy face, they are troubled: thou takest away their breath, they die and return
to their dust.

Finally this section from the Hymn to the Aten:

Thou suppliest his necessities.
When the chick in the egg speaks within the shell,
Thou givest him breath within it to maintain him.
When thou hast made him his fulfilment within the egg, to break it,
He comes forth from the egg to speak at his completed (time);
He walks upon his legs when he comes forth from it.

Compared to this verse of the psalm:

These wait all upon thee; that thou mayest give them their meat in due season.

While these comparisons may seem convincing, both the psalm and the hymn have
many other verses which do not compare with each other. To suggest that the Hymn
to the Aten was the inspiration for the psalm, and then conversely Akhenaten was the
pre-cursor of Christian monotheism is a huge assumption. The Hymn to the Aten is in
itself not unique, and many of the ideas are not new[50] and are adapted from the Middle
Kingdom Coffin Texts and earlier hymns to Amun. He had done what many corporations
do in the modern world: take well-known elements of the traditional religion and re-
brand them to fit his new god. These ideas were then in turn adopted and re-branded
by the Hebrews and then the Christians, and woven into their religion.[51]

Freud, in his *Moses and Monotheism*, reacts to this scenario and presents Moses
as an Egyptian who was close to Akhenaten and, along with the king, adopted the
Aten. He then took the Aten religion after the death of Akhenaten and perfected it
until it was appropriate for the Jewish faith.[52] The religion passed on from Moses was
considered by Freud to be intellectual yet unrelenting;

it increased little by little to every greater clarity, consistency, harshness and intolerance.[53]

He compares the Jewish religion with that of the Aten, drawing on this harshness,
strict adherence to one god and circumcision, as well as no acceptance of an afterlife.[54]
Freud's objective in writing was seen as a means of emphasising the Jewish contribution
to the world, as well as their ability to survive through centuries of oppression.

AKHENATEN AS MOSES

This connection between Akhenaten and Moses was taken one step further by
Ahmed Osman, who presented a theory that Akhenaten was Moses and the familiar
individuals from his reign were characters from the Bible.

The evidence that Akhenaten is Moses is not wholly convincing and his theory has been largely dismissed by the archaeological community. The main reason for this dismissal is because the Biblical record is not supported by archaeological evidence and numerous assumptions are made.

He refers to the Talmud (the compilation of laws and legends), which states that not only did Moses live in the palace but succeeded the throne, and was in fact a king who officiated as high priest to his cult. He uses this as evidence in addition to the one of the cartouches of Aten. He translates the second cartouche as beginning *Im-r-n*, which he interprets as Amran or Imran, the name of the father of the Biblical Moses. As Akhenaten consistently refers to the Aten as his father, Osman believes this is proof that Akhenaten was Moses.[55] However, his translation is not correct, as he has phonetically transliterated the text but not translated it. The cartouches read:

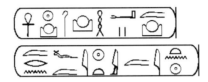

Living sun of the Horizon, ruler of the Horizon, rejoicing in the Horizon in his name (m rn=f) Re the father, Aten.[56]

Osman used part of a word (*m (in) rn (name)*) to prove his theory, which, although it is not a name in ancient Egyptian, he translated as such to match his hypothesis.

He also names individuals working at the Amarna temples of the Aten and claims they are the same individuals mentioned in the Bible; for example, Meryre II was the High Priest of the Aten at Amarna and Panehesy was the chief servitor of the Aten. He translates the name of the official Aper' El to mean 'Hebrew who worships the Lord'.[57] However, he had, earlier in his research,[58] stated that the name Khabiru also means Hebrew, showing there is a discrepancy with his hieroglyphic translations and as these are the basis of his arguments, the whole thing falls apart.

He ascertains that the nurse of Moses was Tiy, Ay's wife, based on her identification as the wet-nurse of Nefertiti and the assumption that Akhenaten and Nefertiti were half-siblings, for which there is no evidence. As Tiy is a wetnurse, he makes the supposition that she has a child, even though this child is not mentioned in the records. He identifies this child as the biblical Aaron[59] who, according to Islamic tradition, was a milk brother of Moses, related through the wet nurse. However, there is no evidence that Ay and Tiy's child was a boy and if it was, the question is raised as to why, when he became king, Ay did not pass the throne to his son, rather than the unrelated general Horemheb.

AKHENATEN THE PACIFIST

A subsidiary myth, which runs alongside that of the spiritualist Akhenaten, is that he was a pacifist, more interested in his god than war.[60] There are none of the typical images of the king riding into battle at the head of his army and while some believe he was too sickly to be a warrior, others believe he had no interest in war, as he was at one with his god and did not believe in violence.

Egypt at the time had a full standing army of thousands of highly trained soldiers, but none of them were deployed for trading expeditions or military campaigns, despite the growing troubles in the Near East with the Hittites. This suggests that they were all idle at Amarna. Excavations there have uncovered a large portion of the city which was occupied by military barracks and police headquarters, and it is clear that there was a heavy military presence at the town of Amarna, the so-called religious utopia. Some authors have really bought into this pacifist scenario and Weigall (1880–1934) was impressed with Akhenaten's spiritual nature:

> for once we may look into the mind of a king of Egypt and may see something of its working, all that is there observed is worthy of admiration.[61]

Can we possibly make these assumptions based on his religious revolution? In less than nine years Akhenaten had completely overhauled the religious beliefs of the country, which would have been a difficult task. The changes Akhenaten instigated and the speed with which they were implemented would have surprised, if not shocked, many people, causing uproar. However, open revolt never seems to have occurred and it needs to be questioned as to why.

Akhenaten effectively banned the worship of gods who had been a part of Egyptian belief systems for 2,000 years, providing a completely different system to follow instead, one where Akhenaten was the head. The relative ease with which he achieved this change suggests two things: either he really possessed 'the gift of the gab' and managed to convince a nation that their gods were ineffective and the way forward was to worship him, or the people were coerced into paying lip service to the new cult, either through bribery or fear. The evidence suggests the latter.[62]

Images of Akhenaten constantly show a military presence consisting of numerous Asiatic and Nubian soldiers acting as his personal bodyguard. Using foreign soldiers was a very good tactic as they were effectively reliant on him for their lifestyle and career but not affected by the changes he made, resulting in no personal vendettas against him. Essentially, they would do as they were told for financial gain. In addition to his bodyguard, Amarna had a very heavy military presence and the network of roads surrounding the city indicates there was a military patrol route in place of an enclosure wall. These patrols would have picked up any ne'er-do-wells in the vicinity, but could also prevent people from leaving except via a monitored route.

This heavy military presence was obviously felt to be necessary, and it has been suggested that the move from Thebes to Amarna was instigated by a rebellion against Akhenaten. This would mean that the soldiers were primarily to protect Akhenaten from personal attack and possibly to punish those who rebelled.

Redford correctly points out that the Amarna culture was very much based on the gift-giving system, more commonly known as bribery, and indeed Amarna art is full of images of the royal couple rewarding favoured courtiers with gifts of gold jewellery.[63]

1. Nebamun hunting in the marshes (eighteenth dynasty). (*British Museum*)

2. Nile view at Luxor.

3. The Holy Family at church of St Sergius, Cairo.

4. Holy Family in Egypt, the Hanging Church, Cairo.

Right: **5.** Red Pyramid internal burial chamber, Dahshur.

Below: **6.** Sphinx of Giza.

7. Medinet Habu; some say the wings depicted frequently in Egyptian art shows a preoccupation with the sky due to extra-terrestrial origins.

8. Sarcophagus from the British Museum. Some believe the preoccupation with boats proves the early Egyptians were space-aliens.

Right: **9.** Alexander the Great. (*Photograph courtesy of photos.com*)

Below: **10.** Roman Amphitheatre, Kom el Dikka, Alexandria. (*Photograph courtesy of Brian Billington*)

11. Qait Bey fortress, Alexandria (*Photograph courtesy of Brian Billington*)

12. Thutmosis III, Luxor Museum.

Right: **13.** Senenmut and Neferure, British Museum.

Below: **14.** Temple of Hatshepsut, Deir el Bahri.

15. Hatshepsut in male attire, Deir el Bahri, Luxor.

16. Hatshepsut as a sphinx, Egyptian Museum, Cairo.

Above: **17.** Incense from the expedition to Punt, Deir el Bahri, Luxor. *(Photograph courtesy of Francesco Gasperetti from Wikimedia Commons)*

Right: **18.** Akhenaten, Luxor Museum, Luxor.

19. Akhenaten in traditional pose, Open Air Museum, Karnak, Luxor.

20. Central Reading Youth Provision Black History Mural, Reading. (*Photograph courtesy of Brian Billington*)

21. Nefertiti, Ashmolean Museum, Oxford.

22. Akhenaten's sarcophagus, Egyptian
Museum, Cairo.

23. Augustus Caesar plaster-cast, Ashmolean Museum, Oxford.

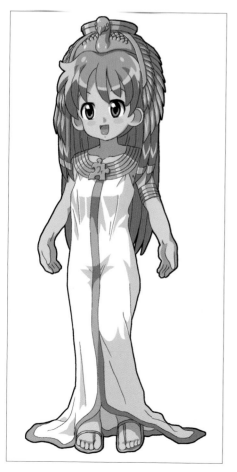

24. Manga Cleopatra. (*Drawing by Kasuga courtesy of Wikimedia Commons*)

Above: **25.** Ptolemaic mummy, Louvre.

Right: **26.** Tutankhamun's death mask, Cairo Museum. (*Photograph courtesy of Clare Banks*)

Above: **27.** Mummy display, British Museum. (*Photograph courtesy of Brian Billington*)

Left: **28.** Halloween display window, 101event.com, London. (*Photograph courtesy of Brian Billington*)

29. Entrance to Egyptian Avenue, Highgate Cemetery.

30. Alexander Gordon's grave, Putney Vale Cemetery. (*Photograph courtesy of Elisabeth Kerner*)

31. Cairo Museum exterior.

32. Luxor Hotel light show, Las Vegas.
(*Photograph courtesy of Paul Dunstan*)

This was a means for Akhenaten to maintain loyalty by keeping favoured individuals wealthy. Bribery and fear should not be necessary if the religion has any basis in truth. Did Akhenaten truly believe in Aten and everything he knew about the god, or was this all about political power?

AKHENATEN THE POLITICIAN

The polar opposite of the spiritual, religious leader that some myths present is a callous, calculating politician. Although Akhenaten caused major religious upheaval with his revolution, he maintained the ideology of kingship, the divinity of the king and the king's role as intermediary between the people and the gods.

As mentioned earlier, before Akhenaten moved the capital to Amarna he is shown as a traditional king, in the pose of smiting his enemies, and even after the move he is shown in the equally traditional activities of overseeing military actions and receiving tribute from foreign dignitaries and vassal states.[64] Other elements of tradition such as the religious processions through the streets were adapted at Amarna, with daily processions through the streets of the king and the royal family. Instead of the god being the focus of these processions, the king and the royal family were, showing their divine status.

Traditional processions enabled the people to get close to their god and these daily chariot rides produced the same result. Therefore, he was more of a traditionalist than the radical he is portrayed to be. He simply took this traditionalism one step too far. It is quite possible that the religious revolution, replacing the pantheon with Akhenaten, was a political rather than a religious act. If the king is the only mortal with access to the god, the entire populace are therefore totally dependent on the king for both political and spiritual nourishment,[65] giving him supreme power over his people as well as revenue from the temples in Egypt.

The total destruction of temples, images and even names was enough to show the populace the power that the new king held and they were no doubt terrified of being found in possession of objects bearing the name of Amun. Some began destroying the signs themselves, or even changing their own names to show allegiance with the new king and his god. In the streets of Amarna the intimidation would have been worse than elsewhere in Egypt, and the inhabitants were not only afraid of the large military presence but also of 'informers' who would try to save themselves by informing on others' religious practices.[66] This is the severest form of control, political dominance disguised as religious zealousness, and is hardly suggestive of a spiritual utopia created by a deeply religious man.

AKHENATEN THE FASCIST

Going one step further than a ruthless politician sees Akhenaten adopted by fascist regimes because of this political prowess and power. His non-Egyptian origins are an aspect of this and studies were carried out which proved he was of Aryan extraction, considered the superior nation on earth. This so-called Aryan blood and his predilection to sun worship were said by Savitri Devi (1905–82) to associate him with Nazi ideology. Devi even wrote *Akhenaten; A play* (1948), which is a parallel between the life of Akhenaten and the fall of Hitler set in the time just after Akhenaten's death. The heroine is Zetut-Neferu-Aton, a fanatic who is based on Devi herself. Zetut-Neferu-Aton is martyred at the end of the play in the name of Aton. Devi later came to be one of the first Holocaust deniers and an important figure in the Neo-Nazi underground. In 1958 Devi wrote her fifth book on Akhenaten, *The Lightening and the Sun*, which compares Akhenaten, Ghengis Khan and Hitler and has a rather shocking dedication:

> To the god-like Individual of our times;
> The man against Time;
> The greatest European of all times;
> Both Sun and Lightening:
> ADOLF HITLER
> As a tribute of unfailing love and loyalty, for ever and ever.

She truly believed that Akhenaten and Hitler were similar in their intelligence, religious and spiritual outlook, even taking it as far as to suggest Akhenaten, like Hitler and herself, was vegetarian and banned blood-sports from Amarna. While Akhenaten's methods may have been harsh, ethnic cleansing was never an issue for him as everyone was created by Aten and therefore all were welcome.

LOVING FAMILY MAN

Another side to the personality of Akhenaten is that of a loving family man, which is normally propagated by those supporting the idea of a monogamous, monotheistic king. This is supported solely by the artwork, which is often referred to as 'realistic' or 'naturalistic'.

However, these images just helped to further separate the king from the ordinary people as they present him as being different from them. This difference is clearly marked by the elongated, gaunt depictions which are adopted by the rest of the royal family too (plate 21), as the chosen ones of the Aten, and the other courtiers are shown in more traditional proportions.[67]

The other element of Amarna art which has led to this myth of Akhenaten being a loving family man is the royal family, shown in very relaxed informal poses, reflecting what are interpreted as intimate family scenes. Akhenaten is regularly depicted with his wife Nefertiti and their six daughters draped over them, and there are images in the Louvre of Nefertiti sitting on Akhenaten's lap (fig. 28) and another where she is leading her husband to her bed, something unique to this period. Many people have taken these family scenes as realistic representations, proof that Akhenaten loved Nefertiti very much and that they were the ultimate happy family. However, it is often overlooked that his secondary wives, Kiya in particular, were also considered important

28. Nefertiti on Akhenaten's lap, Louvre, Paris.

enough to be depicted on official monuments and at least one of his daughters bore him a child. This does go against Akhenaten as a monogamous, religious, family man. These images, like many others from ancient Egypt, are propaganda and presented Akhenaten as how he wanted to be perceived, not necessarily how he lived. Similarities have been made between these images and those of Hitler petting his dog, or Stalin seated with his comforting pipe[68] or the jubilee portrait of Queen Victoria surrounded by her descendants from Russia to Spain.[69] These types of portraits present a united family front to the fractured world, which was exactly what Akhenaten needed to do. He had destroyed the religious beliefs, the temple economy and international relations, but wanted everyone to believe in the utopia he was creating.

COLLAPSE OF AN ERA

This utopia, however, was fragile and did not last long after the death of Akhenaten. As with many aspects of his life, the end of the reign of Akhenaten is poorly documented, but appears to be the final event in a stream of disasters in the personal life of the king, which started in year 12 of his reign (1338 BCE) with the death of his father Amenhotep III, followed in year 14 by his mother Tiye (1336 BCE), if as some scholars believe, there was a long co-regency between Akhenaten and his father. Akhenaten's daughter, Meketaten, also appears to have died in year 12, possibly as a result of childbirth, and soon after this Nefertiti disappears from the inscriptions and is replaced as Great Royal Wife by her daughter Meritaten. It has been speculated that Nefertiti fell out of favour, possibly due to a disagreement with Akhenaten over the Aten. However, a number of images and examples of Nefertiti's name remained after her disappearance, indicating she was not disgraced, but more than likely died. Smenkhkare, Akhenaten's son, or possibly Nefertiti, reigned for three years and died late in year 17 of Akhenaten's reign, and may have ruled independently for a short time.

Akhenaten's two youngest daughters also died during these later years of his reign, although the dates are not clear. This long line of deaths has often been attributed to a plague epidemic sweeping through Amarna. A study of the insect remains from Amarna carried out by Eva Panagiotakopulu,[70] a paleoentomologist from Sheffield University, UK, shows a number of bedbugs, fleas and flies were present at the city, and there is evidence of the plague bacteria in fleas brought to the city on rats of the same type as the European Black Death. Although the spread of this epidemic was due to squalid living conditions, it was probably viewed by the populace of Egypt as punishment for the abandonment of the traditional gods by Akhenaten. The re-establishment of the old traditions would probably have been readily embraced at this time.

As the plague was sweeping through Amarna the building work stopped, either due to funds running out, a lack of conviction to the cause of Akhenaten and his god, or because the plague affected the workmen and their families too. Barry Kemp and his team excavating at Amarna are in the process of excavating the south tombs cemetery used for the burials of the poorer members of the community.

Akhenaten may have been a victim of the plague, dying after the grape harvest of year 17 of his reign, approximately July 1334 BCE. Weigall paints an elaborate picture of his death, although he attributes it to a stroke or fit:

> But in the imagination there seems to ring across the years a cry of complete despair and one can picture the emaciated figure of this "beautiful child of the Aton" fall forward upon the painted palace floor and lie still amidst the red poppies and the dainty butterflies there depicted.[71]

At the death of the king (plate 22) the collapse of the cult of the Aten was inevitable, as the traditional religion had never truly been abandoned. A great deal of everyday life, especially medicine, was tied up in the traditional religion and was not to be easily forgotten. Numerous figurines of such illicit gods as Hathor, Bes and Taweret (household deities) were discovered in homes at Amarna, including in the house of the High Priest of the Aten. This indicates that the inhabitants of Amarna were only paying lip service to the king and his new religion.

Akhenaten, however, did not seem to be that concerned with what would happen after his death as his religion focused on the here and now, even eliminating the elaborate afterlife craved by the officials and workmen at the city. Eternal life was only achieved through worshiping Akhenaten and, in turn, the Aten. This would not have seemed enough for people who had been raised with the idea their ancestors were dwelling with the gods.

Akhenaten knew religion was not stable and there is part of an early speech inscribed at Karnak which displays his opinions on the impermanence of traditional gods:

> Look I am speaking that I might inform you concerning the forms of the gods; I know their temples and I am versed in their writings, namely the inventories of their primeval bodies and I have beheld them as they cease to exist, one after the other, whether consisting of any sort of precious stone ... except for the god who begat himself by himself.[72]

It is clear that Akhenaten believed the gods residing in the statues and images were destined for destruction as all these monuments eventually crumbled away, whereas his god, the Aten, or sun disc, was forever present in the sky and would never fade. He clearly believed the worship of the actual god rather than an image would be far more valuable and worthwhile, and this was indeed the main focus of the worship of the Aten. Sadly, he had not managed to convince all of this and after his death it was not long before Amun was reinstated as the state god and all returned to normal.

AKHENATEN IN WESTERN CULTURE

It is remarkable that a seventeen-year reign 3,400 or so years ago has made such an impact on the Western world, but it has. In fact, the Amarna period in general is the focus of much of the Egyptomania architecture from the early twentieth century, and the sun disc with the arm emanating from it is an iconic Egyptian image (fig. 29) which is even used by the SCA (Supreme Council of Antiquities) in Egypt as their logo.

Akhenaten has also been the focus of artwork and stone work, with Daillion's statue *Archaeology* (1891) in Paris being a prime example. The female 'Archaeology' is holding a small statue in her hand, which is a copy of a statue in the Louvre (fig. 30), showing that archaeology was considered the new science which introduced Akhenaten to the world. The figure 'Archaeology' is personified as Greek, symbolising the passing on of the Egyptian legacy to Greece, which was considered the superior civilisation.[73]

There are scores of novels written about Akhenaten which would be impossible to discuss in their entirety. These myriad novels reflect different aspects of the myth, while also representing the contemporary political issues. Those novels, for example, written just after the First World War present him as a pacifist and spiritual leader, as a reaction to the devastation of the war. The 1920s, and the discovery of the Nefertiti bust, saw Akhenaten and Nefertiti represented as lovers to rival Antony and Cleopatra. In the 1920s and 1930s, following the collapse of the Romanov Dynasty in Russia, the focus in Amarna novels lay in the collapse and devastation of a beautiful and powerful royal house, in addition to parallels with the disappearance of the main protagonists. In the 1970s, after the Watergate scandal and the Cold War, the novels were all about intrigue and corruption, whereas in the 1990s Akhenaten was presented as an erotic and even deviant figure.[74] There are, however, very limited plot

Above: 29. Aten symbol, Wellcome Institute, London. (*Photograph courtesy of Brian Billington*)

Left: 30. Akhenaten, Louvre, Paris.

lines to a classic Amarna novel. One plot has the younger Akhenaten, encouraged by Tiye, contemplating religious matters and follows the trials and tribulations with the formulation of his new religion. The other major plot-line concerns the collapse and aftermath of his revolution. Family life features heavily in both plot lines, and often they can be a verbose description of various pieces of Amarna art with very little creative writing.

The religion of Akhenaten cannot help but be a feature in these novels, but the approaches are very different. Caldecott's *Akhenaten; Son of the Sun* is narrated through the eyes of Akhenaten's brother, who observes religious ideals morph into religious fanaticism, which is viewed with sadness:

> to see an image of a god smashed and the name chipped from a temple wall makes me sad.[75]

Indeed, Akhenaten carries out the desecration in a regimented way as he travels from temple to temple in his chariot, knowing it is a job well-done.

Rider-Haggard, in *Smith and the Pharaohs* (1912–13), has the mummies of the pharaohs come to life in a museum after dark. Akhenaten is found to be lecturing Ramses II on the benefits of monotheism, until Ramses asks him to speak with someone else. Ramses also holds the notion that Akhenaten was a sickly fellow and says to him:

> Your Majesty was rather an invalid, were you not? Of course, in those circumstances, one prefers the nurse whom one can trust.[76]

A somewhat tart response to Akhenaten's criticism of Ramses II's harem of wives. However, the sickliness of Akhenaten is also taken up in *Sinuhe the Egyptian* by Mika Waltari, where Sinuhe is a physician who treats Akhenaten in his last illness. One of the first things that Sinuhe has to treat is an epileptic fit:

> with a shrill cry he sank swooning to the ground, his mouth moving, his limbs twitching convulsively and churning up the sand.[77]

This idea of epilepsy was suggested by Weigall, and then by Smith, on the examination of the mummy in KV55, based on an observed thinning of the skull, although this was later disputed as epilepsy does not leave a mark on the body.[78] However, the main focus of the book is the religious persecution of Aten-worshippers in the years following his death, which included the death of Sinuhe's wife. The persecution is seen from the very beginning of Akhenaten's reverence of the Aton, where he is labelled as mad by his family and courtiers. Even his domineering mother Tiye views his beliefs as nothing more than madness:

> Is my son at all recovered from his madness, or is it time to open his skull? He makes far too much ado about this Aton of his and stirs up the people ...[79]

This book was made into a film in 1953 by Twentieth Century Fox, directed by Michael Curtiz, which cost $4.2 million. Akhenaten was played by Michael Wilding and Bella Darvi, a Polish actress, played Nefer, Sinuhe's love interest. Bella Darvi is depicted in diaphanous robes and the stereotypical black bobbed wig, with a golden diadem. Akhenaten is himself portrayed with a halo, making associations between him and Christ and his followers as the early Christians.

This persecution is adopted in the novel *Moses, Prince of Egypt*,[80] where a number of Aten-worshippers survive the aftermath of the Amarna period, influencing Moses' followers, who in turn tell the Jews of this religion.

As Akhenaten appeals to many people and they feel they can relate to him, the language is often very contemporary in fiction. *King Akhenaton: A chronicle of ancient Egypt* (1928), by Simon Strunsky, is a particularly good example. The main characters, Bek and Neffy (Neferneferuaten), speak to each other as if they were in an American high school:

> You know Bek, it's awful dull here in Thebes since Dad moved out to Aten city.

The Moses connection is also made in this novel, as after the wedding of Bek and Neffy they go to the circumcision ceremony of the infant Moses.

Numerous screenplays have been written about Akhenaten, although not many have ever been produced on the stage or screen. Agatha Christie even wrote a three-act play called *Akhnaton*, which has been described as being a political critique of Nazi Germany in addition to a standard 'family poisoning saga',[81] where Nefertiti and Akhenaten are poisoned by Mutnodjmet, the wife of military bore Horemheb.

It is possible to see that Akhenaten, while being a new discovery in the history of Egyptology, is one that has grasped the imagination of all who learn of him. He is often referred to as the 'first individual', and yet he is a representative of numerous political or religious views. He is presented as black, as the founder of a monotheistic religion, Moses, a spiritual pacifist, a scheming politician and a devoted father and husband.

There are hundreds more myths surrounding Akhenaten which it has not been possible to cover in a book of this length, but include him being the spiritual leader of pagan religions and an icon of spiritualism and mysticism.

However, there is not enough evidence to fully support any of these theories, meaning they all have an element of conjecture and myth about them. People will believe what they want to believe, especially when there is not enough evidence to fully prove or disprove the theories.

Was Akhenaten any of these things? Was he a man worthy of the attention he has obtained? Was he a genius or mentally ill? All of these questions have been answered, but none of them can be proved. Akhenaten will be different things to different people and will remain an interesting yet contentious figure, no doubt for decades to come.

CHAPTER 6

THE MYTH OF CLEOPATRA

The final chapter in the section on people from ancient Egypt is dedicated to Cleopatra VII, the final queen of Egypt before the Romans took control. The name Cleopatra conjures myriad images and scenarios. Everyone has an opinion of this queen, whether it is to regard her as an evil temptress who lured two Roman leaders to destruction; a powerful politician and clever strategist; or a romantic figure and a player in the most tragic love story of all time. The stories of Cleopatra and Marc Antony and, to a lesser degree, Cleopatra and Julius Caesar have gripped imaginations since the Roman period and she has remained a part of Western culture, appearing in movies, books, cartoons and artwork:

> Imagine a woman of sufficient interest to throw future ages into a labyrinth of dreams ... with the mind and a body to captivate a Caesar, a world conqueror ... did such a person exist, or was she only a figment of the imagination?[1]

Many of us are familiar with these varying images of Cleopatra, but how much do we actually know about her and how much of the imagery is mythologising and how much is fact? Who was Cleopatra?

It is difficult to identify who the real Cleopatra is, as there are no contemporary written documents of her life. The earliest record is that of Plutarch, writing 200 years after her death using now lost eye-witness accounts and texts written by Octavian. This record portrays her as a depraved, gluttonous whore, which was further embellished by Horace, Propertius and Virgil. However, we have enough archaeological and written evidence to create a profile of this remarkable woman.

CLEOPATRA IS BORN

Cleopatra VII was the daughter of Ptolemy XII Dionysus, an unpopular king, nicknamed Auletes or 'Flute-Player', who came to the throne in 80 BCE. His mother was a Syrian concubine, and to strengthen his claim to the throne he married his sister, Cleopatra V Tryphaena. Auletes Ptolemy XII had six children from at least two wives. His unpopularity was caused by the debt he plunged Egypt into through his payment of large bribes to the Romans. He was also reputed to be a cruel ruler and a decadent king who revelled in frivolity and became angered if others refused to join him.

His unpopularity grew, and when he died at the age of fifty in 52 BCE, he left his children under the care and protection of a family friend, Pompey, who had remained loyal to him. Rome was demanding repayment for his debts, meaning Egypt was indebted to Julius Caesar, which was not an auspicious start to the reign of Cleopatra VII, his heir. She was nineteen years old married to her half-brother Ptolemy XIII, a boy of only ten years old, both ascending to the throne in 51 BCE. She was given sole power with the understanding that when Ptolemy XIII came of age, he would rule instead. However, one of Cleopatra's first acts was to issue a coin bearing her face, as if her co-ruler did not exist. She then adopted the title 'Lady of the Two Lands', adapted from the kingly title 'Lord of the Two Lands', which was also used by Hatshepsut (see chapter 4), indicating her role was more than simply a queen or consort. Her father's Roman debts needed to be addressed, and to do this she changed the metal content of Egyptian silver and bronze coins by adding other metals. To prevent them being devalued, she stamped the numerical value of the coins onto them. Even at such a young age it was clear to Cleopatra that being in debt to the Romans would only bring trouble.

Cleopatra began issuing decrees and coins independently of Ptolemy XIII, and it soon became apparent she was ruling Egypt alone. She knew this political manoeuvre would not succeed if, like her father, she were unpopular. She therefore started a personal campaign to endear herself to the population by adopting the Egyptian religion and customs, and was the first Ptolemy in three centuries to speak the Egyptian language. In addition to adopting the religion, she adopted the ideology of divine kingship and presented herself as the New Isis, with traditional vulture headdress. Apuleius, in *The Golden Ass*, described her in this guise:

> her long thick hair fell on her neck and she wore an intricate chaplet woven of exotic
> flowers. Just above her brow, was a round disc, shiny like a mirror similar to the moon,
> with vipers on either side of the disc – her robe was linen of many colours, white, crocus
> yellow and red with flowers and fruit along the hem.[2]

The popularity she gained was used against her by the spin-doctors of Ptolemy XIII in an attempt to depose her. The year 50 BCE suffered a bad harvest, resulting in reduced food stocks, and Ptolemy XIII issued a decree in both his and Cleopatra's name stating that all the available grain should be sent to Alexandria, with none deployed to Middle and Upper Egypt. Cleopatra's supporters in these neglected areas saw it as a betrayal and turned against her, forcing her into exile. She fled to Ashkelon on the Syrian coast, north of Gaza, along with her sister Arsinoë, where they stayed for two years, gathering an army. They were positioned on the Egyptian border until 48 BCE, when Julius Caesar travelled to Egypt. He had remained loyal to her father Auletes and had promised him that Cleopatra would remain on the throne.

Politically it was not a good time for Caesar, as he was in a power struggle with Pompey for control of the Roman Empire. After losing the battle of Pharsalos, Pompey fled to Alexandria, pursued by Caesar, to seek Ptolemy's protection. Ptolemy's advisors thought it would be safer to side with Caesar, so when Pompey arrived he was murdered. Three days later, when Caesar entered Alexandria, he was presented with Pompey's head as a gift. Rather than pleasing Caesar, it infuriated him, as Pompey had once been his friend:

> When Caesar saw Pompey's head, he wept and lamented, calling Pompey his fellow-citizen and son-in-law and recounting all the things they had done for one another.[3]

CLEOPATRA MEETS CAESAR

This started a new era in the story of Egypt and Cleopatra, as in his fury Caesar took control of the palace, demanding both Cleopatra and Ptolemy dismiss their armies and meet with him to settle their dispute. Cleopatra was afraid that if she openly entered Alexandria, she would be murdered by Ptolemy's men.

There are a number of different records of how she approached Caesar. The most well-known story, which has developed through the ages into an elaborate myth, is that she smuggled herself into the palace to Caesar inside an oriental rug. This derived from Plutarch (110–15 CE):

> she cloaked herself in a bedding sack and lay down flat. Apollodorus tied the bedding sack with a leather strap and carried it inside to Caesar.[4]

However, the records of Cassius Dio (202 CE) do not mention the bedding sack or rug and claim she simply

> approached the palace at night, keeping her arrival a secret from Ptolemy.[5]

Apparently, when the rug was unrolled, Cleopatra tumbled out and it is said Caesar was bewitched by her charm and became her lover that very night. Lucan (60–65 CE) suggested she 'must have conquered Caesar with drugs',[6] so sudden was their attraction.

However, Julius Caesar had a reputation for being a womaniser and Suetonius records:

> Romans, hide your wives: here comes the bald adulterer. He took out loans, then blew it all on Gallic whores.[7]

Ptolemy XIII was not impressed when he saw Caesar and Cleopatra together the next day and stormed out of the palace, screaming of his betrayal. Caesar had him arrested, but Ptolemy's army, led by the eunuch Pothinus and Cleopatra's sister Arsinoë, laid siege to the palace. In an attempt to diffuse the situation Ptolemy was released, although the war continued for almost six months before Pothinus was killed in battle and Ptolemy XIII drowned in the Nile while trying to flee.

Alexandria quickly surrendered to Caesar, Arsinoë was arrested and Cleopatra VII was restored to her throne. Cleopatra, now a widow, married another brother, Ptolemy XIV, who was only eleven or twelve years old. Cleopatra soon dropped his name from the official documents and coins still only bore her image, indicating Ptolemy XIV was king in name only and Cleopatra ruled Egypt independently.

JULIUS AND CLEOPATRA

Cleopatra's relationship with Julius blossomed and it was one of extravagance. Roman poet Lucan, in his work *Pharsalia*, describes a banquet Cleopatra held for Caesar:

> Cleopatra displayed her magnificence ... ivory clothed the entrance-hall; and Indian tortoise shell, artificially coloured, was inlaid upon the doors and its spots were adorned with many an emerald. Jewels glittered on the couches; the cups, tawny with jasper, loaded the tables and sofas were bright with coverlets of diverse colours – most had long been steeped in Tyrian dye and took their hue from repeated soakings, while others were embroidered with bright gold and others blazed with scarlet ... they served on gold a banquet of every dainty that earth or air, the sea or the Nile affords, all that extravagance, unspurred by hunger and maddened by idle love of display, has sought out over all the earth. Many birds and beasts were served that are divine in Egypt; crystal ewers supplied Nile water for their hands; the wine was poured into great jewelled goblets ... they put on wreaths, twined of blooming nard and ever-flowering roses; they drenched their hair with cinnamon.[8]

In 47 BCE, when she was twenty-three years old and pregnant with her first child, Cleopatra and Caesar went on a boat trip down the Nile. This trip, albeit a pleasure trip, helped repair her relationship with the people of Middle and Lower Egypt by showing they had the support of both the newly re-appointed queen and Rome.

When they returned to Alexandria, Julius Caesar left for Rome, leaving her under the protection of three legions, missing the birth of their son Ptolemy Caesar, nicknamed by the Alexandrian mob Caesarion, meaning 'Little Caesar'. As Caesar was married to Calpurnia in Rome, he never acknowledged Caesarion as his own in the Roman senate and a child of a Roman and a foreigner could never be legitimate in Rome. There are, however, conflicting reports that Caesarion was not born until after the death of Caesar and that it was only during her two-year visit to Rome in 46–44 BCE that she became pregnant. Soon after the birth of Caesarion, a coin was minted in Cyprus which Caesar presented to her when she married Ptolemy XIV, showing Cleopatra, as a goddess, suckling her new-born child.

In September 46 BCE, Caesar celebrated his war triumphs with a large parade in Rome displaying his prisoners, including Cleopatra's sister Arsinoë. Cleopatra was in Rome on a two-year royal visit, residing 'in arrogance'[9] at a villa by the Tiber, and throughout this time Caesar gave her numerous gifts and titles, much to the horror of the Roman people. We know very little about her stay in Rome, other than the odd snippet of information and rumour. She was attended by the 'curious and the fashionable of

31. Cleopatra and Caesarion, Denderah.

Rome', as she was known for her excess and frivolous ways.[10] A statue of her was even erected in the temple of Venus Genetrix and some thought this indicated that Caesar had married her,[11] although as a patrician he was forbidden to marry a foreigner.

Other rumours were circulating that Caesar intended to pass a law allowing him to be polygamous, in order to marry Cleopatra, and change the capital from Rome to Alexandria.[12] No such text has ever been discovered, if it ever existed, although Suetonius states a decree had been drawn up:

> making it lawful for Caesar to marry as many wives as he wished.[13]

DEATH OF CAESAR

This unease eventually led to the murder of Caesar in 44 BCE in the Roman senate by twenty-three dagger thrusts. His great-nephew, Octavian, was named as successor by Julius Caesar over and above Caesarion, who he did not acknowledge as his son. Suetonius (119–21 BCE) recorded that, ten years later, Antony acknowledged Caesarion as Caesar's son,[14] based on a clause in Caesar's will stating Octavian and 'the son who might be born to me' would inherit his estate.[15] Despite this, Caesarion was in danger at the death of Caesar, so Cleopatra left Rome, returning to Egypt. Also around this time, her husband Ptolemy XIV died aged fifteen, possibly poisoned at Cleopatra's command, leaving the throne clear for Ptolemy XV, Caesarion (fig. 31). He became her co-regent, aged three years old.

32. Augustus Caesar, Vatican, Museo Pio Clementino (*Photograph courtesy of Jastrow from Wikimedia Commons*)

The murder of Caesar caused a break in leadership in Rome, meaning that the empire was divided among three men: Caesar's great-nephew Octavian, who later became the Emperor Augustus (fig. 32); Marcus Lepidus; and Marcus Antonius. Marc Antony was another supporter of Ptolemy XII and Cleopatra had met him when her father was alive, in 55 BCE. She was about fifteen years old while he was approaching thirty, and some suggest he had been enamoured of her from this early stage. When she next met him, in 42 BCE, she was twenty-eight years old and was Queen of Egypt, and he had been promoted from cavalry officer to a member of the triumvirate, in control of the eastern sector of the Empire.

ANTONY AND CLEOPATRA

Antony and Cleopatra met in 42 BCE, offshore at Tarsus (in modern-day Turkey). He summoned Cleopatra to question her on her loyalties, but she only agreed to meet him on Egyptian territory. She sailed to him and had him board the ship for the meeting. Plutarch describes this boat, which was designed to dazzle and intimidate:

> a barge with a gilded stern, purple sails and silver oars. The boat was sailed by her maids, who were dressed as sea nymphs. Cleopatra herself was dressed as Venus, the goddess of love. She reclined under a gold canopy, fanned by boys in Cupid costumes.[16]

Cleopatra was very much aware of her strengths, which were her mind and ready wit, although she knew Antony was a pleasure-loving soldier and would be impressed by such a blatant display of luxury, and so she played to this weakness in him. She entertained him on her barge that night and Antony invited her to supper the next night, hoping to outdo her in magnificence. He failed, but joked about it. Like Caesar before him, Antony fell for the Egyptian queen, becoming the second great love in her life. This love was to cause the downfall of both of them.

Antony was instantly enthralled with the young queen and travelled with her to Alexandria, spending the winter of 41–40 BCE there. Their revelry at this time was also recorded by Plutarch (110–15 CE) with a hint of disdain. He records that eight boars were roasted for a dinner of only twelve people, one after another so a perfect meal would be ready whenever Antony and Cleopatra decided to dine,[17] displaying extravagance and waste, which was not received well in Rome:

> She played at dice with him, drank with him, hunted with him: and when he exercised
> in arms, she was there to see. At night she would go rambling with him to disturb and
> torment people at their doors and windows, dressed like a servant-woman, for Antony
> also went in servant's disguise ... However, the Alexandrians in general liked it all well
> enough and joined good-humouredly and kindly in his frolic and play.[18]

The relationship between Antony and Cleopatra was one of frivolity and she shared all of his activities, causing criticism from both the Roman and the Egyptian people, who believed leaders should behave appropriately:

> this capricious, pleasure-loving, fickle, feverish coquette, this ancient Parisienne, this
> goddess of life flutters and rules over Egypt, the silent petrified land of the dead.[19]

However, life was not all frivolity and Cleopatra used her influence for political advantage. She convinced Antony to give up the Alexandrian lifestyle and continue his campaign to annex Parthia, strengthening his position in the Roman Triumvirate, benefitting both Rome and Egypt. While he was away Cleopatra bore him twins, a boy, Alexander Helios (the sun), and a girl, Cleopatra Selene (the moon), who were both acknowledged by their father.[20] It was to be four years until she saw him again.

Octavian Caesar tried to keep Antony and Cleopatra apart by marrying Antony to his sister Octavia during these years of absence. Antony, widowed from his third wife, Fulvia, never claimed to be married to Cleopatra and was therefore technically free to marry Octavia. This did not stop his clandestine meetings with the Egyptian queen and in 37 BCE, on his way to invade Parthia, they enjoyed another rendezvous. He hurried through his military campaign in order to return to her. From then on Alexandria was his main residence, and some say he married Cleopatra in 36 BCE, in Antioch, North Syria. His Roman wife, Octavia, was abandoned in Rome. Shortly after, Cleopatra gave birth to another son, Ptolemy Philadelphus.

In 35 BCE, Octavia wanted to win him back and began a journey to Alexandria with ships, men and supplies. When she reached Athens, she was told to send the goods on and to return home to Rome alone. Plutarch claims that Cleopatra used all of her womanly wiles to convince Antony not to go to his wife.[21]

The Roman people were disgusted by the way Antony treated the virtuous Octavia, and to make matters worse, in 34 BCE Antony made Alexander Helios the king of Armenia, Cleopatra Selene the queen of Cyrenaica and Crete and Ptolemy Philadelphus the king of Syria, all countries in the eastern sector of the Roman Empire.

Although the Roman senate were the only ones authorised to issue a Triumph, Antony decided to hold one himself, in Alexandria rather than Rome. The Triumph had a corps of Roman legionaries leading it with a big C on their shields. If the C stood for Caesar, this was a snub to Octavian, who alone had the right to bear the name Caesar, but if it stood for Cleopatra, this was a bigger insult: Roman soldiers bearing the name of a foreign monarch. The procession went to the Serapeum in Alexandria, where Cleopatra was waiting for him. He alighted from the chariot to greet her before entering the temple to make offerings to Serapis, who brought him the victory, adding further insult to Rome. The Triumph also included a statue of Hapy to be paraded through the streets with a model of the Pharos lighthouse, reminding Rome of Egypt's importance in the world. Octavian used this as an opportunity to build on his propaganda against Antony by emphasising the non-Roman character of the East:

> and at their command, a Queen, followed by a dog-like, devoted Antony, a Roman who had lost all shame.[22]

Octavian continued his campaign of slurs against Antony, claiming him to be a drunk and philanderer, with a list of his Roman lovers.[23] In Antony's mind he was faithful to Cleopatra, his wife, although there is no evidence of a marriage between them,[24] a great insult to Octavian, who had married his sister to Antony. Octavian used numerous anecdotal tales about his behaviour to sully his reputation. For example, one morning in Rome, Antony needed to make a speech in the Forum. He had been drinking at his friend's wedding the night before and had a terrible hangover. He was about to talk when he became nauseous, and then vomited in the forum. This made him repulsive to the refined classes of Rome.

After this campaign, Octavian then changed his methods and presented Antony as a victim of the depraved Cleopatra, a man drugged with wine and sex until he was unable to think for himself.[25] Apian, in his *Civil War* (second century CE), stated:

> The acute interest Antony had once shown in all things suddenly dulled; whatever Cleopatra dictated was done, without regard for the laws of man or nature.[26]

It was clear that Cleopatra was effectively in control of this great man.

In 32 BCE, Antony and Octavia were officially divorced, leading to further political tension in Rome; Octavian decided to rule alone and turned on Cleopatra and Antony, and in 31 BCE Antony's forces fought the Romans in a sea battle off the coast of Actium, aided by Cleopatra and sixty Egyptian ships. When she saw that Antony's large, badly-manned galleys were losing to the Romans' lighter, swifter boats, she fled the scene:

> he allowed himself to be dragged along after the woman, as if he had become a part of her flesh and must go wherever she led him.[27]

The reports continue that she:

> headed for open water in her gilded ship with its purple sails. Soon Antony followed with Caesar hot on his trail.[28]

Although they may have prearranged their retreat, the Romans saw it as proof that Antony was unable to act the part of Triumvir due to the destructive relationship with Cleopatra.

THE END OF A ROMANCE

This was to spell the beginning of the end for Antony, Cleopatra and Egypt. Antony was depressed and regretted his actions, blaming Cleopatra for her betrayal. Cleopatra did her duty and prepared for a Roman invasion alone. Plutarch records that she sent her royal insignia to Octavian in Phoenicia, indicating she would abdicate if he promised that her son would rule after her. He accepted the insignia but refused to make the promise, although Plutarch records he made the promise on the proviso she send Antony away.[29] However, another Roman source claims that rather than the royal insignia being handed over to Caesar, Anthony sent a large sum of money with the request that Cleopatra's children inherit the throne and Anthony remained in Egypt or went to Athens.

CLEOPATRA AND SUICIDE

It is rumoured that at this time Cleopatra started to experiment with poisons to learn which caused the least painful death, in order to prevent her and her son's capture. An anonymous ancient source describes how she coldly watched as condemned men writhed in agony as the poisons took their toll before she decided on the venom of an asp.[30] Even Antony did not trust this new, cold Cleopatra, and he hired a taster to check his food and wine before he ate or drank anything. One evening, before a banquet, she soaked a flower garland intended for Antony to wear in poison and then, during the banquet, proposed a toast where they would drink their crowns. The flowers were placed in the wine, which had been tasted by the taster, and Antony was about to drink it. Cleopatra stopped him and bid a prisoner to drink it, showing that if she wanted to poison him the taster would not prevent her from success.[31]

Octavian reached Alexandria in 30 BCE and was greeted by Marc Antony and the slowly depleted numbers of his army. Antony believed it was better to die in battle than through suicide, and saw this as his last noble act. Antony was on high ground and hoped to see a victorious naval battle. Instead, he saw his fleet raise their oars in surrender to Octavian Caesar. Then, out of fear, the cavalry also deserted him, leaving Antony a defeated man. In his grief he blamed Cleopatra and rushed to the palace, screaming of his betrayal. Cleopatra was terrified and locked herself in her mausoleum, and it is rumoured that she sent word to him that she had died, hoping to calm his anger. Whether she told him this or he heard it somewhere else is unknown. His anger diffused and was replaced by grief, leading him to attempt to commit suicide. He asked his friend Eros to finish the job for him, but Eros fell on his own sword, somewhat more successfully.[32]

When Cleopatra heard that Antony had attempted suicide, she immediately sent a message stating she was not dead, upon which Antony demanded he be taken to her. When he arrived at the mausoleum, Cleopatra was afraid to open the door because of the approach of Octavian and instead she and her two serving women let down ropes from a window and pulled him up. Distraught, Cleopatra laid Antony on her bed and he died in her arms.

Meanwhile, Octavian gained control of the palace and was planning to capture Cleopatra for a victory parade through the streets of Rome. On his arrival at the mausoleum, Cleopatra refused to let him in and negotiated through the barred door, demanding that her kingdom be given to her children. Octavian ordered one man to keep her talking while others set up ladders and climbed through the window. When Cleopatra saw the men, she pulled out a dagger and tried to stab herself, but she was disarmed and taken prisoner along with her children. Horace describes the event with an aura of nobility, despite his Roman attitude to the Egyptian queen:

> Yet, she seeking to perish in nobler fashion, displayed no womanly fear for the dagger's point, nor did she seek out secret shores with her speedy fleet.[33]

While in captivity, Octavian allowed Cleopatra to arrange Antony's funeral and she buried him with royal splendour, but suffered greatly with grief. Plutarch records that she became ill, perhaps due to the damage inflicted on her body when she scratched and beat herself in mourning, and Octavian was worried she would also try to commit suicide and kept her under close guard. She started a hunger strike, but a threat from Octavian that if she did not start eating again, he would harm her children stopped her.

One day he visited her, and she flung herself at his feet and told him she wanted to live. Octavian was lulled into a false sense of security. He did not suspect that she was still planning to die and allowed her to visit Antony's tomb. She threw herself on the coffin and cried:

> My dear Antony, not long ago I buried you with the hands of a free woman, but now I pour libations as a prisoner, under guard so that I will not harm this slave's body by beating it or lamenting and that I may adorn their triumphs over you. Do not expect any further honours or libations; these are your final rites from the captured Cleopatra.[34]

Shortly afterwards, back in her mausoleum, she prepared for dinner and when the servant came delivering figs, the poisonous asp was not noticed. When she reached into the basket, it bit her and killed her, but not before

> she put on her most beautiful apparel, arranged her body in most seemly fashion, took in her hands all the emblems of royalty ...[35]

Although this makes it clear Cleopatra was dressed when she committed suicide, throughout history she has been presented as naked at this time of her life, primarily because this fits in with the idea of an exotic, debauched lifestyle (fig. 33).

POISONOUS ASP

Death by asp venom would not have been as simple as it is presented, and it is thought that she was probably bitten on the veins of her arm rather than on her breast, as the images of her inevitably show (fig. 34). The asp, however, was an appropriate method of death for a queen, due to the royal associations with the snake goddess represented as a cobra, protecting its wearer. However, the idea that she died from a snake bite came from the Roman records, but there is no evidence to prove it. The snake could not be found in the tomb and there were no marks on the queen indicative of a bite.[36]

Plutarch suggests an alternative: that she carried poison in a hollow hairpin, but the asp became more popular as Octavian commissioned a statue of her clutching an asp to her breast, which was paraded through the streets of Rome. Even the precise species of snake is unknown, and the term asp could refer to any type of cobra.[37] Horace describes her death:

> Daring to gaze with serene countenance upon her fallen palace, bravely handling poisonous snakes to draw their dark venom to her body, ever bolder as she determined to die; scorning, it seems the fate of being dragged off as a private citizen in hostile galleys to grace a glorious triumph – she was no humble woman.[38]

In her final moments she wrote a note to Octavian, pleading to be buried alongside her beloved Antony. This note concerned Octavian and he rushed with guards to her mausoleum, but was too late.[39] She was already dead, and he summoned Libyan physicians who were experienced with snake venom to examine and attempt to revive her.[40] Cleopatra was forty years old at her death on 12 August 30 BCE.

The death of Cleopatra saw the end of Egypt as a Ptolemaic country, as it became just another part of the Roman Empire. It was to survive, albeit Romanised, for a further 400 years or so, but Cleopatra was the last queen to rule and live in Egypt.

From this story, it is difficult to know how much can be believed and how much it really tells us about this young queen of Egypt who, like many women before and afterwards, allowed love to lead to bad decisions, and ultimately her downfall. With

Above left: 33. Cleopatra, Louvre, Paris. (*Photograph courtesy of Jastrow from Wikimedia Commons*)

Left: 34. Cleopatra, Metropolitan Museum of Art. (*Photograph courtesy of Userpostdif from Wikimedia Commons*)

no contemporary resources, we need to closely examine those of the first century CE, which are the closest we have to her life time.

NO OIL PAINTING

Although Cleopatra managed to seduce two of the most powerful men in the Roman Empire, she is not believed to have been any great beauty, although she is reputed as being witty, charming, intelligent and seductive and this was what attracted Julius and Antony to her. We have no known accurate portrait of Cleopatra, the images surviving being stylised either as Egyptian, Greek or Roman. In Plutarch's *Life of Marc Antony*, he describes her:

> For indeed her own beauty, as they say, was not, in as of itself completely incomparable, nor was it such that would astound those who saw her; but interaction with her was

captivating and her appearance, along with her persuasiveness in discussion and her character that accompanied every interchange, was stimulating. Pleasure also came with the tone of her voice and her tongue was like a many-stringed instrument, she could turn it easily to whichever language she wished and she conversed with few barbarians entirely through an interpreter.[41]

She is depicted on ancient coins with a long, hooked nose and somewhat masculine features, very different from her Hollywood counterparts, Elizabeth Taylor and Vivienne Leigh, and yet she was clearly a very seductive woman. Henry Houssaye (1848–1911), in his work *Cleopatra, a study*, stated while looking at a profile image of the queen:

> If the nose had not been so pointed, the wayward and ardently voluptuous woman shown in this profile might pass for beautiful.[42]

Some scholars even go as far as denying the accuracy of the profile images on the Cleopatra coins:

> The features which caused Caesar to forget the empire of the world were not spoilt by such a ridiculous nose.[43]

Although her nose may have been somewhat longer than some think is beautiful, it is thought she had unusual eyes, and it is recorded by Dio Cassius that Octavian refused to look Cleopatra in her 'magnificent eyes' and instead chose to stare at the floor in case he was also bewitched by her (plate 23).[44] Lucan (60–65 CE), in *On the Civil War*, comments on:

> her dangerous beauty enhanced by cosmetics.[45]

She may have been considered somewhat frightening to the Romans due to her differences. It was also rumoured in Rome that she wore a wig and, coupled with the use of cosmetics, indicated to them that she was a whore, the only women to dress so.[46]

From the statues of Cleopatra, it is clear she wore her hair in a particular style which is represented frequently. It was long and wavy with kiss curls surrounding her face, and these are sometimes seen under the Egyptian headdresses. The rest of her hair was pulled from her face in a series of small plaits, to be gathered at the nape of her neck in a bun with a broad diadem tied beneath it. However, for decades Cleopatra has been depicted in movies, comics and art work as having a shoulder-length black bob with a headdress of beads hanging to the bottom of the hairline. These images were, however, introduced in the early twentieth century with the Art Deco style, and were fashionable at the time. This was then adopted by Cleopatras in the movies, including Theda Bara, Claudette Colbert, Elizabeth Taylor and Amanda Barry. As these movie images are iconic, they are accepted by many as a true reflection of Cleopatra's time.

AN EDUCATED WOMAN

From Plutarch's description it appears that she was an interesting woman, speaking a total of eight languages, including several African languages, Hebrew and Aramaic, plus her native Greek. She was also the only Ptolemaic ruler to speak Egyptian.[47]

Dio Cassius, writing in 150–235 CE, explains that it was impossible not to fall for the Egyptian queen:

> It was impossible to converse with her without being immediately captivated by her.[48]

There can be no doubt, then, that she was a remarkably intelligent woman, comfortable with conversing with heads of state and high-powered military leaders and a remarkable entertainer. Wertheimer even goes as far as to say that:

> in her presence, boredom, whether by night or day, was out of the question.[49]

However, despite her intelligence it is her sexuality that was the focus of attention and one Roman historian, Lucius Annaeus Florus, writing in the first to second century CE, started the rumours that Cleopatra had even tried to seduce Octavian, so loose were her morals:

> but in vain, for her beauty was unable to prevail over his self-control.[50]

He was one of the Romans who believed she was little more than a prostitute who 'demanded the Roman Empire from the drunken general as the price of her favours'.[51]

ASS'S MILK

We are all familiar with the myth that Cleopatra bathed daily in ass's milk, for which 'they must have milked those asses to a standstill', as quoted in the grossly inaccurate movie *Carry on Cleo* (1965).

Whether this is true is uncertain, but it is recorded that Cleopatra did write a beauty book. She was interested in the study of fragrant and protective unguents and how to mix substances to moisturise and protect the skin from the harsh Egyptian climate. Bearing in mind that one of the gifts of Antony to Cleopatra was the Balsam groves in Judea, which produced the raw materials for perfume and incense, this may have contributed to her interest in the subject as this would have provided a great deal of revenue for Egypt. She was clearly an active businesswoman with the wealth of Egypt in mind, and she even ran her own woollen mill in Alexandria, staffed by her own women,[52] providing an extra income for the capital. Unfortunately, this book has not survived into modern archaeology and is only recorded in a Roman text. The Greeks and Romans saw this obsession with beauty as evidence of her decadent nature. However, in Egypt this was seen as normal, as everyone, both men and women, took care of their skin and wore make-up for both beauty enhancement and medicinal reasons. They were aware of the connection between dirt and disease and in the climate of Egypt, bathing daily was common.

A LOOSE WOMAN

Throughout the Roman propaganda, one of the main criticisms was that Cleopatra was decadent, exotic and wasteful. Lucan (39–65 CE) included this verse into his poem *Pharsalia*:

> Having immoderately painted up her fatal beauty, neither content with a sceptre her own, nor with her brother her husband, covered with the spoils of the Red Sea upon her neck and hair, Cleopatra wears treasures and pants beneath her ornaments.[53]

She is also often associated with pearls, a sign of female lustfulness, and Rabelais in his work *Pantagruel* depicts Cleopatra as an 'onion seller', onions being symbolic of pearls, walking the streets selling her wares.[54] The underlying message is far from subtle.

Pliny the Elder (23–79 CE) comments she owned the two largest pearls in the world, which had been passed onto her from the 'Kings of the East'.[55] These earrings form part of a myth regarding Cleopatra recorded by Pliny but adopted by Renaissance and European artists and authors, such as the work *Di Cleopatra Reina D'Egitti: la vita Considerata* by Paganino Gaudenzio in 1642, where, as a display of her wealth, Cleopatra wagered she could spend ten million sesterces on one banquet. Antony mocked her in the middle of the banquet, and so she called for a goblet of vinegar and dissolved one of her pearl earrings in it, drinking the substance down. She was prepared with the other earring before she was halted in her display by Antony and Plancus.[56]

Although her charisma and charm attracted Julius Caesar and Marc Antony, many commented that it was more to do with her sexual prowess:

> a lecherous ... harlot queen of incestuous Canopus (a Delta town).[57]

It is suggested she had scores of lovers, anyone that she wanted. Wertheimer comments in *Cleopatra; a royal voluptuary*:

> every man who approached her was regarded as her lover.[58]

The Roman records state she sold herself as a prostitute, although the price was often death.[59] Even modern prostitutes practice a technique known as the 'Cleopatra Grip', a method of contracting the vaginal muscles, ensuring this enigmatic queen is always associated with prostitution.

However, the evidence we have indicate she only ever had two lovers, Julius Caesar and Marc Antony, both of whom, on appearance, she loved very much and she was possibly married to Marc Antony. As she held a great deal of power over these men, it was enough to cause envy and bitterness throughout the world, leading to tales of a debauched life of eroticism and pleasure in Egypt.

It is clear from the scanty or biased evidence about the life of Cleopatra that she was a sophisticated, intelligent woman capable of feeling great passion for her lovers, great loyalty to these men and her country, and displayed great political ability from a very young age. Some may say she became all of these things despite her violent family background, filled with power-hungry, unscrupulous men and women, and others may say that it was because of this that she was able to play a man's game in the Roman political arena. George Wilson Knight commented that 'there is in her a streak of mysterious and obscene evil'.[60] However, this 'evil' streak gave her the courage to confront the Romans, but it was a game she inevitably lost and this saw an end to Egypt as an independent country.

CLEOPATRA IN WESTERN CULTURE

Cleopatra has been prominent in Western culture since the time of Plutarch and has inspired writers, artists and film makers to recreate her life in various media. The Romans saw her as an unnatural woman who went against the current culture by choosing her own lovers and exerting political and, worse, erotic power over them and it is this that has coloured the interpretation of Cleopatra. Over the centuries, the imagery and myths of Cleopatra have changed, often reflecting the morals of their time rather than those of her time. However, there are a handful of the events from her life which have taken on the role of myths in Western culture and are consistently reproduced. These are bathing in ass's milk, being delivered to Caesar rolled in a rug, trying out the poisons on criminals and her suicide with the asp. All that changes is the representation.

RENAISSANCE CLEOPATRA

Writers before the time of Shakespeare believed there was a certain nobility in her actions, as dying for love fell into the category of fashionable courtly love, a woman dying for love while her knight risked his life for her. At this time it was believed that a woman who died for love could not be a harlot, as this form of courtly love was the purest.[61] Chaucer presents her as a traditional courtly lady with her knight, Antony, but Boccaccio, writing in the fourteenth century, presents her as the epitome of vice and debauchery:

> She gained glory for almost nothing else than her beauty, while on the other hand she became known throughout the world for her greed, cruelty and lustfulness ... burning with the desire to rule, as some say, [she] poisoned the innocent fifteen-year-old boy who was both her brother and her husband and ruled the kingdom alone.[62]

CLEOPATRA •ANTONIVS •

35. Woodcut from Ulm Boccaccio (1473). (*After Hamer M., 1993*)

In the Ulm Boccacio of 1473 (fig. 35), a woodcut with the legend 'Cleopatra was an Egyptian woman who became the object of gossip for the whole world' beneath summed up the general opinion held at the time. The woodcut shows Antony and Cleopatra at a banquet in one image and Antony with a sword in his chest in the second image. Cleopatra has her sleeves rolled up, displaying an asp on each arm, showing her own manner of death, but whether she killed Antony or not is unclear.

In these pre-Shakespeare days, it is recorded that before she died, Cleopatra admitted all her wrongdoings and rendered Antony innocent.[63] From the Roman period through to modern times, albeit only in isolated civilisations today, men would lay the blame for their sexual desires upon women, as if were there were no women, they would not feel desire. This explains why Cleopatra was solely blamed for Antony's behaviour, even though he made the decisions himself – it had to be because of the seductive powers of Woman, rather than his own choices.[64] Confessing such sins and taking the guilt away from the man almost absolved her of her sins in death, although the general male view at the time was:

the only good woman is a chaste woman and the only chaste woman is a dead one.[65]

This myth of Cleopatra as a guilty, wanton, temptress has remained prominent throughout the centuries. Elizabethan writers saw Antony and Cleopatra's suicides as a morality tale about fidelity and passion, and by the time Shakespeare wrote *Antony and Cleopatra* (1608) it was a tale of the dangers of excessive love, creating a tragic heroine from this passionate, powerful queen.

The seventeenth and eighteenth centuries portray her as a weak and passionate woman who got caught up in politics beyond her understanding, reflecting the politics of the time that saw the education of women as superfluous. She is often portrayed as an icon of feminine manipulation and commercial seduction:

without any moral dignity.[66]

The Romantics focused on the passion surrounding her death, seeing the drama that it created, whereas the Victorians viewed her as a murderous, wanton woman. However, she was not always presented in a negative fashion and the Dutch artist Jan de Braij of Haarlem painted a portrait of his family who he had lost in the plague of 1663–64, depicting his parents as Antony and Cleopatra in an opulent, decorated room. It has baffled art critics, as dressing up was normally to associate the sitter with a famous and noble person from history, but why one would want to represent your mother as Cleopatra was not apparently obvious,[67] although it has been suggested that it displays Cleopatra within a family context as a symbol of domesticity. The Palazzo Labia in Venice has a banquet scene painted by Giambattista Tiepolo (1696–1770), and it is thought that Cleopatra is based on the lady of the house, Maria Labia, although she is represented both as a queen and a whore.[68] The painting is thought to be influenced by the earlier banquet scenes at the Palazzo Spada in Rome by Fransesco Trevisani. Tiepolo so enjoyed this banquet image that different versions can be located in Melbourne, Paris, London and Stockholm. Such banquet scenes were popular in art throughout the seventeenth and eighteenth century, only to be largely abandoned in the nineteenth century.

In the nineteenth century, there was an increase in the number of paintings and sculptures of Cleopatra, with almost every aspect of her life depicted at one time or another. In particular, there was an increase in the number of images of her death during this period, inevitably shown topless, holding a snake to her breast, often accompanied in her grisly task by her two servants. Hans Markat (1840–1884), in his *Der Tod der Kleopatra*, shows one servant already dead and the other with her head bowed as Cleopatra looks to the ceiling as the asp bites her breast. Jean-André Rixens' (1846–1924) *Death of Cleopatra* shows a deathly pale Cleopatra laid out on an ornate Egyptian-style bed, with one of her servants already dead across her legs while the other attends to her. Guido Cadnacci (1668), in two paintings, deviates from the deathbed by having her seated in a throne as she dies, and in *The Death of Cleopatra* she is surrounded by a number of serving girls who look on in interest. The statue *The Death of Cleopatra* by Mary Edmonia Lewis also shows Cleopatra in a *nemes* headdress and voluptuous gown, seated on a throne, with her head thrown back in her final death throes.

TWENTIETH-CENTURY CLEOPATRAS

By the twentieth century and the introduction of the moving image, Cleopatra was portrayed in a decadent fashion, as befitting Hollywood. She is an It Girl, doing her own thing regardless, surrounded by beauty and wealth, as befitting her station as queen.[69] Over twenty-five films have been made about Cleopatra in the twentieth century, each bringing a different aspect of the queen to life. One of the earliest renditions was that of Theda Bara in 1917, who played the role as 'divinely, hysterically, insanely malevolent',[70] following the Victorian image of Cleopatra. This remained popular until the Cecil B. de Mille movie in 1934, where Claudette Colbert took on the role. The script was sold to her with the words, 'How would you like to play the wickedest woman in history?' With the first kiss between Claudette and her Anthony, three members of the crew fainted due to the passion with which it was delivered. Cleopatra was not presented as a working woman, but rather one on the road to discovery through true love, and while the men are hard at work, she 'must go and dress',[71] presenting her as an ideal wife and lover, but not a businesswoman.

At the time of the movie release, there were a number of pieces of Cleopatra-associated merchandise to be sold in cinema shops, such as gowns and accessories similar to those seen in the movie. Goods were marketed for all pockets and the Five and Ten Cent stores stocked a Cleopatra perfume, advertised as 'alluring and lasting'. Even Colbert's appearance in the movie was sold, with either a haircut to achieve the Cleopatra Bangs (fringe) or cheap hair-curlers to do the job yourself, should your budget not reach a hair salon. This was the first movie to have such associated merchandise.

Also in 1934, Vivien Leigh took on the role of Cleopatra, in a rendition of Bernard Shaw's *Caesar and Cleopatra*, where she is portrayed as young, frightened and childlike. She is led in all she does by Julius Caesar. However, one of the most famous movies was Joseph Mankiewicz's *Cleopatra* (1963), where the title role was immortalised by Elizabeth Taylor and women worldwide fell in love with Marc Antony, portrayed by Richard Burton. The movie cost an amazing $44 million, the equivalent of $307 million in today's currency, nearly bankrupting Twentieth Century Fox, as the hype and publicity exceeded the success of the film. However, it eventually made its money back and is now considered a classic.

Cleopatra has also entered into children's entertainment, including Miss Piggy from the Muppets in the role of 'Cleopigtra, the Queen of Denial' (the Nile), in episode 409 of *The Muppet Show*, as well as a hardback book in 1982 where Miss Piggy and Kermit travel back in time to ancient Egypt. Other children's books incorporating the mythology of Cleopatra include the 2005 Scooby Doo book *The Curse of Cleopatra*.

In adult novels Cleopatra is a popular theme, and again each author presents her in a different way. Some authors choose to create a full biography of the queen from her own viewpoint, such as *The Memoirs of Cleopatra* (1997), whereas others will focus on a small element of her life, like McCullough's *Antony and Cleopatra* (2007), building her life into the wider context of Roman politics, or George Bernard Shaw's *Caesar and Cleopatra* (1898). Other authors view Cleopatra through the lives of others, and for her brief appearance in Moran's *Cleopatra's Daughter* (2009), she is portrayed as totally mortal in her emotions and actions. Her daughter claims:

> Unlike a real goddess she was mortal and I could read in the muscles of her body that she was afraid. When someone knocked on the door she tensed.[72]

This human fear and mortality is displayed even more when Antony is brought to the mausoleum dying:

> "No" She said "I can't... if I open this door, any one of your soldiers could seize us for ransom."[73]

Her cameo role in *Pyramids* re-enacts the carpet scene, when Ptraci in the novel is carried to King Pteppic:

> The crew moved aside, leaving a grinning Alfonso to cut the strings around the carpet and shake it out. It unfurled swiftly across the floor in a flurry of dust balls and moths and eventually, Ptraci, who continued rolling until her head hit [P]Teppic's boot.[74]

This unfortunate outcome would be a toned-down rendition of the same scene in *Carry on Cleo* where Henghist Pod, while pretending to be Caesar, is a little heavy handed when unrolling the carpet, sending Cleopatra (Amanda Barrie) hurtling into a table laden with food. As she stands up she is covered in spilled food, with crustaceans attached to her clothing and her wig askew.

INTERNATIONAL CLEOPATRA

It is not just in Europe and the United States that Cleopatra has gripped the imagination of artists, as even in Japan Cleopatra has inspired artists, both traditional and graphic. There are numerous references, for example, to Cleopatra in Japanese Manga (plate 24), some following the story of Shakespeare and others simply using her image.

In 2008, a beachside sculptural exhibition of famous women was held in Mina-Mi-Satsuma in Japan, comprising eighty sculptures of women who had the greatest impact on world history. They ranged from the Queen Cleopatra to Valentina Tereshkova, the first woman in space. The statue of Cleopatra showed the queen wearing a *nemes* headdress, seated on a chair, leaning on her arm, staring into the distance, clearly deep in thought. Her seductiveness is emphasised by the exposure of her left breast, as her tunic has slipped off her shoulder. It is clear that in Japan she is viewed as an honourable, influential figure, rather than the negative image promoted by Rome and adopted by Europe.

Even in 2010 the name of Cleopatra is inspiring, and an auction house in Newcastle, UK, is using the name of Cleopatra to sell a mummified hand. It was presented to

General Bowser in Egypt in 1794 and was labelled then as belonging to Cleopatra.[75] Sadly, there is no proof it is hers, or if the hand is royal. It is a left hand, with manicured nails and the remains of a ring. However, labelling it as Cleopatra's hand is likely to raise more money than 'unknown woman'.

AFROCENTRISM

The black community also view Cleopatra as an honourable woman, and Afrocentrists claim Cleopatra was black. There are two points of uncertainty in Cleopatra's family tree, with the identity of her mother and grandmother unknown. Afrocentrists believe they were black, and with one black member of the family this would make her black too.[76] Although none of the classical authors mention that she was black in their records, this is claimed to be because:

> classics has kept Cleopatra's Africanity and Blackness a secret and questionable.[77]

However, the Macedonian Greeks were fair skinned and although there are two family members whose origin is unknown, it is highly likely that she was fair-skinned or dark like modern Egyptians, rather than black. As one scholar puts it, 'If she was black, no one mentioned it.'[78]

In 2008, for a television series on Cleopatra, Sally-Ann Ashton of Cambridge University helped to create reconstruction images taken from a combination of statues and coins of the queen. The result indicates that she was not the porcelain-skinned Caucasian portrayed in the majority of art. Ashton claimed Cleopatra:

> probably wasn't just completely European. You've got to remember that her family had actually lived in Egypt for 300 years by the time she came to power.

Most Egyptologists and scholars accept Cleopatra was not white, but are not convinced there is enough evidence that she was black and emphasise the absence of evidence is equally, not proof.

Regardless of the reputation held by Cleopatra, it is interesting that she is another aspect of ancient Egypt which is fundamental to Western culture. It is clear, however, that there is no consistency regarding the myths. Even during the Roman period, the reports did not agree. Every aspect of her life has contradictory reports, some the result of myth and legend and others the result of propaganda, depending on the motivation of the author.

Cleopatra has always been and no doubt always will be used to fit an author's political or personal agenda. Without a record of her life from an Egyptian contemporary viewpoint, she will always be a Cleopatra of someone else's making: 'an empty figure without an existence of her own.'[79]

In order to answer the question 'who is Cleopatra?' one needs to look at every representation and reference to her, but one will still come to conclusion that Cleopatra is a myth; she is whoever the author wants her to be to fit into the political context. What would Cleopatra herself make of the different representations of her character? Anne Rice immortalises the moment when Ramses II, the reanimated mummy who knew Cleopatra when alive, witnessed a waxwork in Madam Tussaud's in London:

> His composure crumbled at the first sight of Roman soldiers. He recognised the figure of Julius Caesar instantly. And then in disbelief he stared at the Egyptian Cleopatra, a wax doll which bore no resemblance to the bust he had cherished or the coins he still possessed. But her identity was unmistakable as she reclined on her gilded couch, the snake coiled in her hands, its fangs just beneath her breast. The stiff figure of Mark Antony stood behind her, a characterless man in Roman military dress.[80]

How inaccurate are our representations? We will never know as the true Cleopatra is lost to us and no doubt, as with many legends, the reality would be disappointing.

SECTION 3

THE MYTH IN THE MODERN WORLD

CHAPTER 7

MUMMYMANIA

Mummies have fascinated the West and have been a part of Western culture for centuries, albeit in varying ways. Even though there are few mysteries surrounding the mummies of ancient Egypt, there are myriad myths surrounding them and the power they hold. The myths of the mummies are the opposite of other Egyptian myths, which are associated with wealth, exoticism and wisdom, whereas mummies are inevitably dirty and unpleasant, representing evil.

Needless to say, none of the myths surrounding mummies are based in fact as a mummy, by its very nature, is a dead body whose tissues have been preserved using natron, giving them an unusual appearance. Despite this mummies are an integrated part of Western culture, with the myths believed by many rooted in literature and legend. Unlike other myths discussed in this book, the myth and reality of mummies cannot be studied in isolation of each other as their very origins *are* the myths.

MUMMY MEDICINE

Mummies have interested the West since the earliest times and were even used as medicine (plate 25). In the twelfth century CE, Abd el-Latif discusses how mummia, a type of bitumen, flowed from the mountain in Persia and when it mixed with water gave off an odour which was considered beneficial when inhaled. However, it had been used from earlier periods and Avicenna (980–1037 CE), a Persian physician, claims it was used for treating abscesses, eruptions, fractures, concussions, paralysis, epilepsy, vertigo, blood from the lungs, throats, coughs, nausea and disorders of the liver and spleen. It was mixed with herbs before being ingested[1] and was considered very effective. Mummy as a medicine was so popular that Queen Victoria was sent some by the King of Persia for her health, and one wonders if her long life could be attributed to it. Mummy was still used until the early twentieth century in Egypt, where it was mixed with butter as a cure for bruises.[2]

When Shakespeare was writing, he changed mummia from an effective medicine to an effective poison and he refers to mummies and mummia in *Romeo and Juliet*, *The Merry Wives of Windsor* and *Othello*, where mummia was part of the magic potion that impregnated the handkerchief. This was popular fiction at the time and would have been familiar to the audience. It was also adopted in Walt Disney's *Snow White and the Seven Dwarfs* (1937), where it is included as one of the evil stepmother's magic potions.

In 1564, Guy de la Fontaine, the physician of the King of Navarre, went to Alexandria to buy mummies in bulk for medicine. He was rather suspicious of the smell and discovered they were all less than four years old, and were the mummies of criminals and unclaimed dead.

Such fakes had been created due to demand from about 1200 onwards. Petrie told of a tourist that bought a mummy from Aswan which was eventually identified as the body of an English engineer who had died there. This entrepreneurial idea was adopted in Rice's *The Mummy*, where Henry Stratford, the gambling drunk, was murdered and ended up 'floating in the bitumen',[3] turning him into a lovely mummy for tourists to buy. In reality, this industry did not deter people from buying these gruesome souvenirs.

In 1888, Graham Hamrick decided to make some mummies using his own patented mummy-making elixir. He bought two female bodies from the West Virginia Hospital for the Insane. They formed part of P. T. Barnam's curiosity exhibition and toured the world until their popularity waned and they returned to Virginia. Although there is no proof they are the same mummies, there are two mummies displayed in glass-topped wooden coffins at the Barbour County Historical Museum, strangely enough in the bathroom. There is a charge of $1 to see them.[4]

MUMMY PRODUCTS

Although used for medicine until the twentieth century, in the nineteenth century 'mummy brown' became a very popular paint colour, made with crushed mummy. It is thought that this practice may have originated in the twelfth century.[5] One artist, Alma Tadema, witnessed a mummy being ground up for paint, and he and Edward Burne-Jones held an impromptu funeral by burying a tube of paint.[6]

For a while in the nineteenth century, Augustus Stanwood, an American paper manufacturer, used mummy wrappings to make brown paper which was sold to butchers and grocers to wrap food. When there was an outbreak of cholera the paper was no longer made and used, although whether this was outbreak due to the paper was never proved.

UNWRAPPING MUMMIES

From the seventeenth century, while mummy as medicine was still popular, it became common for the rich to purchase mummies, either in Egypt or from antiquities sellers abroad, to display in their town houses.

It was considered an influential social event to have a public unwrapping, where ladies were known to faint at the 'ghastly sight' and men looked on in scientific interest. These events were followed by food and drinks. From an archaeological point of view, unwrapping a mummy is nothing short of vandalism, destroying the wrappings and exposing the mummified tissue to the damp western air, often causing it to disintegrate. The earliest recorded unwrapping was in September 1698, when Benoit de Maillet (1656–1738), the consul in Cairo of Louis XIV, unwrapped a mummy for a group of French travellers. He did not record anything other than a few of the amulets which were discovered on it.[7] In 1718, C. Hertzog, an apothecary, unwrapped a mummy and recorded some of his findings before he ground it down to be sold as medicine.

Such public unwrappings became so popular that one held by Thomas Pettigrew (1791–1865) in Charing Cross in April 1833 was so crowded with antiquarians, excavators, Egyptologists, Members of Parliament, artists, authors, peers, princesses, military officers, statesmen and diplomats that when the Archbishop of Canterbury showed up, he was turned away. However, he had a private showing at a later date.[8] A mummy has not been unwrapped in the West since 1975 at Manchester, with the unwrapping of Mummy 1770.

Some people were so fascinated by the process of mummification that they requested mummification upon death. Alexander, 10th Duke of Hamilton, for example, asked Pettigrew to mummify him upon his death. This was carried out, and he was placed in a specially purchased Egyptian sarcophagus inside a mausoleum in the grounds of Hamilton Palace. The tomb was then found to be structurally unsound and he was moved to the local graveyard. Due to sub-soil movements, attempts to locate the sarcophagus have failed.

Jeremy Bentham, the founder of University College, London, was mummified upon his death, and he stipulated in his will that he should attend every board meeting, even after his death in 1832. He currently sits in the cloisters of the university in a glass-fronted case for all to see, and has been there since 1852. The mummified head is in storage and a wax substitute has been placed on the shoulders of the body.

The main attraction of unwrapping mummies was to obtain knowledge, but sadly they lost more in the process than they learnt. This fascination with what mummies can tell us leaked over into the fiction of the nineteenth century, where the reanimated mummies were engaged in conversation. In Edgar Allan Poe's *Some Words with a Mummy* (1850), as part of an experiment during an unwrapping, electricity was applied to a mummy, Allamistakeo, using a battery. His first speech was a rebuke to those present about the terrible behaviour he had suffered at the hand of the scientist at their behest. A conversation then ensued where the benefits of the modern era were discussed. For every modern wonder, Allamistekeo countered it by asking if the modern people are able to construct similar monuments as found in Egypt, using his contemporary tools. The winning question was whether:

> the Egyptians had comprehended, at any period, the manufacture of either Ponnonner's lozenges or Brandreth's pills.

The mummy was obviously unable to answer in the affirmative, meaning the discussion was won by the modern-day questioners. It is clear, however, that the superior knowledge and abilities of the ancient Egyptians were acknowledged throughout the story. The entire conversation was carried out in Egyptian and Poe commented that he regrets that American printing presses did not have a hieroglyphic font, otherwise he would have written the conversation in hieroglyphs for the readers as well.[9]

Christians were particularly interested in what mummies could tell of their experiences of the biblical stories.[10] There were some contradictions in the Bible regarding mummification, with Jacob and Joseph being mummified (Genesis 50:26), showing a shared belief in life after death. Contrary to this, however, the Bible also comments that the dead should be allowed to decay in the earth to release the soul (Genesis 3:19). Accordingly, the Christian corpses were simply empty shells with no need for treasures, which almost justified the removal of the amulets and jewels. They were viewed as the ultimate in waste, as they had no need for the riches they were buried with.[11]

THE CURSE OF THE MUMMY

Since the end of the nineteenth century, the curse of the mummy has been very prominent and has dominated Egyptology. However, at this time there were two curse theories: the curse of the mummy and the curse of Tutankhamun, which is attributed to his malice at those involved in his excavation. In the mummy's curse in general, the possession or presence of mummies is enough to kick-start the curse.[12] There are, however, cross-overs within the myths. The curse of the pharaohs is essentially that any archaeologist who disturbs any Egyptian tomb will be struck down with the curse which is often claimed to have been written somewhere on the tomb walls, or on an object within the tomb. The curse of the mummy, however, is attached to the body or the coffin and wherever these items are moved to, the curse becomes apparent.

THE ORIGIN OF THE CURSE

Although many people believe the curse originates in strange experiences and events, this is not the case. The origin of the curse in the West lies within fiction.

A very early curse story can be found in a children's book from 1827 written by a twenty-five-year old English author, Jane Loudon Webb. She was inspired by watching a mummy unwrapping by Belzoni in the wake of the publication of *Description de l'Égypte* and the new wave of Egyptomania. In her tale *The Mummy; a Tale of the 22nd Century*, the mummy came back to life to strangle the hero,[13] following the style of Shelley's *Frankenstein* with a man-made monster. In fact, the idea of a revitalised mummy which causes harm is a common theme in early mummy stories. One anonymous story, *The Mummy's Soul* (1862), has an archaeologist unwrapping a female mummy which then crumbles away. He takes some of the dust, along with an ancient insect which is later revived by his servant. It drains the blood of his wife so she 'resembles the mummy in the tomb'. He is bitten by the insect and puts up a fight, killing it by hitting it with the vase containing the mummy's ashes. These intermingle with his blood and the mummy is revitalised.

Jane Austin (1868) wrote *After Three Thousand Years*, where the main character, Millard Vance, takes a scarab with diamond eyes and green enamel wings from a princess's mummy for his sweetheart. It is inscribed with a curse and she refuses to wear it, although in the end she is won over and she is found dead with it around her neck. The scarabs had pierced her neck with its claws, killing her. Millard Vance laments:

> I never have quite forgiven myself for stealing [the mummy's treasure], or for burning her.[14]

Louisa M. Alcott (1869) wrote a very similar story, *Lost in a Pyramid* or *The Mummy's Curse*,[15] where the main character, Forsyth, was lost in the pyramid of Cheops. In a plan to be found by their guide Jumal, Forsyth and Niles decide to light a fire with the only material available, a mummy in a wooden coffin. Within the wrappings, clasped in the mummy's hands, was a golden box, which Forsyth takes. He discovers a piece of papyrus, with a curse written in hieroglyphs which he deciphers, and some seeds. His fiancée Evelyn wants to plant the seeds, but he forbade it and threw them on the fire. One, however, did not burn and she planted it. It grew into a flower that sapped the life of his bride-to-be, as it was one of the most deadly poisons known to the Egyptians.

Sir Arthur Conan-Doyle also wrote about mummies and was a great believer in the curse theory. He wrote two short stories in 1890 about a cursed mummy and in one of these, *Lot No. 249*, he is the first author to use a live mummy to act violently on the behest of another.[16]

CURSE OF TUTANKHAMUN

Since 1922, Tutankhamun's tomb has been the focus of the majority of the curse stories (fig. 36). The untimely death of Lord Carnarvon in 1923 (fig. 37) really caught the media's attention, and this interest has not waned in all these decades. Lord Carnarvon initially travelled to Egypt in 1903 due to poor health as the winter weather in Egypt was better than his native UK. At the time of his death, he was under a great deal of stress due to political strife between Carter and the authorities and was not in the best of health.[17] He was bitten by a mosquito, and while shaving he nicked the top off, instigating septicaemia, lowering his immune system further. He died on 5 April 1923, of pneumonia. Some have said that the mosquito bite was in the same place as a scab on Tutankhamun's face, providing a link between the two men[18] and fodder for the curse theorists who are constantly looking for coincidences.

Certain 'strange events' are constantly quoted as proof of the existence of the curse. The first was reported by Arthur Weigall, who stated that on the day the entrance of the tomb of Tutankhamun was discovered, Howard Carter's pet canary was devoured by a cobra, the symbol of royal protection, believed by some to represent the spirit of Tutankhamun,[19] giving a dire warning to the archaeologist. Apparently at the exact

36. KV62, Tutankhamun, Valley of the Kings.

37. Lord Canarvon's grave, Beacon Hill. (*Photograph courtesy of Brian Billington*)

time of Canarvon's death, the lights in Cairo inexplicably went out, although this is not unusual in Cairo, even today.

However, there are inconsistencies with reports regarding the exact time the power went off, throwing doubt on the significance of this event. Lord Canarvon's death certificate states he died at 01.45 a.m., whereas in his memoirs his son, the 6th Earl, stated that the lights went off shortly after 02:00 a.m., quarter of an hour after the death. As he left his bed, he grabbed a handy torch from his bedside, indicating that perhaps out of habit, a torch was kept nearby for power-cuts. The *Daily Express* reported that the electricity went off just prior to his death, at 01:40 a.m. Although only a few minutes out, it is impossible to say the lights went out at the *exact* time of death.

Canarvon's three-legged dog Susie is also reported to have howled and died in the UK at the time of his death. Again, there are inconsistencies with the timing. As mentioned, Carnarvon died at 01:45 a.m. in Cairo. Susie stood up, howled and keeled over dead at 03.55 a.m. in the UK. The 6th Earl of Carnarvon, in his memoirs, states that the UK was two hours ahead of Cairo, meaning Cairo time was 01.55 a.m. when Susie died, ten minutes after the death of Lord Carnarvon. However, in 1923 GMT (Greenwich Meantime) was in fact two hours behind Egyptian time, so the dog died at 5:55am, Cairo time, and not 1:55am, a full four hours after the death of Lord Canarvon.[20] Once these inconsistencies are investigated, the evidence is not as compelling.

After his death, psychics and spiritualists appeared with tales of their premonitions and warnings issued to the doomed Earl. One of these was Cheiro (Count Louis Harmon), a psychic who warned Carnarvon with a message he claimed was received through automatic writing from Makitaten, a daughter of Akhenaten. At this time, with the discovery of KV55 (the Amarna tomb), the Egyptological world was absorbed with the Amarna period and this gave the message further poignancy:

> It was to the effect that on his arrival at the tomb of Tutankhamun he was not to allow any of the relics found in it to be removed or taken away. The ending of the message was that if he disobeyed the warning he would suffer an injury while in the tomb – a sickness from which he would never recover and that death would claim him in Egypt.[21]

The Earl was not deterred from continuing work in the tomb. Although it is not recorded where Carnarvon obtained the mosquito bite that was to kill him, it does not appear to have been in the tomb.

Carnarvon is also reported to have visited a palm-reader and psychic, Velma, on more than one occasion and was given a further warning:

> I see great peril for you ... most probably – as the indications of occult interest are so strong in your hand – it will arise from such a source.[22]

On a second meeting, Velma looked into a crystal ball and described a vision pre-empted by the words:

> To Aton ... only god ... Universal father.

Here, again, is the Amarna connection, even though Tutankhamun restored the traditional religion of Egypt. A curse during his reign would surely invoke Amun rather than Aten. The vision in the ball apparently cleared, revealing an image of a golden mask being placed over the head of a king, which Velma believed represented the burial of Tutankhamun. Then the image changed to that of Carter and the team carrying out their work amid a number of spirits in the tomb who

> demanded vengeance against the disturbances of the tomb.

Amid the chaos of this stood Carnarvon. This vision was recognised as a dangerous omen and Carnarvon apparently told Velma that he had felt a strong impulse to give up, but was determined to continue with his work in the tomb regardless.[23]

There are mixed reports on how these warnings were received by Howard Carter, who would also have been affected by the curse as it was essentially his project. Sir Thomas Cecil Rapp (1893–1984), the British Vice-Consul to Cairo at the time, wrote in his unpublished memoirs:

> He [Carter] was suffering too from a superstitious feeling that Lord Canarvon's death was possible nemesis for disturbing the sleep of the dead, a nemesis that might also extend to him. But he was to survive for seventeen years.[24]

However, in the words of Carter himself the opposite view is presented. One source states he commented:

> all sane people should dismiss such inventions with contempt.[25]

In the mind of believers in the curse, this bold statement is guaranteed to end in an unpleasant death.[26] Another source quotes Carter as saying:

> It has been stated in various quarters that there are unusual physical dangers hidden in Tutankhamun's tomb – mysterious forces, called into being by some malefic power, to take vengeance on whomsoever should dare to pass its portals. There was perhaps no place in the word freer from risks than the tomb.[27]

In every novel or movie where the curse of the mummy is mentioned, there is always a clairvoyant or psychic, normally a woman, who warns the archaeologists of their folly and their fate. If this woman does not materialise, there will be a warning written somewhere in the tomb in order for the archaeologist to ignore it. Peter's *The Curse of the Pharaohs* is a prime example of this. As the archaeologists are about to enter the tomb, an anonymous voice in the crowd shouts:

> Desecration! Desecration! May the curse of the gods fall on him who disturbs the king's eternal rest.[28]

Later in the book, an imam emphasises the danger the archaeologists were in:

> I bring no blessing but a warning. Will you risk the curse of the Almighty? Will you profane the dead?[29]

From the beginning of the book, Amelia Peabody makes it clear she does not believe in the curse and believes someone is using the superstitions of the locals to protect a murderer.

Practically every aspect of the death of Carnarvon was used as proof of the curse, including his last words:

> A bird is scratching my face. A bird is scratching my face.

This brought to mind a First Intermediate Period tomb inscription which claims Nekhbet, the vulture goddess, will scratch the face of anyone who does anything to a tomb.[30] However, it is not taken into account that as an Egyptologist it is possible Carnarvon was familiar with this inscription and, coupled with the press and psychics telling him he was cursed and would die, in his last moments of delirium a connection was made. This 'last word' scenario is another that is used in novels, and in Peter's *Curse* Arthur Baskerville, when gaining consciousness after being attacked, murmurs:

> The beautiful one has come ... Sweet of hands, beautiful of face; at hearing her voice one rejoices.

Emerson points out these were the titles of Nefertiti.[31] In fiction, as in real life, Akhenaten and the Amarna period are invoked as being more recognisable to the reader.

THE CURSE CONTINUES

Even in 1972, new cases of curse victims were making front-page news. At this time, the first exhibition of the treasures of Tutankhamun was touring the world. It was reported that the flight crew who transported the artefacts all had bad luck. One of the crew was playing cards on the case containing the mask (plate 26), and he kicked it and joked, 'Look, I'm kicking the most expensive thing in the world.' Sometime later, he broke the same leg. Another member of the crew was divorced shortly after.[32]

CURSES WRITTEN IN TOMBS

Apparent inscriptions in tombs are quoted *ad infinitum*, with some sources claiming a curse was written in the tomb of Tutankhamun:

Death will slay with its wings whoever disturbs the peace of the pharaoh.

This was apparently written on a clay tablet in the antechamber of Tutankhamun, catalogued along with all the other objects, and was translated by Alan Gardiner.[33] However, there is no record of this tablet, no photographs and no notes regarding it, and it is assumed it has been intentionally 'lost'.

However, the origin of this curse was not Tutankhamun's tomb but an American occult novelist, Marie Corelli, who wrote to *The New York Times* in 1923 stating she had discovered an old book on ancient Egypt with this curse:

Death comes on wings to him who enters the tomb of pharaoh.[34]

She never disclosed the title of the book and it has never been discovered. However, the press claim this was written above the door to Tutankhamun's tomb, or on magical bricks within and another on the mud-brick entrance to the treasury of the tomb:

It is I who hinder the sand from choking the secret chamber. I am for the protection of the deceased and I will kill all those who cross this threshold into the sacred precincts of the royal king who lives forever.[35]

Sometimes this inscription is said to be written on the underside of a candle near the Anubis figure in the tomb. A further inscription is said to be written on the rear of the *ka* (spirit) statue guarding the door to burial chamber:

It is I who drive back robbers of the tomb with flames of the desert. I am the protector of Tutankhamun's grave.[36]

There are, therefore, clearly a number of inconsistencies as to where this curse was recorded and this is because no such inscriptions are in Tutankhamun's tomb, but they have been quoted so often they are often considered fact and accepted by many.

Although there was no such curse in the tomb of Tutankhamun, there are some tombs which do have a curse text as a deterrent to robbers. The curses all refer to people entering the tomb to cause harm, as seen with the sixth-dynasty tomb of Harkkhuf in Aswan:

As for anyone who enters this tomb unclean, I shall seize him by the neck like a bird, he will be judged for it by the great god.[37]

One such tomb is the fourth-dynasty tomb of the Priestess of Hathor, Lady of the Sycamore, Nesysokar, buried at Giza:

O anyone who enters this tomb,
who will make evil against this tomb:
May the crocodile be against him on water,

And the snake against him on the land
May the hippopotamus be against him on water
The scorpion against him on land.[38]

Her husband, Pettety, has a similar curse written in his tomb, except he calls on the crocodile, lion and hippo to protect him:

Listen all of you! The priest of Hathor will beat twice anyone of you who enters this tomb or does harm to it. The gods will confront him ... the crocodile, the hippopotamus and the lion will eat him.[39]

The tomb of Ursa, who lived a century before Tutankhamun, also has a curse carved upon the walls:

He who trespassed upon my property or who shall injure my tomb or drag out my mummy, the sun-god shall punish him. He shall not bequeath his goods to his children; his heart shall not have pleasure in life; he shall not receive water (for his ka to drink) in the tomb; and his soul shall be destroyed for ever.

The majority of the tombs which bear such a curse are quite specific in who will be punished by a deity rather than the deceased. They are aimed at people who mean to steal or cause harm to the mummy; this does raise the question as to whether archaeological science counts as 'harm' or not.

DROPPING LIKE FLIES?

The death or misfortune of anyone connected with the tomb has been consistently attributed to the curse. Some of these claims are somewhat ludicrous, with the death of Charles Kuentz, Pierre Lacau, Bernard Bruyere and Alan Gardiner over forty years later being attributed to it. The ages of the individuals and their general health is rarely taken into account, despite the fact that in the 1920s many people travelled to Egypt, like Carnarvon, for their failing health. Some of the protagonists were still alive in the 1960s, aged over eighty years old, and their deaths were not unexpected.

Carnarvon died in 1923, aged fifty-seven, of pneumonia and septicaemia, and Howard Carter, the chief archaeologist, died in 1939 aged sixty-five. A number of people who had close contact with the objects in the tomb died after 1940, including Harry Burton, who photographed the objects (1940, aged sixty); A. Lucas, the Director of the Chemical Laboratory of the Egyptian Government Antiquities Service, who treated the objects (1950, aged over seventy-nine); R. Engelbach, the Chief Inspector of Antiquities (1946, aged fifty-eight); Dr Derry from Cairo University, who examined the mummy (1969, aged eighty-seven); Jean Capart (1947, aged seventy) who showed the treasure of Tutankhamun to Queen Elizabeth of

Belgium, although the Queen seemed to be fine; Gustave Lefèbvre from the Institute of France and the Chief Curator of Cairo Museum, who was responsible for the organisation of the exhibition, died in 1957, aged seventy-eight; Charles Kuentz (after 1939, age unknown); Pierre Lacau, who was ninety-two when he died in 1965; Bernard Bruyere was over eighty when he died, sometime after 1965; and Alan Gardiner, who was responsible for translating the inscriptions, died in 1963, aged eighty-four. None of these deaths are particularly early, or even close in time to the opening of the tomb.

Many books advocating the curse theory often leave out the ages of many of these people, as it is not that compelling when it is noted many of them were over sixty when they died and many over eighty, as one Egyptologist states:

> It cannot be denied, however that death was peculiarly selective in his choice of victims and surprisingly long in coming for those who were perhaps closest to the work.[41]

Any misfortunes or illness of others connected to the tomb are also been attributed to the curse. George Bénédite, the Head of the Department of Egyptian Antiquities at the Louvre, suffered a fall and a stroke after leaving the tomb on a visit. Arthur Mace, the Assistant Keeper of the Department of Egyptian Antiquities at the Metropolitan Museum in New York, died shortly after visiting the tomb, aged fifty-three, of pleurisy. Some authors add intrigue to this death by stating that he died in the same hotel as Canarvon,[42] whereas he actually died at home in England.[43] He contracted pleurisy long before the discovery of the tomb and therefore this cannot be seen as a direct result of the curse.[44]

George Gould, the son of an American financier, collapsed with a high fever after entering the tomb on a visit in 1923 and died of pneumonia.[45] Lord Canarvon's younger brother, Aubrey Herbert, died in 1923 and Canarvon's wife, Lady Almina, died in 1929 as the result of an insect bite, showing it was a common cause of infection. Carter's secretary, Richard Bethel, died that year too,[46] in unusual circumstances at the Bath Club. His father, distraught with grief, committed suicide shortly afterwards. Although he had never visited the tomb, it is still cited as the cause of death. Then, tragically, on the way to the funeral, an eight-year-old child was run over by the hearse. The Egyptian Ali Kemel Fahmy Bey was shot by his wife in the London Savoy Hotel shortly after visiting the tomb, and even this has been attributed to the curse.

When listed in such a format, it does seem like an awful lot of people died who were involved in the tomb, or visited the tomb, but in the grand scheme of things hundreds of people visited the tomb and have been involved with the artefacts and the body of Tutankhamun and survived well into old age.

DEATH BY MUMMY

Tutankhamun is not the only contender for the curse of the mummy and in Vandenberg's *The Curse of the Pharaohs,* he entitled one of his chapters 'Suicide for the Advancement of Science,' where he states that long before Carter and Carnarvon, Egyptologists were dying, or losing their faculties, in the name of Egyptology. The curse

> always struck men who had spent long years in Egypt and were somehow involved in excavation.[47]

Some of his examples included Heinrich Brugsch (1827–1894), who became delusional the longer he stayed in Egypt. Apparently, he left Egypt rather abruptly to take up Lepsius' position in Berlin at the university, even though Lepsius was still in the post. He threatened that if he were not given the post he would take a similar post in Paris, although none had been offered.[48] Rather than blaming the curse for Brugsch's failings, surely it would have been more sympathetic to offer help or support for what was clearly a mental disorder.

Vandenberg also claims Champollion, who died in 1932, soon after his return from Egypt, of an unidentified paralytic disorder at only forty-two years old. This similar affliction was said to have affected Emery in 1971; he suffered paralysis on the right side and lost the ability to speak. The next day he died, and it was recorded in the newspaper *Al Ahram*

> This strange occurrence leads us to believe that the legendary curse of the pharaohs had been reactivated.[49]

However, it sounds like Emery suffered a stroke, which at the age of sixty-eight is not so unusual. He also claims that many Egyptologists die of fever and delusions, sudden terminal cancers and circulatory collapse, quoting the deaths of Belzoni in Sierra Leone in 1823, George Möller at aged forty-four in 1921 and James Henry Breasted in 1935[50] as proof.

SCIENTIFIC STUDIES

In 1934, Winlock drew up statistics demonstrating that the curse of Tutankhamun was fabrication. His findings were that twenty-six people were at the opening of the tomb and only six died within a decade. There were twenty-two at the opening of the sarcophagus and only two died, and of the ten at the unwrapping of the mummy not one succumbed to death.

He also added a list of some of the victims and corrections to the claims made by the press at the time. He reported that George Gould was ill before he even travelled to Egypt, Arthur Weigall was only allowed in the tomb as a member of the general public and had nothing to do with the tomb itself, Ali Fahmy Bey only visited the tomb as a tourist and was not involved in the excavation, workmen in the British Museum handling objects from the tomb were said to have fallen dead, although there had never been any Tutankhamun artefacts in the British Museum and he made a general comment that many people visiting Egypt at the time were elderly and suffering with their health,[51] so the curse was not responsible for their deaths.

In 2002, a further scientific study was carried by an Australian scientist, Mark Nelson. The study investigated the length of time between exposure to the tomb and death. They listed twenty-five people as potentially susceptible to the curse: those present at the opening of the third door (17 February 1923), the opening of the coffins (3 February 1926) and the unwrapping of the mummy (11 November 1926).

The study showed that of these twenty-five exposed individuals, the mean age of death was seventy years old and the average length of time between exposure to the tomb and death was between thirteen and fifteen years, indicating that scientifically there is no proof of a curse causing the death of those present in the tomb.[52]

BIOLOGICAL WARFARE

This myth of the curse and lists of apparently superstitious deaths has led to research into germs, diseases or bacteria being present in the tombs and contributing to these deaths. Various theories have developed:

- Tutankhamun died of an infectious disease and the bacteria was still alive.
- The bat droppings in the tomb cause breathing problems which could aggravate previous condition.
- Radiation as a natural protection against the tomb became popular in the 1960s.[53]
- Simply paranoia and misinterpretation of some tragic or natural events.

These studies have raised a lot of interest and even Carter considered it, but in regard to the tomb of Tutankhamun he commented:

> out of five swabs from which cultures were taken, four were sterile and the fifth contained a few organisms that were undoubtedly air-infections unavoidably introduced during the opening of the doorway and the subsequent inspection of the chamber and not belonging to the tomb and it may be accepted that no bacterial life whatsoever was present. The danger, therefore to those working in the tomb from disease germs, against which they have been so frequently warned is non-existent.[54]

A number of studies were carried out in the 1990s[55] on ancient Egyptian mummies and various forms of the aspergillus bacteria were discovered: *aspergillus nigers*, *aspergillus ochraceus* and *aspergillus flavas*. The theory originally suggested by Dr Ezzedin Taha in 1962 demonstrated that *aspergillus nigers*, with symptoms of skin rashes and laboured breathing common with those who worked with Egyptian papyri, could be the cause of such health problems with archaeologists in general.[56]

It is believed if the bacteria were disturbed when the tombs were opened, they could be inhaled by the archaeologists, causing illness, organ failure and even death if the individual is already weakened. Kramer's findings were supported by Merk, who studied rocks and dust from the tombs and found spores of two forms of aspergillus and cephalosporium, both dangerous to humans.[57] Hradecky also studied food from earthen pots at various Egyptian grave sites and discovered the bacteria which is thought could remain potent for thousands of years.[58]

Although this is plausible, further examinations of the deceased archaeologists would need to be carried out in order to prove it. Some scholars believe that the Egyptians actually placed such substances within the tombs in order to cause harm to anyone entering into them. Some use Lord Canarvon's teeth as proof of this. These fell out or chipped every few days, which some have interpreted as a sign of deep infection[59] or slow gradual poisoning.[60]

There is little to no evidence of poisons placed in the tombs, although Zahi Hawass commented that when he entered the twenty-sixth-dynasty tomb of the vizier Zedkhonsuefankh under King Apries:

> At that moment of discovery, I felt as though arrows of fire were attacking me. My eyes were closed and I could not breathe because of bad smell [sic]. I looked in to the room and discovered a very thick yellow powder around the anthropoid sarcophagus. I could not walk and did not read the name of the owner. I ran back out because of this smell. We brought masks for the workers who began to remove the material. I found out it was hematite, quarried nearby in Baharia.[61]

Although there clearly was a noxious substance within the tomb, it is impossible to tell if it was placed there intentionally. It is not the only tomb which has left the archaeologists feeling unwell. Sami Gabra, who was excavating in the ibis necropolis of Tuna el Gebel in the 1940s, reported that his team all had violent headaches and shortness of breath, which they blamed on a curse of the ibis-headed god of wisdom. Gabra, on the other hand, believed it to be noxious gases and simply evacuated the tomb, leaving it open for a few days before returning to work.[62]

Such ideas of poisons in the tombs as a deterrent to tomb robbers have been widely considered. Some researchers believe there could be a type of nerve gas which could kill instantly.[63] Vandenberg used this theory to explain why Horemheb did not desecrate Tutankhamun's tomb – because he was afraid of the poison used. Although an interesting idea, the question arises as to why there are not more dead tomb-robbers in entrances to tombs where they were overcome by fumes, and in special regard to the objects in the tomb of Tutankhamun, they seem to be reused from earlier burials, which would have required exhumations to obtain.

The ancient Egyptian knowledge of the power of radiation is another theory adopted by some researchers. It is obtainable from uranium core, available in roughly the same areas as gold mines, as well as in some forms of granite. Professor Bulgarini in 1949 believed the burial chambers could have been lined with stone heavy in uranium, creating a radioactive field, so when entered by archaeologists they died of radiation poisoning.[64] As yet this is not supported by the archaeology and is not widely accepted, although it became very popular as a line of study in the 1960s.

When Jasmine Day was interviewing museum patrons for her research on mummies, she asked about these theories. One woman had seen a television programme about noxious gases as the cause of the curse and stated that all the information about the curse should be released. She believed archaeologists were withholding information about this. This is a constant mantra with fringe theorists: that there is a conspiracy to withhold the truth. This itself is a myth which could be attributed to the apparent perceived exclusivity of Egyptology.[65] This exclusivity is decreasing with the thousands of television shows, books and news reports which keep Egyptology and the discoveries in the limelight.

CURSED COFFINS

The danger to archaeologists is not limited to being present in the tomb or disturbing the rest of the deceased. The curse was also believed to be attached to coffins, which have been blamed for all manner of accidents and disasters.

A mummy board was allegedly on the Titanic, leading to the disaster. The mummy board apparently belonged to a priestess from the Amarna period and was being transported by Lord Canterville from England to New York. It was shipped in a wooden crate stored behind the command bridge. Vandenberg believes the presence of the mummy turned the captain's mind, causing him to make wrong decisions, which led to the disaster. Apparently the mummy had an amulet of Osiris behind her head, which was inscribed with:

> Awake from the swoon in which you sleep and with a glance of your eyes will triumph over everything that is done against you.[66]

Clearly another curse, although what Lord Canterville had done against her, other than buy her a ticket on a doomed vessel, is uncertain.

This connection with mummies and shipwrecks was introduced in a story of a shipwreck in 1699 caused by a consignment of mummies aboard.[67] Mummies smuggled out of Egypt were thought to cause storms at sea, and were often thrown overboard in order to prevent them.[68]

Museums bear the brunt of these cursed objects as they are institutions which objectify and display mummies (fig. 38). Museums represent new tombs for the deceased and many museum displays in the modern world present funerary assemblages together, creating a tomb environment with which to invoke the curse. In movies and cartoons, museums are often shown with complete tombs recreated, including a sarcophagus and mummy.[69] Museums are often reputed to be haunted by such Egyptian mummies. For example, during the 1930s and 1940s guards patrolling the Field Museum in Chicago heard a scream from the Egyptian department. They found no intruders but one mummy, originally upright, was leaning his head against

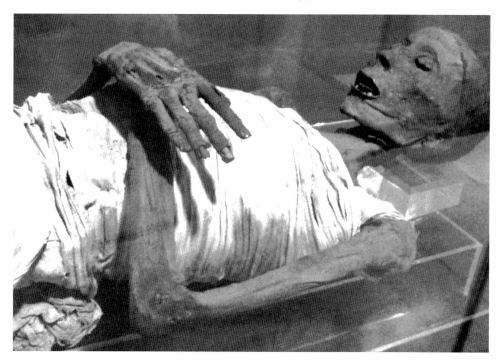

38. Mummy from the Saite Period. Rositcrucian Museum. (*Photograph courtesy of Keith Schengili-Roberts from Wikimedia Commons*)

a display case, although one report states it was face down on the floor. There was some confusion as to the identification of the mummy, as it was described as Harwa, the naked mummy, whereas the only naked mummy in the exhibition was of a child. It was well-known that lovers hid in the museum at night because of the reduced security and probably bumped into a display case, knocking the mummy over, and making a noise before they ran.[70]

In 1927, the British Museum Sculpture Gallery was reported to be haunted. One of the glass cases held an empty sarcophagus, but viewed through a particular case it showed a superimposed reflection of a face, which probably was a reflection of another anthropoid coffin.[71] One of the most famous, however, is the British Museum cursed mummy board, referred to as the 'unlucky' mummy, although it is no longer on display. While on display, the mummy board would frighten night-watchmen by making strange noises. Before it was given to the British Museum it was unlucky for anyone who owned it, whereas once it was in the museum it was only unlucky to those who were disrespectful. One lady who was rude to it fell down the stairs and sprained her ankle, whereas a journalist who wrote about it in jest apparently died a few days later, although how he died is not stated.

It was originally purchased in the 1860s by a group of Englishmen, all of whom were injured or died, including Douglas Murray who, shortly after, lost an arm when his gun exploded. However, further fuel to this story was added when both the cab and the ship that transported the mummy board were wrecked and the house the mummy board was originally stored in was burnt down. According to *The New York Times* in 1923, at the height of cursemania, it was stated that any photographs of the face appeared to be contorted with agony.

The connections started getting a little spurious when the man who photographed it shot himself, a sign of depression not a curse, and a woman connected to it had terrible family losses and was almost lost at sea.[72] The mummy board has since been 'exorcised' and apparently a green mist left the face, and since then nothing bad has happened.

Despite these dangerous associations with museums, most museums with an Egyptian collection will use the image of a mummy or coffin to advertise any exhibition about Egypt, even if it is not about mummification, or even if the exhibition is not about Egypt. Museums have a responsibility when displaying mummies to initiate a suitable response. With numerous discussions regarding the display of human remains, it is essential that the humanity of them is emphasised rather than objectifying them. This can sometimes be difficult due to the nature of archaeology, where the name and any personal details of the mummy may be lost but the goods and jewellery buried with them are available, meaning that the humanity of the mummy is not possible to present (plate 27). It is important that mummies are identified as the humans they are rather than objects affected by, or instigators of, the curse.

REANIMATED BODY PARTS

The reanimated mummy is one that dominates books, movies, cartoons and myths, and it is so powerful an idea that the curse of the mummy can be present in a single body part. One tale concerns the mummified hand of Makitaten, the daughter of Akhenaten,[73] the same individual who warned Cheiro that Carnarvon would die if he took anything from the tomb.

As Cheiro owned the mummified hand, it seems strange that she did not mention the violation of her own corpse. This hand belonging to the princess would, at times, become reanimated and would ooze blood. Cheiro soaked it in pitch and shellac to staunch the bleeding, but this only worked temporarily. He had totally objectified the mummy by trying to use it as a paper weight and cremated it the day before the tomb of Tutankhamun was discovered, and it was only then that the princess visited the psychic. This account of the mummy's hand is remarkably similar to Theophile Gautier's short story *The Mummy's Foot* (1840). The hero buys the beautifully preserved foot in a curiosity shop and uses it as a paperweight. He is awakened one evening to hear it hopping around the desk. The princess to whom it belonged to returns to claim it, and then whisks the hero to Egypt to meet the ancestors.[74]

This gruesome element of ancient Egyptian souvenirs was big business and mummy parts were cheaper to buy than a whole mummy, and were therefore more widely available. They were also considered interesting curiosities and at Ripley's Believe it or Not in San Francisco, they gave a mummy hand on display a background story to make it more appealing. They claimed it once wore a cursed golden disc causing the death of the person who acquired it, Walter Ingram.[75]

Reanimated body parts are a key inclusion in books and cartoons, as an element of abject horror as well as the power of the Egyptians themselves. This power is adopted by Lumley in *Khai of Ancient Khem*. The High Priest, Anulep, had the ability to reanimate the dead and control them:

> "Dead, eh, boy? Dead and falling into decay, returning to dust. Ah, but they have known the touch of the Dark Seven! They are not incorruptible, no – but neither are they wholly dead – not yet. Look!" And from a pocket he took a tiny golden whistle which he put to his lips. He blew a single note an eerie, undulating note... and at once the air was full of a leathery creaking, the suffocating stink of death and motion![76]

Not all of the reanimated mummy stories are so gruesome, and in *The Mummy* Ramses II is not really reanimated, as he never died. When his tomb was discovered by Lawrence Stratford and the mummy was brought into daylight, due to the elixir he had taken in life, the sunlight reanimated his body in the most beautiful way imaginable:

> This is the most beautiful man I had ever seen ... Skin like the skin of any other human being, only smoother, perhaps softer and full of more high colour – like that of a man who had been running, the cheeks faintly flushed.[77]

However, this elixir of immortality causes all to go drastically wrong as people desperately want to get hold of a vial. The biggest mistake was when Ramses came across the desiccated and badly damaged mummy of Cleopatra in the Egyptian museum and brings her back to life using the elixir. However, she had been dead too long and did not reanimate properly, causing death and destruction wherever she went. This book would make a fabulous mummy movie, but as yet it has not been produced. It is greatly influenced by *The Ring of Thoth*, where Sosra had lived for thousands of years after taking an elixir. His love interest refuses to take it and then, when he sees her mummy in a museum millennia later, he decides to take the antidote to the elixir and join her in death.

Television has been a great advocate of the reanimated mummy, and in the Egyptian special of the UK afternoon television chat show *The New Paul O'Grady Show*,[78] a reanimated mummy was the main gag, as it lay calmly on the couch while the Egyptologist explained about the mummification process, only to sit up and attack the host of the show. Mummies are now almost as synonymous with *Scooby Doo* as they are with ancient Egypt. The earliest introduction of a mummy in the show was in 1969, in *Scooby Doo and a Mummy Too*, which focuses on the curse of the mummy. Anyone confronted with the mummy is turned to stone. The mummy is displayed with grey skin reminiscent of bandages, wearing a *nemes* headdress and a kilt, and is terrifying in appearance. This type of representation was consistently used in the movies, often caked in blood or mud.

The mummy in *Scooby Doo and Mummy's the Word* (1980) is not as terrifying, and is simply a bandaged form. The mummy lives in a pyramid with the door at ground level. The lower levels of the pyramid have a river complete with crocodiles, which the gang use in an attempt to escape. When Scrappy Doo unwraps the mummy it loses its substance, resulting in a pile of bandages. However, as the mummy chases them out of the pyramid his footprints are visible in the sand. It is clear that the mummy is not malevolent, but rather just wants them to leave his home, and once they have gone he goes back inside and slams the door.

The idea that mummies are made simply of bandages is an interesting one, as many people are aware there is a more complex process behind mummification, but often in cartoons and movies, to make a mummy all one has to do is wrap a person in bandages. This is picked up in the *Futurama* episode 'A Pharaoh to Remember', where the dead king is simply wrapped in bandages in preparation for burial. The idea that a mummy is constructed simply of bandages makes for comedy unwrapping, where one bandage can be pulled and the mummy will spin like a top. This idea of single bandage unwrapping was adapted in 1993, when a mummy sticky tape dispenser was produced where the mummy was unwrapped as the sticky tape was used.

The mummies buried in the pyramids in Djelibeybi[79] are miraculously brought back to life, but rather than being 'mummies' with the associated characteristics, they are simply mummified humans with the same personalities. Luckily for them, the embalmer was a perfectionist and insisted on only the best materials:

> "You shouldn't talk to me of calico and wear. What happens if someone robs the tomb in a thousand years' time and him in calico, I'd like to know. He'd lurch halfway down the corridor, maybe throttle one of them, I'll grant you, but then he's coming undone, right? The elbows'll be out in no time, I'll never live it down."

However, the material of the bandages was to be the least of the reanimated kings' worries:

> It is astonishingly difficult to walk with legs full of straw when the brain doing the directing is in a pot ten feet away.

As is the nature of fiction, historical fact is unimportant. In the mummification process the brain was not preserved in a jar, but instead was thrown away; however, if this was used then the joke would not work in the story.

MUMMIES IN THE MOVIES

When something as intriguing as mummies has been at the forefront of Western imagination for hundreds of years, it is hardly surprising that Hollywood has adopted the theme. Between 1899 and 1924 over forty mummy films were produced, but it was the six mummy-themed films made between 1932 and 1955 which outlined the basic plots which were to inspire the later films. All of the early films show mummies as being 'different' from us, and more often than not evil.

Many of the earlier mummy films are based on the Tutankhamun curse, or *The Ring of Thoth* (1890) by Conan Doyle. Other films followed a similar plot, where a mummy kills those who pillaged the tomb of his beloved princess, pursuing a modern woman who is the reincarnation of his dead love. The mummy is inevitably killed before he or his master can kill this modern day woman.[80] An alternative plot is that a tomb is despoiled by archaeologists or treasure hunters, which invokes the curse. A mummy is reanimated and goes on the rampage, murdering all in his path, often indiscriminately. Many films and, subsequently, books use the plot of the mummy trying to revive a dead lover or attempting to attain immortality.[81] By the 1940s, adults were desensitised to horror movies and mummies were relegated to the children's matinee shows demonstrating an element of farce, which in modern movies like *The Mummy*, a remake of the 1932 Boris Karloff movie *The Mummy*, and *The Mummy Returns*, appealed to both adults and children.

Cinema turned the curse from criticism of grave-robbing into a celebration of it,[82] as mummies were the considered to be the opposite of everything that was good and right and were always presented with dirty, tatty bandages which may have been a direct contrast to the obsession with cleanliness prevalent in the West at the time.[83]

SYMPATHY FOR MUMMIES

Over the years the representation of mummies has changed, from these frightening creatures intent on killing to creatures we should sympathise with. As mummies have become a major inclusion in children's cartoons, the frightening element was removed or toned down to appeal to the market. A perfect example of this empathy can be found in Tim Burton's poem *Mummy Boy*,[84] about a little boy who was a mummy:

He wasn't soft and pink
with a fat little tummy;
he was hard and hollow,
a little boy mummy.
"Tell us, please, Doctor,
the reason or cause,
why our bundle of joy
is just a bundle of gauze."
"My diagnosis," he said
"for better or worse,
is that your son is the result
of an old pharaoh's curse."
That night they talked
of their son's odd condition

they called him "a reject
from an archaeological expedition."
They thought of some complex
scientific explanation,
but assumed it was simple
supernatural reincarnation.
With the other young tots
he only played twice,
an ancient game of virgin sacrifice.
(But the kids ran away, saying, "You aren't very nice.")
"Look it's a píñata,"
said one of the boys,
"Let's crack it wide open
and get the candy and toys."
They took a baseball bat
and whacked open his head.
Mummy Boy fell to the ground;
he finally was dead.
Inside of his head
were no candy or prizes,
just a few stray beetles
of various sizes.

This poem appeals to our sympathies as it focuses on the humanity of the mummy, presenting him as a child that wanted to make friends. Other examples of this can be seen in the children's cartoons *Tutenstein*[85] and *L'il Horrors*. *Tutenstein* tells the story of Tutankhensetamun, who was reanimated in a museum using electricity from lightning, rather like Shelley's Frankenstein. The first moment when it is realised that he is alive, all one can hear is an aggressive and terrifying growling. When he appears he is covered in very tatty bandages, but to reduce the terrifying element of the mummy, he is a small boy with a small boy's needs and indeed the first thing he needs to do is to use the bathroom. The characterisation, however, for Tutenstein is straight from the Bible and Herodotus, showing an arrogant and pompous ruler.[86] Even though he is an unpleasant character, he is one which the audience can feel empathy. In *L'il Horrors* the characterisations are very different, but still attract empathy. Cleo is a mummy child at boarding school. She is a bit of an airhead and is not threatening in any way and speaks regularly about vibes, bringing New Age connections into this show.

Once an audience is empathetic to the plight of the mummy, the natural progression is encouraging the audience to relate to the mummy. This is easily achieved with children by presenting mummies in a way they can associate with. This is achieved in the *Magnificent Mummies*, the story of a family of mummies – Daddy Mummy, Mummy Mummy, Tut and Sis – who befriend a travelling archaeologist, Sir Digby Digger. The mummies, while living in a very human way, are presented in a stereotypical manner, with dirty bandages

39 Upright coffins, British Museum. (*Photograph courtesy of Brian Billington*)

covered with cobwebs and living within a pyramid. The family eat at a dining table, but the children are told off by their parents for making a mess, something all children will be able to relate to. Children enjoy the concept of mummies as they go against the realities of their life and they are attracted to unpleasant things, dirt and disruption.[87] At bedtime, the whole Mummy family step into their coffins, which are displayed vertically against the wall. They cross their arms over their chests in a stereotypical manner.

It is interesting that the coffins are placed vertically here, as in tombs they were always horizontal. However, they are represented vertically in museums (fig. 39), on television shows and in movies, leading many people to think this is the normal position for an Egyptian coffin. However, in museums they are in this position to enable the visitor to see as much of the decoration as possible, displaying the coffin to its best advantage, whereas in movies and television the coffins need to be vertical in order to enable to mummy to stumble out of it.

A particularly interesting feature of cartoons is the animation of mummy cases, which are given the power of movement or speech. Often in movies it is the shifting of the coffin lid which alerts the audience to the presence of the mummy, but in cartoons like *Bananaman*[88] for example, benevolent coffin cases, bizarrely, are able to talk and laugh with animated facial features. These animated coffins are normally empty and the animation is of the coffin itself rather than a mummy inside. The benevolence of the original mummy transfers to the coffin.

The gradual changes in the meanings of mummies have been instigated by changing representations in the press, change in the response to mummies and changes in how mummies are treated by professionals.[89] They have been presented in three main ways: evil baddie who kills people, the friendly clown and the evil but ineffectual creature[90] who inspires sympathy.

A perfect example is Tutankhamun himself, a young man who died at only eighteen years of age and was left alone in the tomb for 3,500 years. The sympathy wanes once we realise how many treasures are associated with him.[91] It suddenly seems more important to retrieve these treasures than let him rest in peace.

Mummies are an interesting element of the myth of Egypt, as while they are a feature of ancient Egyptian funerary beliefs, the myth is completely fabricated in the West and built upon with superstitions, imagination and politics. Even those with no interest in ancient Egypt include the myth of the mummy in their lives. There are many people who believe the curse is real, and I once had two students who were very interested in Egyptology and went on a two-week trip to Egypt. They were very much looking forward to visiting the Valley of the Kings, but when I asked them about their trip they told me they did not go in any of the tombs because they were scared of the curse and were just happy to be there. They truly believed the curse made entering a tomb a foolish and reckless activity.

Mummies are included in daily language, with the elderly or particularly thin people being compared to mummies and mummies compared to old people. Homer Simpson in *The Simpsons* (1991) tells Mr Burns:

You are a senile buck-toothed old Mummy.

40. Hobby Craft display, October 2010, Swindon. (*Photograph courtesy of Brian Billington*)

41. Mummy Mural at Holborn Station, showing it is the 'British Museum Stop'. (*Photograph courtesy of Sunil060902 from Wikimedia Commons*)

Many parents have also been bombarded with hundreds of terrible mummy jokes:

- What kind of music do mummies like? Wrap music.
- What is the mummy's favourite musical programme? Name that tomb.
- What was a favourite saying in ancient Egypt? A fool and his mummy are soon parted.
- Why was the Egyptian confused? Because his daddy was a mummy.

A constant joke is also associated with the wrapping of a mummy and the use of bandages. If someone is injured and is wrapped in bandages, they will inevitably be compared to a mummy.

Since the 1960s mummies have joined the Halloween market in the United States, and this has spread throughout the English-speaking world, where they are sold en masse to 'scare' people (fig. 40). It is interesting that mummies have been coupled with imaginary creatures such as zombies, witches and vampires, even though they are, in fact, 'real'. Mummies are also the simplest costume for a parent to throw together at the last minute (plate 28). All that is needed is a couple of rolls of toilet paper. Even teenagers have not been forgotten and the Backstreet Boys video for 'Everybody' (1997), which is very *Scooby Doo* in nature, had the Boys stranded in a haunted house, which in addition to werewolves and vampires included mummies in the basement emerging from an iron-maiden type coffin, with trailing yellowing bandages. It is clear that mummies are here to stay (fig. 41), and it will be exciting to see how they are presented and received in the decades to come.

CHAPTER 8

EGYPTOMANIA IN THE WEST

The preceding chapters have investigated various myths surrounding Egypt, and although they have different origins they have one thing in common. They are all existent in the minds of Westerners and show that Egyptian history, myths and legends are very much a part of Western culture. Even mentioning the word 'Egypt' brings to mind images of decadence, wealth, exoticism, curses, intelligence and mysticism. Everyone seems to have their own opinion about Egypt and its history, and people and Western culture would be lost without it. However, like most things in the world, Egypt goes in and out of fashion. As different discoveries were made over the years, Egypt became popular in the media before waning until the next major archaeological event.

Each of these periods of popularity spurred a period of 'Egyptomania' where Egyptian elements were included in jewellery, furniture, architecture, television shows, literature and movies. Egyptomania can be divided into specific interests, such as Tutmania (an interest in Tutankhamun) and Mummymania (an interest in mummies). The first real period of Egyptomania followed the publication of *Les Description* in 1809–1828, when there was an introduction of Egyptian style in the West, including architecture, art, literature and an increased interest in collecting artefacts from Egypt itself, which led to increased tourism to Egypt. The next revival of Egyptian motifs followed the decipherment of hieroglyphs in 1822 by Jean-Francois Champollion, followed by the opening of the Suez Canal in 1869, which was shortly followed in 1922 by the discovery of Tutankhamun's tomb. In the 1970s, with the first tour of the Tutankhamun artefacts, there was a further sweep of Egyptomania in the West. At the moment, in the opening decades of the twenty-first century, with another tour of Tutankhamun's artefacts, Egypt is very popular, with hundreds of TV documentaries, books and 'gifts' being created, including such items as Egyptian-themed USB portable storage devices, soft toys and household linen. You name it, it can be Egyptianised. So what makes an object Egyptianised?

Generally, an Egyptianised object is not an original artefact, and if it is the mount should be modern with Egyptian design elements. A perfect example of the difference can be seen in the obelisks in Paris and London. Both are genuine ancient obelisks, but only the London one includes Egyptianising elements. The French obelisk is mounted on a block which displays how the obelisk was transported and re-erected but does not incorporate Egyptian elements, whereas London's Cleopatra's Needle is

42. Sphinx as part of Cleopatra's Needle, London. (*Photograph courtesy of Brian Billington*)

mounted using lots of Egyptian motifs, flanked by two bronze sphinxes (fig. 42). Even the benches along the Embankment have Egyptianising characteristics, made up of sphinxes and camels.[1] Copies of genuine artefacts are not seen as Egyptianising, unless they have other elements included. However, it is surprising how many Egyptianising elements can be seen in the Western world.

WORLDWIDE EGYPTOMANIA

The first period of Egyptomania followed Napoleon's expedition to Egypt and spread throughout the Western world, even reaching Russia, Brazil and Australia. Egyptomania reached Russia via Italy and France[2] and, contrary to the rest of the Western world, the discovery of Tutankhamun had no impact on Russian Egyptianisation.[3]

Brazil's interest in Egypt was inspired by Napoleon's expedition, which intrigued King Dom Pedro I, who purchased the first Egyptology collection in 1824. This is now housed at the National Museum.[4] A second wave of Egyptomania in Brazil was introduced after the opening of the Suez Canal. The Egyptianising elements in Brazil were manifested primarily in the artwork, although obelisks became a popular architectural addition.

However, as would be expected, the focus of a great deal of the Egyptianising monuments after *Les Description* was in Paris. It was government-funded and commemorated Napoleon's military role in Egypt, as well as associating ancient Egyptian accomplishments with him.[5] Even the Arch de Triomph has Egyptian elements with the triumphal procession of the armies, transporting a sphinx resting on an obelisk in a cart, during the Italian campaign.[6]

Throughout the world similar elements are used on architectural structures, including cavetto corniches, torus mouldings, battered walls, sphinxes, pyramids and obelisks. These are used to adorn buildings, fountains, tombs, bridges, homes and furniture.[7] Each element used had different meanings for those using them, and these were often in conflict with the original Egyptian meaning. For example, in the United States obelisks represented justice and truth, American expansionism, commemoration for various events and a connection with the positive aspects of Egyptian history.[8] The sphinx is also popular in Egyptianised monuments, where it was a sign of kingship or divinity in ancient Egypt, whereas in the modern world it was used for protection, to feed the vanity of shop owners, represent stability, and was even used on a brothel sign in Paris.[9] While the sphinx has been consistent in Egyptianising architecture, the sex changed from the Greek female to the Egyptian male,[10] showing an ambiguity in the meaning.

FUNERARY ELEMENTS

As many of the archaeological finds from Egypt are funerary in nature, funerary artefacts and characteristics were intriguing to people in the West. Funerary furniture was replicated, with scantily clad women in Egyptian wigs, or pharaohs in kilts for furniture legs.[11] The funerary elements were generally not considered easily adapted for domestic architecture[12] and were adopted for cemeteries throughout the Western world, with a prominence in Europe and United States.

Sometimes those who chose to have an Egyptianising funerary monument had some connection with Egypt, either through profession or interest. In the cemeteries of Paris, for example, many of the people who were part of Napoleon's expedition are buried with Egyptianising tombs comprising corvette corniches, winged sun discs, lotus, papyrus plants and pylon-shaped structures which are juxtaposed with Christian motifs. However, in most situations the connection between the interred and Egypt appears to be more obscure.[13] For many the choice was led by fashion, and it has been suggested that the continuity of Egyptian history and the durability of their monuments were considered an appropriate reason for associating them with the dead.

The Mount Auburn Cemetery, Cambridge, Massachusetts, has an Egyptian-style gateway which is not associated with an individual burial. The wood used to construct the original gateway was painted to look like granite, but in 1842 it was rebuilt using real granite. The gateway is based on the pylons of Karnak and Denderah temples,[14] and emphasises the continuity of the time.

Egyptianising monuments in cemeteries, however, do follow fashions. From the seventeenth century onwards obelisks and pyramids became the Egyptian

43. Wilson Mausoleum, Hampstead Cemetery. (*Photograph courtesy of Elisabeth Kerner*)

monument of choice, although mastabas and Egyptian-style chapels were common in the eighteenth century. A prime example of such a chapel was the mausoleum at Blickling Hall in Norfolk (1794) for the Count and Countess of Buckinghamshire. These funerary structures have reached as far as South Africa, where a pyramid tomb was built by Dr Johann Friedrich Häsner (1764–1821) for his wife, who died in 1817 in childbirth. The pyramid was plastered and stands over 3 metres tall.[15]

One of the most famous cemeteries is Highgate Cemetery West, London, which was founded in 1839, covers 37 acres and has an entire Egyptian Avenue (1859), entered via a corbelled arch with four reed columns (plate 29) and a colossal obelisk. The Avenue is a covered walkway of mausoleums with doorways decorated with torus mouldings, which leads to the Circle of Lebanon, a circular avenue of mausoleums placed around a huge Lebanon cedar in the centre. Outside of this area dedicated to Egyptianising architecture, there are numerous Egyptianised tombs, with all the expected elements such as torus mouldings (fig. 43), corbelling (plate 30), obelisks and pyramids. Some are a juxtaposition of Egyptian and classic designs, for example a pylon-styled monument with a Roman urn placed on the top (fig. 44).

Other funerary structures were adapted from their original form into Egyptianised monuments. The catacombs in Paris are one such structure. They were converted from a quarry in 1786, and at the turn of the nineteenth century they were opened up and more burials were transferred here. Napoleon wanted the burials here to be 'decorative', and between 1810 and 1811 a number of obelisks were painted onto the roof supports within the catacombs and outnumbered the Christian crosses.[16]

44. Egyptian Mausoleum, Highgate Cemetery.

It was not just the rich and influential who chose Egyptianising elements on their funerary monuments. Dorothy Eady, better known as Omm Sety, who died in Abydos, Egypt in 1981, had built an underground tomb in her back garden for her interment:

> It's a lovely underground room made of red brick, lined with cement and covered with slabs of concrete, In the west wall I have carved a nice little false door, just as they did in the ancient tombs. Then I also carved an offering prayer asking for 1,000 jars of beer, 1,000 loaves of bread, 1,000 oxen, 1,000 geese, 1,000 jars of wine, perfume and every good and pure thing.[17]

Unfortunately, the health department would not allow her to be buried there and she was buried in a cemetery nearby.

PUBLIC BUILDINGS

The durability of Egyptian monuments was incorporated into a number of public buildings in the West, although in the first half of the nineteenth century Egyptianising monuments in American decoration were rare because ancient Egypt was not considered as appropriate an association in America as Greece and Rome.[18] Because of this, there was a proposal (1891–1900) in the United States Senate to build a Parthenon which was 50 per cent larger than life size, with a central walkway to the Capitol Building, with rooms leading from it representing the eight great civilisations, which did include Egypt. The processional way was to have a scaled-down Sphinx and Giza Pyramids, which would serve as auditoriums or store rooms. However, despite these grand ideas, all that was built was the 'Hall of the Ancients', with columns based on the hypostyle hall at Karnak and the temple of Hathor at Denderah.[19]

Despite Greece and Rome being considered more appropriate, there were a number of Egyptianising monuments built in the United States, such as the New Jersey State Penitentiary, Trenton, built between 1832 and 1836. The high enclosure wall was decorated with corvetto cornicing and niches for flagpoles, resembling the pylon of Edfu temple. The entrance to the prison comprised two pylon towers with a portico between them. They are described with an inscription of Amenhotep III taken from *Les Description*. Another similar building was the New York City Halls of Justice and House of Detention, known as The Tombs. This building was connected with prison reform and came across as terrifying and gloomy rather than decadent and glamorous. Law courts in nineteenth-century England also used the same designs in order to represent immortality, grandeur and justice intended to intimidate the criminals and reassure the law-abiding citizens.

Reverend Van der Lingen, a student of Egyptology and hieroglyphs, commissioned the Gymnasium Primary School north of Cape Town, South Africa, in 1858, which was constructed using Egyptianising elements. The entrance was a large pylon gateway,

45. Cairo Museum exterior detail.

with torus mouldings and a corvette cornice, with the window frames decorated with cornicing, the winged sun disc, a Hathor head and a sphinx. It has been compared to the Egyptian Hall in London, although the school was not as elaborate, as it was plain white stone. The school was still functioning as such in 1968 and was declared a national monument.[20]

Museums also have incorporated Egyptianising elements, such as the Egyptian Museum in Cairo (fig. 45). Although a museum dedicated to Egyptian artefacts, the figures above the main entrance are pure Egyptianising as they are not replicas of known artefacts (plate 31). The museum was built in 1897 and opened in 1902.

The Louvre Museum, Paris, has the ultimate in Egyptianising monuments with the rather contentious glass pyramid constructed in the courtyard. Despite concerns at the time of opening, the pyramid is now considered as much a part of the landscape of Paris as the Eiffel Tower. The architect Ieoh Ming Pei always stated that the pyramid was not Egyptian in design but was rather about the transparency and space it incorporates,[21] but this is not how it is viewed by most visitors to Paris.

PUBLIC MONUMENTS

The stability and continuity of Egyptian culture and monuments was quite a powerful image, and therefore Egyptianising forms were used in suspension piers and bridges from the 1820s in Europe,[22] the United States and even as far as St Petersburg, Russia, over the Fontanka Canal.[23] At the time there was a great deal of suspicion about these new types of bridges, and in order to assuage these fears the engineers drew on the reputation of Egypt as a land of wisdom.[24] This wisdom gave people confidence in the bridge, almost as if it was endorsed by the wise men of old. However, they never openly stated this was what they were doing, and it is very difficult to prove this was the case.

Egyptianised monuments were also frequently used to commemorate events and make public statements, and are often juxtaposition between Christian and Egyptian motifs. In 1780, the Fountain of the Pyramid was constructed in Praça XV Square in Rio de Janeiro, with a church tower supporting a pyramid. The Fountain of the Saracuras, also in central Rio de Janeiro (1795), incorporated an obelisk mounted by a Christian cross.[25]

In Paris, Napoleon commissioned fifteen public fountains, six of which were designed to honour him and his role in Egypt. The Fontaine du Fellah, for example, displays a statue of Antinous, a Roman Egyptianising statue from Hadrian's villa, carrying water jugs. This combination of a peasant dressed in the royal *nemes* headdress was a cross-over of traditional ideas.[26]

RESIDENTIAL STRUCTURES

Egypt became popular among the rich and many wished to live in Egyptianised houses, which may have included an Egyptian room to display their collections of

46. Antinous statue, Buscot Park, Oxford.
(*Photograph courtesy of Tracy Walker*)

antiquities, as well as their 'modern' Egyptian-influenced furniture. One of the earliest examples was Thomas Hope's house in Duchess Street, London, built in 1807. The outside of his house was neoclassical in design and showed no indication of the Egyptianised objects within, which he designed as a means of proving the Egyptian origin of all civilisation. He combined genuine artefacts with Egyptianised furniture in pale yellow, blueish green, black and gold. These objects are now currently in the Victoria and Albert Museum and Buscot Park, Oxfordshire. Buscot House was built between 1780 and 1783 for Edward Loveden Townsend. The Egyptianised objects made for Thomas Hope are primarily in the hall, including a suite comprising an ebonised and gilt couch, a pair of chairs and a pair of ebonised and gilt torches. Buscot House also has Egyptianised objects in the garden in the form of Antinous Osiris statues (fig. 46) wearing a *nemes* headdress and Greek-style sphinxes.

Egyptianised monuments in gardens were not uncommon, and in the eighteenth century the 'Anglo-Chinese' gardens[27] normally contained Antinous statues, sphinxes or pyramids, which were used as ice-houses. Lovely examples include the ice-house in Cascine Park in Florence, built in 1796,[28] and the Potsdam Pyramid in Germany built between 1791 and 1792, with its pylon-style door with cabalistic inscriptions and hieroglyphic friezes.[29] Even the garden of Catherine the Great at Tsarskoye Selo, Russia, constructed in the 1770s, included a pyramid, used as the burial place for her favourite dogs.[30] Other gardens in Russia from the eighteenth century started to house Egyptian lions modelled on those in Rome, which remained in style for a few decades.[31]

In the first half of the twentieth century, there was an influx in the construction of Egyptianised residential buildings, especially in the United States. For example, there were a number of apartment complexes in Los Angeles with names such as King Tut Court, Osiris, Amasis and Amun-Ra Apartments. One group of apartments, the Egyptian Court Apartments, constructed in 1926 in San Diego, are decorated with a frieze of flowers across the entrance, copied from the Malkata palace of Amenhotep III. The apartment complex even has a central garden with a pond reminiscent of the palaces of ancient Egypt, although these are flanked by two small shops.[32]

A summer residence called the Egyptian House in Wesley Hills, New York, was built in 1915 on 600 acres of land. The owner spent a great deal of time in Egypt for his health and wanted to recreate this in New York. The house comprised kiosks and gazebos on two corners of the terrace, with a Luxor temple-style colonnade between the main house and the guest house.[33] Also in New York, the Temple for the Knights of Pythias was constructed in 1927. The building is covered in Egyptian motifs, such as winged Horus of Behdet signs and *khekher* friezes. There are four colossal glazed-tile statues of seated pharaohs in a New Kingdom style,[34] with *nemes* headdresses and false beards. The entrance comprised a pillared portico with bound reed columns adorned with two winged sphinxes above the door. In 1958, it was purchased by the New York Institute of Technology, and was used as the main college campus. In the latter part of the twentieth century, people once more wanted to live in the luxury of an Egyptian house and in 1986 it was converted into a residential building with eighty-eight apartments.

Modern residential houses are still constructed in Egyptian style; in 1977 Jim Onan in Wadsworth, Illinois, created a six-storey house in the form of a 16-metre-tall pyramid. This was plated in 24-carat gold and is the largest gold-plated object in the world. It is part of a wider complex with subsidiary pyramids forming a three car garage, a colossal standing statue of a king, a sphinx avenue leading to the entrance and a sacred lake. The inside of the house is decorated with Egyptian-style images and was opened to the public, charging admission of $20 per person.[35] Today, the site is more an Egyptian-themed gift-shop, open for tours only once a week.

EGYPT AND THE FREEMASONS

Egypt and the Freemasons have long been associated, and there are theories suggesting they were formed in Ancient Egypt. This theory originated with manuscripts dating to 1390, following the development of man from Adam to the modern day, which had Abraham in Egypt teaching the seven liberal arts and sciences. This was enhanced by Sarah Belzoni, writing a paper on Freemasonry (1844) in the tomb of Pharaoh Osirei in the Valley of the Kings, where she describes the tomb paintings, assuming they are performing mason rituals. This paper was greatly received and led to theories that the Freemasons were in fact responsible for building the pyramids and obelisks.[36]

However, the Freemasons' official birthday is on 24 June 1717 and rather than having lodges to meet in, most Freemasons would meet in local bars and taverns. The Freemasons spread quickly from England throughout Europe, Turkey, China, Indonesia and America. The founder of Egyptian Freemasonry was Count Cagliostro from Palermo, who, it was reported, obtained his secret knowledge while in the subterranean chambers of the Egyptian pyramids. Even at this time, some people believed the pyramids to be a store of ancient knowledge. Cagliostro died in prison in 1795, condemned as a 'propagator of Egyptian Masonry', and his book on Egyptian masonry had been publically burned. The Egyptian connections started early, with a seal of the Lodge in Naples bearing a sphinx, pyramid and sun disc with emanating rays as its symbol, although the Egyptian motifs did not become popular until the end of the eighteenth century.[37]

In 1766, Carl Friedrich Köppen (1734–1797) wrote the *Crata Repoa*, which was a seven-stage tract based on Egyptian ideas, rituals and dietary taboos. Stage one saw the initiate questioned by a hierophant and experiencing an ordeal of the four elements before being taught the secrets of hieroglyphs, while dressed in Egyptian clothes, with a pyramid-shaped hat, apron and collar. The second degree was a test of love and a test involving a snake, before progressing to the third degree, where he enters a room filled with coffins and embalmed bodies. Here he was introduced to the hierogrammatic writing system, before being led to the fourth degree by a rope. He was given an unpleasant drink and change of clothes and at the recital of the password he entered the fifth degree, where he was given another password and familiarised with alchemy. In the sixth degree he learned astrology and became a prophet in the seventh degree.[38]

Mozart's *The Magic Flute* (1791) was also thought to bring such Masonic concerns to public view as the opera concerns mysteries of Isis and initiation within a pyramid, and the sets of Freidrich Schinkel (1781–1841) were completely Egyptian in design. Mozart had been admitted to the Vienna lodge in 1784.

The first Egyptianised Masonic lodge was built in Strasbourg in 1779. From this date onwards, there an increase in pyramids used to house conference rooms or Masonic lodges with Egyptianised themes. In 1806 the Sovereign Pyramid was created in Toulouse which had an altar flanked by Osiris and Isis, the latter having close associations with the Masons. At this lodge, the initiates are said to have worn Egyptian-style robes for their ceremonies.[39]

In 1824, the Masonic Temple in Douai was decorated with numerous Egyptian frescoes,[40] and in 1840 the Lodge in Valenciennes, between Belgium and France, had a façade based on temple images from *Les Description*,[41] and the temple in Boston, Lincolnshire was based on a combination of Denderah, Edfu and Philae. It was important to the Freemasons to try to accurately reproduce Egyptian elements rather than create a pastiche, and in addition to using *Les Description*, various papyri of the Book of the Dead were referred to. In 1879, the Venerable Master of the Lodge claimed:

> Going back into the distant past, we have borrowed from ancient Egyptian wisdom what, according to supreme divinity, was regarded as the essence of life.[42]

However, by the 1920s the Masonic interest in Egypt had waned and Egyptianising lodges were no longer built, as with further study of their history they generally believed now

47. Carreras Cigarette Factory, London. (*Photograph courtesy of Brian Billington*)

that Freemasonry did not originate in Egypt, but rather in England in the late eighteenth century. However, the Egyptian connection is still alive, and the obelisk standing in Washington D.C. and the pyramid and the triangle with the radiant eye which adorn the one dollar bill in the United States are testament to the Masonic forefathers of America: George Washington, Thomas Jefferson and Benjamin Franklin.[43]

COMMERCIAL BUILDINGS

Various businesses use elements of ancient Egypt in order to sell their products and there are numerous businesses called Pyramid, Sphinx, or Cleopatra. Some companies use Egyptian images in their advertising, as the glamorous, erotic images sell products. At the end of 2010 in the UK, at least two companies have used Egypt to sell their products: Go Compare home insurance used an Egyptian tomb, with the archaeologist reading the inscriptions from the wall, which talks about home insurance, and Easyjet, who were celebrating their fifteenth birthday, used an image of an adapted golden mask of Tutankhamun wearing a party hat, even though their flights to Egypt were a relatively recent addition to their flight schedule.

Even if the names of the companies are not associated with Egypt, their buildings sometimes have Egyptianising elements. The Carreras Cigarette Factory in Mornington Crescent (fig. 47), London, was built by Arcadia works and opened in November 1928.

The design was based on the temple of Bubastis,[44] dedicated to the cat-headed goddess Bastet. The columns, however, were influenced by Amarna tombs. The factory was vast, covering four hectares over five floors, and is the largest factory of its kind in the world. The outside of the building was rendered with Atlas white cement, which was sand-coloured to add to the Egyptian theme. The coloured sections on the pillars were created using Venetian glass.

The original stairs leading to the entrance of the building had a serpentine handrail, in reference to the Cleopatra myth. Above the door was a Horus of Behdet symbol, which was covered up during the Second World War as it was considered too similar to Third Reich symbols, and therefore not appropriate.[45] The cats that currently flank the doorway of the factory are replicas, as the originals have long since been parted. One is in the factory of Carreras of Jamaica Ltd in Spanishtown, Jamaica, and the other is outside the Tabacofina-Vander Elst Museum, Antwerp, Belgium.[46]

The opening ceremonies of the cigarette factory were an impressive event and the organisers sprinkled sand on ground in front of the building and there was a procession of the cast of *Aida*, who performed in front of the factory, followed by a chariot race and a procession of 'Egyptian Types'.[47] In 1962, Carreras had moved on and the new owners turned the cigarette factory into offices. Sadly, many of the Egyptian features were removed or covered over, and it was renamed Greater London House.

Another factory built at approximately the same time was the Hoover Factory in London, which was completed in 1932 and is a wonderful example of an art nouveau building. The whole building was flooded with natural light as the northern, eastern and western light is utilised in the construction. This was an innovation in twentieth-century architecture. The building is reminiscent of the façade of the temple of Sety I at Abydos. The building was closed in 1980, but was renovated in the early 1990s for Tesco. The original plans were used for renovations[48] and sadly, at the time of writing the building stands empty.

At the end of the twentieth century, Egypt was still incorporated into commercial buildings and Sainsbury's Homebase, Earls Court, London, was completed in 1988. The external walls were decorated with relief carvings of ten Egyptian gods, with those furthest away from the entrance gilded and coloured, whereas others are only partially coloured or plain.[49] The entrance was originally flanked by decorated pillars and a carved sphinx, which were demolished on the order of Lord Sainsbury.[50] The carvings took eight carvers seven months to complete and were a veritable work of art, although some critics claimed it was the most hated building in London.[51]

Jumping onto the Egyptian bandwagon, the Egyptian Hall in Harrods, completed in 1992, was designed by William Mitchell with advice from James Putman of the British Museum. The Egyptian Hall on the upper floor contains scenes of everyday life and funerary scenes, whereas in the lower hall there are images of the *Opet* and *hebsed* festivals. These images were mostly based on a combination of Old Kingdom and Amarna art, which has maintained its popularity through the decades.[52]

The images are a real juxtaposition of modern myth and ancient facts. For example, there is a statue of a seated king surrounded by text from Shelley's 'Ozymandias', a combination of myth and history. There is a procession of royal children, reminiscent of the procession of Ramses II's children, with the modern twist on this being the small handprint above each child.[53] The cartouches at the end of the escalator say in hieroglyphs 'Egyptian Hall within Harrods 1991', whereas the other cartouches say 'Al Fayad', the owner of Harrods at the time. Despite the escalators and decorations costing £20 million,[54] they were purely for entertainment rather than education as none of the motifs are labelled or dated and are there purely for their aesthetic characteristics.

EGYPT AND ENTERTAINMENT

At the start of the twentieth century, cinema and movies were becoming big business and many organisations wanted to tie in movies with the decadence and exoticism of ancient Egypt. This led to numerous Egyptianised cinemas and play houses being constructed throughout the Western world. One of the earliest was the Egyptian Hall in Piccadilly, London, which opened in 1812 as a Natural History Museum. It was built by William Bullock and it housed his collection. In 1816, Bullock sold the collection and opened the Hall as an exhibition space, which was used primarily for art, although in 1821 Giovanni Battista Belzoni exhibited the Sety I tomb here. It was renovated into a cinema in 1896,[55] when it was used to show some of the very first films or animated photographs. In 1905, the Egyptian Hall was knocked down and blocks of flats were built there instead.

This started a run of Egyptianised cinema building throughout Europe. The Louxor Palais du Cinéma in Paris, although constructed before the discovery of Tutankhamun, certainly profited from it. It was built between 1920 and 1921, with an elaborate entrance comprising a portico with papyrus bud-columns, with winged sun-disks above the door. The Egyptian theme continued throughout the interior, with the frame around the screen including an image of a winged Nekhbet and a frieze above the screen with Egyptian figures walking in procession. Between 1928 and 1930, four Egyptianising cinemas were constructed in London: the Luxor in Twickenham, Astoria in Streatham and two Carltons in Upton Park and Islington. The only one still standing, albeit in a dilapidated and abandoned state, is the Carlton in Islington. The construction was quite plain and unadorned at street level, although the canopy over one of the entrances comprised a lotus frieze. There are two large papyrus columns in the higher central section, which were brightly painted. The interior of the Islington Carlton was a combination of modern and classical design, with the Egyptian elements only existing on the outside.

This was the same for the Carlton in Upton Park, where there was an Egyptian exterior and a modern or classical interior. This cinema had an inset entrance with twin columns, one of palm and one of papyrus. There was a corvette cornice around the top of the structure, with a winged sun disk and ureaus adorning the centre. The Luxor cinema in Twickenham had both an Egyptian façade and Egyptian interiors. The external façade had six palm-capital columns and two winged pharaoh heads with *nemes* headdress. Even the souvenir programme had Egyptian motifs in the cover.

The Astoria in Streatham had an Italian façade and Egyptian interior, and was described in the *Clapham and Lambeth News* in June 1930 as:

> A vast auditorium adorned with Egyptian painting and glass mosaics ... the general design
> is based upon Egyptian traditions in pleasing tones of red, green, gold ... while the flank
> walls of the circle are enriched with highly coloured bas reliefs of Egyptian scenes.[56]

In addition to cinema, Egyptianising elements are included in any structures involved in entertainment where images of exoticism and decadence add to the entertainment experience. Zoos and parks did not escape this decorative style, in both Europe and the United States. Memphis (Tennessee) Zoo and Aquarium has an elaborate pylon gateway built in 1990–91. This pylon is approached by a sphinx avenue comprising various animals, including, rather bizarrely, an image of Snoopy. The hieroglyphs on the pylon spell out words like kangaroo and shark. The Detroit Zoo has Egyptianised paintings on the hippopotamus building and giraffe house.[57]

The Antwerp Zoo in Belgium has an Egyptian temple to house the giraffes, which was built in 1857. It has a typical pylon entrance and a readable inscription which states, 'In the twenty-third year of the reign of Her Majesty, the royal Daughter Victoria, Lady Most Gracious, this building was erected.'[58] The elephant house itself was designed as an Egyptian temple and was built in 1855–56 and is decorated internally and externally. It was restored in 1988. It also bears another inscription:

> in the year of the Lord 1856, under His Majesty the King, sun and life of Belgium,
> son of the Sun, Leopold I, this house was made to delight Antwerp and educate its
> inhabitants.[59]

The Pharaoh's Lost Kingdom Adventure Park in Redlands, California, was completed in 1996, with massive structures within the park of pyramids which rise above the walled park. The entrance has a large sphinx, and to enter the park visitors have to walk through the paws of the sphinx. The amusement park itself comprises Egyptian colonnades, colossal statues, sculpted creatures and a pyramid grill.[60]

In addition to zoos, amusement parks also have Egyptian themes, with many fairs in the nineteenth and early twentieth centuries including Egypt. One such fair was the Crypte des Pharaons at Luna Park in Paris in 1907. This was a juxtaposition of Egyptian and Islamic elements, although the ubiquitous pylon flanked with two obelisks and a colossal sphinx were of course present,[61] as it was a form clearly identified with Egypt, endurance and stability. What this attraction was is uncertain, but a lot of effort had clearly gone into creating the elaborate pylon entrance, with a staircase leading from it.

There were two very important fairs in the United States in the late nineteenth century which seemed to be the start of any widespread interest in Egyptomania in America. One was the Centennial Exhibition in 1876, a world fair to celebrate the centenary of American independence, and the second was the World's Columbian Exhibition in 1893, celebrating the 400th anniversary of Christopher Columbus landing in America. The Centennial Exhibition had an Egyptian court in the main building dominated by a temple façade made of wood comprising palm pillars, winged sun-discs and cornicing, as well as two plaster heads of kings. The hieroglyphic inscription across the top of the façade was authentic and read:

> The Viceroy has made for the Centennial Celebration, at the city of Philadelphia, a temple.[62]

Beyond this façade was a 'bric-a-brac' area, where there were numerous products from the Middle and Far East including silks, gold, silver and furniture. There were also a few casts of Egyptian objects from the Bulaq Museum comprising a few busts, some bas reliefs and a model of the Great Pyramid.

The Chicago Fair in 1893 was much more elaborate, with a reconstruction of a street in Cairo, in addition to a miniature version of Luxor Temple in full Technicolor, with two obelisks flanking the pylon gateway. One obelisk was inscribed with the name of Ramses II and the other with the name of the United States' President, Grover Cleveland. Within the temple were reconstructions of the recently discovered royal mummies of Tuthmosis III, Senusret and Sety I. There were daily processions of the Apis Bull with actors dressed as Egyptian priests through the temple. There were also exhibitions of antiquities discovered by Petrie, as well as seventy-five of the Fayuum portraits and a number of bronze statues.[63] Perhaps the extravagance of the later exhibition reflected an increased interest in ancient Egypt by the American public, which justified more expense as it would bring the visitors to the fair.

48 The Luxor Hotel foyer, Las Vegas. (*Photograph courtesy of Lasloravga from Wikimedia Commons*)

At the end of a day's entertainment, what could be better than relaxing in a decadent Egyptian-style hotel and the ultimate in luxurious, sumptuous structures is the Luxor Hotel and Casino in Las Vegas. The structure is dominated by a giant pyramid, which was chosen over the Mayan U-shape, for the very practical reason that it would make a larger casino, as well as being able to make the claim that they had built the first pyramid in the desert for 6,000 years. The pyramid stands thirty stories tall and the light on the top 'invokes' pyramid power (see chapter 2). In front of the pyramid is a giant multi-coloured sphinx, which is 50 per cent larger than the Sphinx at Giza.[64] At night, there is a light show from the sphinx's eyes (plate 32). It was originally to be marketed as 'Egypt Land', and in the original version it was possible to take a cruise along a narrow Nile inside the pyramid, passing replicas of some of the monuments (fig. 48). The casino also includes a nightclub, the Ra Club, which is based on the movie Stargate and heavy-metal music. The door is guarded by two over-life-sized warrior maidens, and inside the walls are covered in art deco metal panels, as well as colossal statues of a winged figure with hippopotamus head and a kneeling winged figure wearing a *nemes* headdress.[65]

ARTWORK

In the same way as architects and engineers were influenced by ancient Egypt, so were many artists, and at the turn of the nineteenth century Egyptian themes appear in the work of Edwin Long (1829–91), Lawrence Alma Tadema (1836–1912), Edward Poynter (1836–1919) and Jean-Andres Rixens (1870s). Popular themes were historical and biblical recreations,[66] using *Les Description* as a resource, for images of monuments and landscapes.

Such religious reconstructions include Poynter's *Israel in Egypt* (1867), showing slaves working on the monuments, really emphasising the barbarianism of Egyptian kings as introduced by Herodotus. In Poynter's composition, he included many features of the temples of Thebes, Edfu and Philae in addition to the pyramids. The story of Cleopatra was also a very important element and there are numerous artworks associated with the story of Anthony and Cleopatra. Some focus on the romance but others, like Alexandre Caberel (1887), present the ruthlessness of Cleopatra as she tests poisons on prisoners, apparently with complete callousness, while many artists represent her suicide by asp. Many of the women depicted in the Egyptian-influenced paintings of the nineteenth century depict the exoticism of ancient Egypt, with subjects depicted wearing ostrich feathers, exotic costumes and adorned with elaborate jewellery. Many of these Egyptian-inspired paintings were created without the artists having visited Egypt, resulting in errors of representation; for example, many of Alma Tadema's domestic paintings showed the dwellings decorated with funerary scenes that would only be depicted in tombs or funerary temples.[67]

Such Egyptian scenic images were adopted for the theatres for stage design[68] as Egypt became popular in this genre too. These stage designs focused on the vastness of the landscape, providing a sense of depth and space to the sets. Egypt was even to become the theme of some of the Russian ballets, including Theophile Gautier's

Roman de la momie (1858).[69] However, Egyptian plays were not a new thing and had, in fact, been performed for 100 years already at this time, including John Sturmy's *Sesostris, or Royalty in Disguise* (1728), *Busiris, King of Egypt* (1730) by Edward Young and Charles Marshes's *Amsis, King of Egypt* (1731).[70]

Modern artists are still influenced by Egypt, and Brazilian painter and sculptor Eduardo Vilela creates painted clay dioramas or paintings with ancient Egyptian inscriptions and artefacts. Flowing water is a constant theme in his painting, either in the form of the river or water flowing from a jug, with the main subject floating on it. The subjects were frequently taken from the Amarna period, including Akhenaten, Nefertiti and a sun disc with rays emanating from it.[71]

EGYPT IN THE MEDIA

Throughout the book, we have been introduced to dozens of movies, television shows, cartoons and novels about certain aspects of ancient Egypt.

Egypt is such a part of everyday life and language that in television shows, references are made to Egypt in order to present an idea. For example, in an *Only Fools and Horses* feature-length episode, 'Sleepless in Peckham', the Trotter brothers' mother's funerary monument was enhanced with an obelisk which, Derek comments, makes hers:

The Ferrari of shrines.

This draws on the idea of Egyptian elements displaying decadence and wealth and was clearly the finishing touch to this fibreglass funerary monument. This decadence is further emphasised in the *Blackadder III* episode 'Sense and Sensibility', where Prince George visits the theatre to watch a play about ancient Egypt, with a murder scene as the finale. This play did not make a difference to the plot, other than adding to the decadence of Prince George and of the time. In *Peep Show* series one, episode 3, Mark Corrigan tries to impress his boss Alan Johnson by talking about his book, *The Business Secrets of the Pharaohs*, showing his intelligence through the achievements of the pharaohs. All of these themes, presented by these one-liners, are inherent within the mind of the audience and they do not need to be explained further.

Controversial opinions are also addressed in movies, which some may see as supporting evidence for the theory. One such controversial theory is that of the ancient Egyptians being visitors from another planet, as suggested originally by Von Däniken (see chapter 2). These theories were also adopted by fringe theorists, with a particularly interesting piece of research being *The Sirius Mystery* (1979) by Robert Temple, where he argues that travellers from Sirius came to Egypt and were the source of Egyptian civilisation. He bases the research primarily on the Egyptians' apparent knowledge of the star Sirius B, which is only visible through a telescope. This idea was adopted by the producers of *Stargate* (1994), originally released as a movie and then a spin-off television series, which was about a gateway to alien worlds, each of which had some Egyptian connection.

Literature has also not escaped and while some authors write a book about Egypt as a one-off vanity piece, such as Rice's *The Mummy*, Learner's *Sphinx*, or Wilbur Smith's *River God* series, many Egyptian-themed novels are part of series covering entire periods of Egyptian history. Christian Jacq, for example, started by writing a series about the life of Ramses II, progressing onto a series about Deir el Medina and the Hyksos. Michelle Moran has written a number of individual stories about Egypt, including *Nefertiti's Sister*, *Cleopatra's Daughter* and the *Heretic Queen*, all focusing on the lives of women in ancient Egypt, whereas Luban, in the *Pharaoh's Barber*, wrote of a servant in the house of Thutmosis III. There are also the numerous Amelia Peabody books, where Elizabeth Peters writes about Egypt in the turn of the twentieth century from the point of view of two archaeologists, who not only excavate but fight crime too.

The novels from the twentieth century alone are endless and yet this genre became popular in the nineteenth century as a way for readers to get lost in an exotic and mystical country, whether in the past or the present. There are two types of historical novel written about ancient Egypt: those which are vanity projects designed to show the author's knowledge of ancient Egypt, often with two dimensional characters and uninspiring dialogue, and others are those which take the idea of Egypt and its history and create a story within it, perhaps with reference to the known kings, queens and events without them being the focus of the plot. The biographical historical novels are plenty and are rarely done well, as they are extremely formulaic in nature, meaning the reader knows exactly what will happen. As Montserrat observed:

> In Philip Larkin's autobiographical novel Jull (1946), a schoolmaster spends an evening marking thirty schoolboy's essays on 'The Supernatural in Macbeth'. It was a very dull evening: thirty boys with the same resources and knowledge produce thirty very similar essays. Reading forty novels about Akhenaten is a similar experience.[72]

Akhenaten here can be substituted with Hatshepsut, Ramses II or Cleopatra and would still ring true. The outstanding novels are those from a different angle; for example Luban's *The Pharaoh's Barber*, Moran's *Nefertiti's Daughter*, Lumley's *Khai of Ancient Khem* and Carmichael's *Amulet of Amon-Ra*. All have taken popular stories and written about something else that was happening at the time.

There is something other-worldly about Egypt which draws a reader in and ensures there will be hundreds more novels published before the end of the twenty-first century. This can be said for all aspects of the myth of Egypt and Egyptomania. Over the next century, as over the last, there will be periods where it is fashionable to like Egypt and Egyptianised things and this will be displayed and manifested in new and exciting ways. New theories about all of the ideas presented in these pages will be presented, proved or debunked and still people will be interested in this enthralling country. Why is Egypt so enthralling? I do not think it is possible to answer that, as Egypt is a myth. Almost all we believe about it comes from a myth, but these myths keep Egypt popular and keep the research active. Egypt means something different for everyone and no doubt always will.

SECTION 4

REFERENCES

NOTES

Introduction

1 Rice 1997, 197
2 Rice 1997, 203
3 Hornung 1999, 55
4 Rice 1997, 200
5 2010, 4
6 2010, 114
7 Peters 2006, 44
8 Collins 1998, 369
9 Day 2006, 69
10 Day 2006, 2

Chapter 1: The Myth of the Nile

1 Lichtheim 1975, 186–9
2 Weeks 2009, 8
3 Lurker 1974, 57
4 Lichtheim 1975, 204–9
5 Lichtheim 1976, 188
6 Little 1965, 18
7 Tafla 2000, 166
8 Collins 2002, 15
9 Lichtheim 1975, 204–9
10 Faulkner 1998, 235
11 Arbel 2000, 106
12 Collins 2002, 18
13 Tafla 2000, 162
14 Pankhurst 2000, 26
15 Collins 2002, 22–3
16 Pankhurst 2000, 30
17 Collins 2002, 23
18 Pankhurst 2000, 34
19 Collins 2002, 218
20 Said 1993, 273
21 Sélincourt 1954, 139
22 Arbel 2000, 107
23 Collins 2002, 29
24 Jules Verne
25 2006, 60
26 Edwards 1888, 12–3
27 Manley 1991, 14

28 http://www.nile-cruises-4u.co.uk accessed November 2010
29 Jules Verne
30 http://www.luxoregypt.org/English/Activities/Niletrip/Pages/Dhabia.aspx, accessed November 2010
31 Nightingale 1987, 67
32 Manley 1991, 128
33 Kerisel 2001, 31
34 Booth 2009, 142–58
35 Lichtheim 1976, 193
36 Cornelius 2003, 253
37 Champion 2003,167
38 William Golding quoting an Egyptian sailor in Manley 1991, 129
39 Edwards 1888, 195

Chapter 2: Myths of the Pyramids

1 Edwards 1947, 267
2 Collins 2009, 53
3 Spell 267, in Edwards 1947, 280
4 Jackson & Stamp 2002, 87
5 Sakovitch 2002, 56
6 1968, 97
7 Collin 1998, 15–6
8 Mendelssohn 1974, 59 & 82
9 Manley 2003, 62
10 Bauval 1999, 311
11 Edwards 1981, 56
12 Jackson & Stamp 2002, 79
13 Bauval & Gilbert 1994, 224–5
14 Bauval 1999, 375
15 http://autospeed.celeonet.fr/khufu/spip.php?article21, accessed November 2010
16 Edwards 1981, 56
17 Jackson & Stamp 2002, 120
18 Vivant Denon (1802) quoted in Humbert 2003, 25
19 Nightingale 1987, 170
20 Manley 2003, 43
21 Jackson & Stamp 2002, 132
22 Quoted in Cott 1987, 50
23 Jackson & Stamp 2002, 172
24 Jackson & Stamp 2002, 173–4
25 Jackson & Stamp 2002, 119
26 Edwards 1947, 298
27 Hornung 1999, 155
28 Hornung 1999, 157
29 Jackson and Stamp 2002, 169
30 Jackson & Stamp 2001, 164
31 Legon 1989, 54–5
32 Legon 1989, 57
33 Bauval & Gilbert 1994, 117
34 Doernenburg 1997
35 1994, 124
36 1994, 143
37 Hornung 1999, 158
38 Jackson & Stamp 2002, 175–6
39 Collins 2009, 24

40 Petrie quoted Jackson and Stamp 2002, 181
41 Collins 2009, 189
42 Collins 2009, 214
43 http://www.andrewcollins.com/page/news/caves1.htm
44 Bauval 1999, 389
45 Zivie-Coche 1997, 102
46 Zivie-Coche 1997, 17
47 Jackson & Stamp 2002, 52
48 1974, 55
49 Mendelssohn 1974, 129
50 Jackson & Stamp 2002, 54–57
51 Hawass 2006, 159
52 Jackson & Stamp 2002, 55–57
53 Edwards 1947, 252
54 Jackson & Stamp 2002, 62
55 Jackson & Stamp 2002, 33
56 Jackson & Stamp 2002, 78
57 Hornung 1999, 159
58 Wodzińska 2007, 143
59 Redding 2007, 171
60 Hawass 2006, 163
61 Manley 2003, 56
62 Hawass 2006, 169
63 Jackson & Stamp 2002, 59
64 1968, 43–44
65 http://www.enterprisemission.com/mission.html
66 Sélincourt, 1954, 179
67 Lowdermilk 1991, 47
68 Coppens
69 Collins 1998, 96
70 Collins 1998, 71
71 Collins 1998, 103
72 Collins 1998, 122
73 Collins 2009, 57
74 http://lofi.forum.physorg.com/Pyramid-construction-method-solved._8178.html, accessed
   November 2010
75 Edwards 1947, 276
76 Edwards 1947, 245
77 Jackson & Stamp 2002, 55
78 Sélincourt, 1954, 178–9
79 Edwards 1947, 262
80 Jackson and stamp 2002, 177
81 Schul and Pettit 1976, 177–8
82 Schul & Pettit 1976, 195
83 Schul & Pettit 1976, 197
84 Schul & Pettit 1976, 8
85 Burnett 2003, 68
86 Jackson & Stamp 2002, 121
87 Constance Sitwell 1927 in Manley 1991, 91
88 1980, 22
89 1980, 112
90 1980, 72
91 1989, 8
92 Jacq 1997, 3–4

93 Jacq 1997, 12
94 1989, 109
95 1989, 138
96 1989, 185

Chapter 3: The Myth of Alexandria

1 Vrettos 2001, 6
2 Finneran 2005, 130
3 Empereur 2002, 27
4 Vrettos 2001, 5
5 Finneran 2005, 33
6 Ricks 2004, 343
7 Vrettos 2001, 7
8 Fahmy 2004, 299
9 Forster 1923, 15
10 Empereur 2002, 62
11 Ray 2007, 152
12 Keeley 1996, 80
13 Forster 1923, 18
14 Book 4, Chapter 195
15 Forster 1973, 20
16 Finneran 2005, 62
17 Vrettos 2001, 32
18 Vrettos 2001, 33
19 Empereur 2002, 39
20 Maehler 2004, 6
21 Empereur 2002, 40
22 Empereur 2002, 25
23 Maehler 2004, 3
24 Empereur 2002, 54
25 Watts 2010, 2
26 Finneran 2005, 97
27 El-Abbadi 1990, 150
28 El-Abbadi 1990, 153
29 El-Abbadi 1990, 159
30 El Abbadi 1990, 169
31 Butler 2003, 259
32 Vrettos 2001, 80
33 Finneran 2005, 99
34 Socrates in Dzielska 1995, 18
35 Finneran 2005, 99
36 Watts 2010, 240
37 Vrettos 2001, 214
38 Empereur 2002, 120
39 Butler 2003, 273
40 Hassan-Gordon reported in Butler 2007, 245
41 Vrettos 2001, 74
42 2010, 18
43 Davis 2009, 95
44 Forster 1923, 73–4
45 Vrettos 2001, 8
46 Davis 2009, 171
47 Finneran 2005, 24
48 Ricks 2004, 346

49 Ricks 2004, 340

50 Silk 2004, 353

51 Voltaire in Dzielska 1995, 3

52 Quoted in Dzielska, 11

53 Claudio Pascal 1989 quoted in Dzielska 1995, 16

54 Dzielska 1995, 25

55 Ricks 2004, 343

56 Bickerton 2009, 6

57 Davis 2009, 11

58 Roessel 2004, 326

59 Ricks 2004, 348

60 Keeley 1996, 136

61 Empereur 2002, 31

62 Bickerton 2009, 195

63 Davis 2009, 105

64 Roessel 2004, 328

65 Dzielska 1995, 2

66 Dzielska 1995, 15

67 Roessel 2004, 323

68 Learner 2010, 24

69 Davis 2009, 14

70 1923, 54

71 Durrell in a letter to Diana Gould in 1969

72 Liddell 1952, 238

73 Forster 1923, 98

74 Empereur 2002, 134

75 Al Abaddi in Butler 2003, 258

76 Butler 2003, 266

77 Butler 2003, 269

78 Butler 2003, 267

79 Vrettos 2001, 217

80 Prime Minister al-Nahhas quoted in Colla 2007, 230

81 Roessel 2004, 324

82 Finneran 2005, 140

83 Butler 2003, 260

84 Butler 2003, 265

85 Roessel 2004, 323

86 Learner 2010, 153

87 Roessel 2004, 324

88 Roessel 2004, 331

89 Vrettos 2001, 220

90 Fahmy 2004, 281

91 Fahmy 2004, 305

92 Forster 1923, 59

Chapter 4: The Myth of Hatshepsut

1 Ray 2001, 46

2 Tyldesley 1996, 137

3 Ray 2001, 56

4 Robins 1993, 45 & Dodson 2000, 78

5 Bunson 1991, 108–9

6 Tyldesley 1996, 177

7 Tyldesley 1996, 191

8 Ray 2001, 57

9 Tyldesley 1996, 184

10 Tyldesley 1996, 181

11 Tyldesley 1996, 182

12Tyldesley 1996, 191

13 Kreszthelyi 1995, 88

14 Ray 2001, 42

15 Ray 2001, 47

16 Forbes 2005, 31

17 Ray 2001, 55

18 Tyldesley 1998, 138

19 Tyldesley 1996, 145

20 Ray 2001, 50

21 Clayton 1994, 107

22 Ray 2001, 50

23 Tyldesley 1996, 147

24 Ray 2001, 55

25 Tyldesley 1996, 161

26 Hawass 2006, 40

27 Robins 1993, 53

28 Tyldesley 1998, 233

29 Bickerstaffe 2002, 76–7

30 Ryan 1990, 38–9

31 Ryan 1990, 58

32 Hawass 2006a, 41

33 Hawass 2006a, 43

34 Ryan 1990, 58

35 Ryan 1990, 58

36 Hawass 2006, 43

37 Hawass 2007

38 Hawass 2007a

39 *Science Daily* 2007

40 http://hollywood-spyblogspotcom/2010/07/pharaoh-new-epic-tv-series-set-inhtml, accessed November 2010

41 http://wwwdaughterofracom/theprojecthtml, accessed November 2010

42 1989, 96

43 'Ruth' in Whitman 1997, 21

44 Pita 2009, 16

45 McGraw 1953

46 Carmichael 2009

Chapter 5: The Myth of Akhenaten

1 Montserrat 2003, 126

2 Hornung 1992, 43

3 Montserrat 2003, 122

4 Weigall 1911, 54

5 1947, 29

6 Watterson 1999, 76

7 Ghalioungui 1947, 41

8 Aldred 1991, 232

9 Watterson 1999, 76

10 Burridge 1996, 127

11 Hawass et al, 2010

12 Harrison 1966, 113

13 Montserrat 2003, 124

14 Ghalioungui 1947, 30
15 Reeves 1999, 165
16 Aldred 1991, 231
17 Ghaliongui 1947, 45
18 Montserrat 2000, 165
19 Fletcher 2001, 67
20 Reeves 2001, 169
21 Aldred 1991, 234
22 Aldred 1991, 236
23 Montserrat 2003, 124
24 Montserrat 2000, 119
25 Hornung 1999, 186
26 Weigall 1911, 26
27 Montserrat 2000, 122
28 Montserrat 2000, 116–7
29 Champion 2003, 172–3
30 Hawass et al. 2010
31 Watterson 1999, 48
32 Hawass et al. 2010
33 2004
34 Robins 1991, 72
35 Hornung 1995, 36
36 Watterson 1984, 156
37 Reeves 1999, 154
38 Montserrat 2003, 122
39 Hornung 1992, 48
40 Reeves 1999, 145
41 Reeves 1999, 146
42 Aldred 1991, 248
43 Hornung 1992, 49
44 Reeves 1999, 146
45 Montserrat 2003, 124
46 Pritchard 1958, 227–30
47 Reeves 2001, 139
48 Montserrat 2000, 36
49 Weigall 1911, 118
50 Reeves 1999, 144
51 Montserrat 2000, 107
52 Montserrat 2000, 108
53 Freud 1937, 22
54 Freud 1937, 26
55 Osman 1999, 184
56 Hornung 1999, 76
57 Osman 1999, 185
58 1999, 183
59 Osman 1999, 180
60 Weigall 1911, 229
61 Aldred 1991, 303
62 Hornung 1999, 50
63 Redford 1994, 165–6
64 Montserrat 2003, 125
65 Reeves 1999, 146
66 Reeves 1999, 155
67 Reeves 1999, 149

68 Reeves 1999, 147
69 Montserrat 2000, 45
70 1994
71 1911, 257
72 Reeves 1999, 140
73 Bryan 2003, 191
74 Montserrat 2000, 140
75 1986, 142
76 Montserrat 2000, 150
77 1949, 58
78 Ghalioungui 1947, 31
79 1949, 323
80 Fast, 1958
81 Montserrat 2000, 162

Chapter 6: The Myth of Cleopatra

1 Foss quoted in Lovric 2001, 2
2 Vrettos 2001, 97
3 Jones 2006, 54
4 Jones 2006, 57
5 Jones 2006, 56
6 Jones 2006, 71
7 Jones 2006, 49
8 Lovric 2001, 74
9 Cicero, 106–43 BC, quoted in Jones 2006, 87
10 Foss 1997, 94
11 Alfano 2001, 277
12 Walker & Ashton 2006, 58
13 Foss 1997, 97
14 Walker & Ashton 2006, 58 & Jones 2006, 79
15 Chauveau 2002, 32
16 Lovric 2001, 64
17 Jones 2006, 104
18 Jones 2006, 105
19 Henriche Heine 1838 quoted in Lovric 2001, 22
20 Samson 1985, 131
21 Chauveau 2002, 55
22 Vrettos 2001, 130
23 Walker & Ashton 2006, 61
24 Walker & Ashton 2006, 75
25 Walker & Ashton 2006, 63
26 Jones 2006, 103
27 Plutarch quoted in Lovric 2001, 68
28 Florius, second century AD, Jones 2006, 164
29 Jones 2006, 81–2
30 Walker & Ashton 2006, 20
31 Jones 2006a, 75
32 Jones 2006, 184
33 Walker & Ashton 2006, 68
34 Plutarch Jones 2006, 188–9
35 Dio Cassius from *Roman History* quoted in Lovric 2001, 86
36 Cassius Dio, AD 202, Jones 2006, 195
37 Jones 2006a, 133–4
38 Walker & Ashton 2006, 69

39 Jones 2006, 193
40 Walker & Ashton 2006, 53
41 Jones 2006, 32–4
42 Lovric 2001, 32
43 Anatole France 1899 quoted in Lovric 2001, 33
44 Lovric 2001, 26
45 Jones 2006, 68
46 Hughes-Hallett 1990, 179
47 Samson 1985, 105
48 Quoted in Lovric 2001, 36
49 Quoted in Lovric 2001, 50
50 Lovric 2001, 85
51 Jones 2006, 106
52 Foss 1997, 132
53 Quoted in Lovric 2001, 73
54 Lovric 2001, 47
55 Quoted Jones 2006, 107
56 Walker &Ashton 2006, 65
57 Propertius, 50–15 BC, Lovric 2001, 47 & Walker & Ashton 2006, 64
58 Quoted in Lovric 2001, 46
59 Aurelius Victor quoted in Lovric 2001, 52
60 Quoted in Lovric 2001, 8
61 Hughes-Hallett 1990, 119
62 Hamer 1993, 30–1
63 Lovric 2001, 15
64 Hughes-Hallett 1990, 129
65 Hughes-Hallett 1990, 131
66 Eduard Hülsmann 1856 quoted in Lovric 2001, 46
67 Hamer 1993, 24
68 Hamer 1993, 48
69 Lovric 2001, 15
70 Bette Davis
71 Hamer 1993, 124
72 2009, 2
73 2009, 11
74 1989, 363
75 http.//newsbbccouk/local/tyne/hi/front_page/newsid_9107000/9107449stm, accessed 1st
   November 2010
76 Jones 2006, 281–4
77 Shelley Haley in Jones 2006, 285
78 Foss 1997, 82
79 Chauveau 2002, 2–3
80 1989, 135

Chapter 7: Mummymania

1 Dodson & Ikram 1998, 64
2 Dodson & Ikram 1998, 65
3 1989, 378
4 http://www.roadsideamerica.com/story/2930, accessed November 2010
5 Day 2006, 25
6 Day 2006, 36
7Dodson & Ikram 1998, 69
8 Dodson & Ikram 1998, 71
9 Hornung 1999, 167

10 Day 2006, 32

11 Day 2006, 29–30

12 Day 2006, 4

13 Collins & Ogilvie-Herald 2002, 84

14 Day 2006, 47

15 1868 quoted in Montserrat 1998, 72–85

16 Lupton 2003, 27

17 Reeves 1995, 62–3

18 Weigall 1923, 243

19 Weigall 1923, 232

20 Collins & Ogilvie-Herald 2002, 88–9

21 Collins & Ogilvie-Herald 2002, 80

22 Velma 1927 quoted in Frayling 1992, 244

23 1927 in Frayling 1992, 245

24 Collins & Ogilvie-Herald 2002, 81

25 Nelson 2002, 1484,

26 Day 2006, 76

27 Collins & Ogilvie-Herald 2002, 91

28 1981, 20

29 1981, 100

30 Collins & Ogilvie-Herald 2002, 85

31 2006, 242–3

32 El Mahdy 1999, 131

33 Vandenberg 1975, 19

34 El Mahdy 1999, 129

35 Forbes 1998, 549

36 Forbes 1998, 549

37 Dodson & Ikram 1998, 72

38 Hawass 2006, 170–1

39 Hawass in Day 2006, 17

40 Weigall 1923, 233

41 Reeves 1995, 63

42 Vandenberg 1975, 26

43 Forbes 1998, 549

44 Hoving 1978, 228

45 Vandenberg 1975, 26 & Reeves 1995 62–3

46 Vandenberg 1975, 26

47 Vandenberg 1975, 47

48 Vandenberg 1975, 50

49 Vandenberg 1975, 44

50 1975, 64–7

51 Hoving 1978, 229

52 Nelson 2002, 1,482

53 El Mahdy 1999, 130

54 Collins & Ogilvie-Herald 2002, 92

55 Kramer, 1999

56 Vandenberg 1975, 157

57 Viegas 1999, 2

58 Collins & Ogilvie-Herald 2002, 93

59 Hoving 1978, 221

60 Collins & Ogilvie-Herald 2002, 95–6

61 Hawass 1999, 2

62 Dodson & Ikram 1998, 73

63 Vandenberg 1975, 174

64 Vandenberg 1975, 177 & 184
65 Day 2006, 153
66 Vandenberg 1975, 183
67 Lupton 2003, 26
68 Day 2006, 45
69 Day 2006, 119
70 Day 2006, 34
71 Day 2006, 49
72 Weigall 1923, 236
73 1934 quoted in Frayling 1992, 245–54
74 Lupton 2003, 25–6
75 Day 2006, 135
76 Lumley 1980 116
77 1989, 92
78 Series 4, 2006
79 Pratchett 1989, 99 & 256
80 Day 2006, 67
81 Day 2006, 177
82 Day 2006, 66
83 Day 2006, 9
84 1997
85 Directed by La Duca 2003
86 Day 2006, 126
87 Day 2006, 121
88 'Mummy's Curse', Series 2 episode 5 (1984)
89 Day 2006, 169
90 Day 2006, 116
91 Day 2006, 171

Chapter 8: Egyptomania in the West

1 Price & Humbert 2003, 17
2 Whitehouse 2003a, 59
3 Price & Humbert 2003, 14
4 Bakos 2003, 232
5 Bryan 2003, 202–3
6 Bryan 2003, 188
7 Price & Humbert 2003, 3
8 Price & Humbert 2003, 5
9 Price & Humbert 2003, 18
10 Bryan 2003, 187
11 Humbert 1989
12 Elliot et al. 2003, 105
13 Price & Humbert 2003, 5
14 Fazzini & McKercher 2003, 141
15 Cornelius 2003, 253
16 Bryan 2003, 188
17 Cott 1987, 166
18 Fazzini & McKercher 2003, 145
19 Fazzini & McKercher 2003, 139
20 Cornelius 2003, 247
21 Humbert 2003, 36
22 Fazzini & McKercher 2003, 135
23 Whitehouse 2003a, 66
24 Fazzini & McKercher 2003, 136

25 Bakos 2003, 234–5
26 Bryan 2003, 184
27 Humbert 2003, 27
28 Rosati 2003, 221
29 Humbert 2003, 29
30 Whitehouse 2003a, 60
31 Whitehouse 2003a, 63
32 Fazzini & McKercher 2003, 147–8
33 Fazzini & McKercher 2003, 145
34 Fazzini & McKercher 2003, 151
35 Fazzini & McKercher 2003, 150
36 Hamill & Mollier 2003, 212–3
37 Hornung 1999, 118
38 Hornung 1999, 120
39 Humbert 2003, 30
40 Hamill & Mollier 2003, 210
41 Hamill & Mollier 2003, 214
42 Hamill & Mollier 2003, 217
43 Hornung 1999, 125
44 Elliot et al. 2003, 105
45 Elliot et al. 2003, 107–8
46 Price & Humbert 2003, 11–12
47 Elliot et al. 2003, 107
48 Elliot et al. 2003, 110–1
49 Elliot et al. 2003, 115
50 Price & Humbert 2003, 19
51 Elliot et al. 2003, 116
52 Elliot et al. 2003, 117
53 Elliot et al. 2003, 119
54 Elliot et al. 2003, 118
55 Elliot et al. 2003, 111
56 Elliot et al. 2003, 113
57 Fazzini & McKercher 2003, 152
58 Price & Humbert 2003, 9
59 Price & Humbert 2003, 20
60 Fazzini & McKercher 2003, 157
61 Bryan 2003, 198
62 Delamaire 2003, 124
63 Delamaire 2003, 131
64 Fazzini & McKercher 2003, 154
65 Fazzini & McKercher 2003, 156
66 Whitehouse 2003, 43
67 Whitehouse 2003, 50
68 Whitehouse 2003, 45
69 Whitehouse 2003a, 69
70 Montserrat 2000, 139
71 2006
72 Montserrat 2000, 141

BIBLIOGRAPHY

Aldred C. 1991: *Akhenaten: King of Egypt*. London. Thames and Hudson.

Alfano C. 2001: 'Egyptian influences in Italy' in Walker S. & Higgs P. (Eds) 2001: *Cleopatra of Egypt*. London. British Museum Press.

Arbel B. 2000: 'Renaissance Geographical Literature and the Nile' in Erlich H. & Gershoni I. (Eds) *The Nile; histories, cultures, myths*. London. Lynne Reinner Publishers.

Bakos M, 2003: 'Egyptianising motifs in architecture and art in Brazil' in Humbert J-M. & Price C. (Eds) *Imhotep Today; Egyptianising Architecture*. London. UCL Press.

Bauval R. & Gilbert A. 1994: *The Orion Mystery*. London. William Heinemann Ltd.

Bauval R. 1999. *Secret Chamber; The Quest for the Hall of Records*. London. Arrow Books Ltd.

Bickerstaffe D. 2002: 'The Discovery of Hatshepsut's "Throne"' in *KMT*, Vol. 13 No. 1 pp. 71–7.

Bickerton D. 2009: *The Desert and the City*. New York. Eloquent Books.

Booth C. 2009: *The Curse of the Mummy and other Mysteries of Ancient Egypt*. Oxford. OneWorld Publications.

Bradman T. & Chatterton M. 1997: *Magnificent Mummies*. London. Henemann and Mammoth.

Bryan C. 2003: 'Egypt in Paris: 19th Century Monuments and Motifs' in Humbert J-M. & Price C. (Eds) *Imhotep Today; Egyptianising Architecture*. London. UCL Press. pp. 183–205.

Bunson M. 1991: *The Encyclopaedia of Ancient Egypt*. New York. Gramercy Books.

Burnett C. 2003: 'Images of Ancient Egypt in the Latin Middle Ages' in Ucko P. & Champion T. (Eds) *The Wisdom of Egypt; changing visions through the ages*. London. UCL Press. pp. 65–100.

Burridge A. 1996: 'Did Akhenaten suffer from Marfan's Syndrome?' in *Biblical Archaeologist* 59:2 pp. 127–8.

Burton T. 1997: *The Melancholy Death of Oyster Boy and Other Stories*. London. Harper Collins.

Butler B. 2003: '"Egyptianising" the Alexandrina: The contemporary revival of the ancient Mouseion/library' in Humbert J-M., Price C. (Eds) *Imhotep Today: Egyptianising Architecture*. London. UCL Press. pp. 257–281.

Butler B. 2007: *Return to Alexandria*. Left Coast Press. Walnut Creek.

Caldecott M. 1986: *Akhenaten Son of the Sun*. Mushroom ebooks.

Caldecott M. 1986: *Hatshepsut; Daughter of Amun*. Bath. Mushroom Publishing.

Carmichael l. 2009: *The Amulet of Amon-Ra*. Texas. CBAY Books.

Champion T. 2003: 'Beyond Egyptology; Egypt in 19th and 20th century Archaeology and Anthropology' in Ucko P. & Champion T. 2003: *The Wisdom of Egypt; Changing Visions Through the Ages*. London. UCL Press. pp. 161–185.

Chauveau M. 2002: *Cleopatra; beyond the myth*. London. Cornell University Press.

Cheiro 1934: 'A Mummy's hand that came to life' in Frayling C. 1992: *The Face of Tutankhamun*. London. Faber & Faber. pp. 245 54.

Christie A. 1937: *Death on the Nile*. London. Harper.

Clayton P. 1997: *Chronicle of the Pharaohs*. London. Thames and Hudson.

Colla E. 2007: *Egyptology, Egyptomania, Egyptian Modernity*. Duke University Press. Durham.

Collins A. & Oglivie-Herald C. 2002: *Tutankhamun; the Exodus Conspiracy*. London. Virgin.

Collins A. 1998: *Gods of Eden*. London. Headline.

Collins A. 2009: *Beneath the Pyramids; Egypt's Greatest Secret Uncovered.* Virginia. 4th Dimension Press.

Collins R. 2002: *The Nile.* London. Yale University Press.

Coppens P. 'On the wings of a Kite'. http://www.philipcoppens.com/kite_obel.html Accessed October 2010.

Cornelius I. 2003: 'Egyptianising Motifs in South African Architecture' in Humbert J-M. & Price C. (Eds) *Imhotep Today; Egyptianising Architecture.* London. UCL Press. pp. 247–255.

Cott J. 1987: *The Search for Omm Sety.* New York. Doubleday and Co.

Davis L. 2009: *Alexandria.* Random House Group Ltd.

Day J. 2006: *The Mummy's Curse: Mummymania in the English-Speaking World.* Oxford. Routledge.

Delamaire M-S. 2003: 'Searching for Egypt: Egypt in 19th century American World Exhibitions' in Humbert J-M. & Price C. (Eds) *Imhotep Today; Egyptianising Architecture.* London. UCL Press. pp. 123–134.

Dodson A. 2000: *Monarchs of the Nile.* Cairo. American University in Cairo Press.

Dodson A. & Ikram S. 1998: *The Mummy in Ancient Egypt.* London. Thames and Hudson.

Doernenburg F. 1997: 'The Orion Theory' http://doernenburg.alien.de/alternativ/orion/ori00_e.php, accessed November 2010.

Dzielska M. 1995: *Hypatia of Alexandria.* London. Harvard University Press.

Edwards A. 1888 (1993): *A Thousand Miles Up the Nile.* London. Parkway.

Edwards I. E. S. 1947 (1993): *The Pyramids of Egypt.* London. Penguin Books.

Edwards I. E. S. 1981: 'The Air-Channels of Chephren's Pyramid' in Simpson W. K. & Davis W. M. (Eds) *Studies in Ancient Egypt, the Aegean and the Sudan: Essays in honor of Dows Duha on the occasion of his 90th birthday, June 1, 1980.* Boston. Department of Egyptian and Ancient Near Eastern Art, Museum of Fine Arts.

El Daly O. 2005: *Egyptology; the Missing Millennium.* London. University College London Press.

El Mahdy C. 1999: *Tutankhamun: Life and Death of a Boy King.* London. Headline.

El-Abbadi M. 1990: *The Life and Fate of the Ancient Library of Alexandria.* Paris. UNESCO.

Elliot C., Griffis-Greenberg K., Lunn R. 2003: 'Egypt in London; entertainment and commerce in the 20th century metropolis' in Humbert J-M. & Price C. (Eds) *Imhotep Today; Egyptianising Architecture.* London. UCL Press. pp. 105–121.

Empereur J-Y. 2002: *Alexandria: Jewel of Egypt.* London. Thames and Hudson.

Fahmy K. 2004: 'Towards a social history of modern Alexandria' in Hirst A. & Silk M (Eds). 2004: *Alexandria: Real and Imagined.* London. Kings College. pp. 281–306.

Fast H. 1958: *Moses; Prince of Egypt.* Ibook inc.

Faulkner R. O. 1998: *The Ancient Egyptian Pyramid Texts.* Oxford. Clarenden Press.

Fazzini R. & McKercher M. E. 2003: 'Egyptomania and American Architecture' in Humbert J-M. & Price C. (Eds) *Imhotep Today; Egyptianising Architecture.* London. UCL Press. pp.

Finneran N. 2005: *Alexandria; a City and Myth.* Stroud. Tempus Publishing.

Fletcher J. 2004: *The Search for Nefertiti.* London. Hodder & Stoughton.

Forbes D. 1998: *Tombs, Treasures, Mummies.* Sebastepol. KMT communications.

Forbes D. 2005: *Maatkara Hatshepsut; the female pharaoh* in *KMT* Vol. 16 no. 3 pp. 26–42.

Forster E. M. 1923: *Pharos and Pharillon.* Richmond. Hogarth Press.

Foss M. 1997: *The Search for Cleopatra.* London. Michael O'Mara Books.

Frayling C. 1992: *The Face of Tutankhamun.* London. Faber & Faber.

Freud S. 1937: *Moses and monotheism; an outline of Psycho Analysis.* London. The Hogarth Press.

George M. 1997: *The Memoirs of Cleopatra.* London. Macmillan.

Ghalioungui P. 1947 A Medical Study of Akhenaten in *ASAE* 47 pp. 29–46.

Hamer M. 1993: *Signs of Cleopatra.* London. Routledge.

Hamill J. & Mollier P. 2003: 'Rebuilding the Sanctuaries of Memphis: Egypt in Masonic Iconography and Architecture' in Humbert J-M. & Price C. (Eds) *Imhotep Today; Egyptianising Architecture.* London. UCL Press. pp. 208–220.

Harrison R. G. 1966: 'An anatomical Examination of the Pharaonic Remains Purported to be Akhenaten' in *Journal of Egyptian Archaeology* 52 pp. 95–119.

Hawass Z., Gad Y. Z., Ismail S., Khairat R., Fathalla D., Hasan N., Ahmed A., Elleithy H., Ball M., Gaballah F., Wasef S., Fateen M., Amer H., Gostner P., Selim A., Zink A., Pusch C. M. 2010: 'Ancestry and pathology in King Tutankhamun's Family' in *The Journal of American Medical Association* Vol. 303 No. 7 pp. 638–47.

Hawass Z. 1999; 'Finding the Tomb of the Pharaoh's Vizier in the "Valley of the Mummies"' on www.Egyptvoyager.com/drhawass_findingthetomb-2.html accessed September 2007.

Hawass Z. 2006: *Mountains of the Pharaohs*. Cairo. Cairo University Press.

Hawass Z. 2006: 'Quest for the Mummy of Hatshepsut: could she be the lady in the attic of the Egyptian Museum Cairo?' in *KMT* Vol. 17 no. 2 pp. 40–3.

Hawass Z. 2007: 'Press Release: CT-scans of Egyptian Mummies from the Valley of the Kings' http://guardians.net/hawass/, accessed September 2010.

Hawass Z. 2007a: 'Identifying Hatshepsut's Mummy' http://guardians.net/hawass/, accessed September 2010.

Holland T. 1988: *Sleeper in the Sand*. Little, Brown and Company.

Hornung E. 1992: 'The Rediscovery of Akhenaten and His Place in Religion' in *JARCE* XXIX pp. 43–9.

Hornung E. 1999: *Akhenaten and the Religion of Light*. London. Cornell University Press.

Hornung E. 2001: *The Secret Lore of Egypt; its Impact on the West*. London. Cornell University Press.

Hoving T. 1978: *Tutankhamun: the Untold Story*. New York. Touchstone.

Hughes-Hallett L. 1990: *Cleopatra; Histories, Dreams and Distortions*. London. Bloomsbury Publishing Ltd.

Humbert J-M. 2003: 'The Egyptianising Pyramid from the 18th to the 20th century' in Humbert J-M. & Price C. (Eds) *Imhotep Today; Egyptianising Architecture*. London. UCL Press. pp. 25–39.

Jackson K. & Stamp J. 2002: *Pyramid; Beyond Imagination*. London BBC Worldwide Ltd.

Jacq C. 1997: *Beneath the Pyramid*. London. Pocket Books.

Jones P. 2006: *Cleopatra; a Sourcebook*. Norman. University of Oklahoma Press.

Jones P. 2006a: *Cleopatra; The Last Pharaoh*. Cairo. Cairo University Press.

Keeley E. 1996: *Cavafy's Alexandria*. Chichester. Princeton University Press.

Kerisel J. 2001: *The Nile and its Masters; Past, Present and Future*. Rotterdam. A. A. Balkema p. 31.

Kramer G. 1999: 'The Curse of the Open Tomb' http://www.catchpenny.org/curse.html accessed in November 2010.

Kreszthelyi K. 1995: 'Proposed Identification for "Unknown Man C" of DB320' in *KMT* Vol. 6 No. 3. p. 88.

Learner T. S. 2010: *Sphinx; a Secret for a Thousand Years*. London. Sphere.

Legon J. 1989: The Giza Ground Plan and Sphinx in Discussions in *Egyptology* 14, pp. 53–60.

Lichtheim M. 1975: *Ancient Egyptian Literature. Vol. I*. Berkeley. University of California Press.

Lichtheim M. 1976: *Ancient Egyptian Literature. Vol. II*. Berkeley. University of California Press.

Liddell R. 1952: *Unreal City*. London. Peter Owen Limited.

Little T. 1965: *High Dam at Aswan: the Subjugation of the Nile*. Methuen.

Lovric M. 2001: *Cleopatra's Face; Fatal beauty*. British Museum Press. London.

Lowdermilk R. 1991: 'Reinventing the machine Herodotus said built the Great Pyramid' in *KMT* Vol. 2 No. 4 pp. 45–53.

Lumley B. 1980: *Khai of Ancient Khem*. London. Grafton.

Lupton C. 2003: '"Mummymania" for the masses – is Egyptology cursed by the mummy's curse?' in Macdonald S. & Rice M. (Eds) *Consuming Ancient Egypt*. London. University College London Press. pp. 23–46.

Lurker M. 1974: *The Gods and Symbols of Ancient Egypt*. London. Thames and Hudson.

Maehler H. 2004: 'Alexandria, the Mouseion and cultural Identity' in Hirst A. & Silk M. (Eds). 2004: *Alexandria: Real and Imagined*. London. Kings College. pp. 1–13.

Manley B. (Ed) 2003: *The Seventy Great Mysteries of Ancient Egypt*. London. Thames and Hudson.

Manley D. 1991: *The Nile*. London. Cassell.

Mann T. 1958: *On a Balcony*. Harper Perrenial.

McCullough C. 2007: *Antony and Cleopatra*. London. Harper Collins.

McGraw E. J. 1953: *Mara, Daughter of the Nile*. London. Puffin (Penguin Books).

Mendelssohn K. 1974: *The Riddle of the Pyramids*. London. Sphere Books Ltd.

Montserrat D; 1998: 'Louisa May Alcott and the Mummy's curse' in *KMT* 9 Vol. 2 pp. 70–5.

Montserrat D. 2000: *Akhenaten; History, Fantasy and Ancient Egypt*. London. Routledge.

Montserrat D. 2003: 'The Enigma of Akhenaten' in Manley B. (Ed) *The Seventy Great Mysteries of Ancient Egypt*. London. Thames and Hudson. pp. 122–6.

Moran M. 2009: *Cleopatra's Daughter*. London. Quercus.

Nelson M. R. 2002: 'The mummy's curse: historical cohort study' in *British Medical Journal* 325.

Nightingale F. (Sattin A.) 1987: *Letters from Egypt; A journey on the Nile (1849–1850)*. London Parkway.

Osman A. 1990: *Moses: Pharaoh of Egypt*. London. Paladin.

Panagiotakopulu E. 2004: 'Pharaonic Egypt and the origins of plague' in *Journal of Biogeography* 31 p. 269–75.

Pankhurst R. 2000: 'Ethiopia's control of the Nile' in Erlich H. & Gershoni I. (Ed) *The Nile; Histories, Cultures, Myths*. London. Lynne Reinner Publishers. p. 26.

Peters E. 2006: *The Curse of the Pharaohs*. London. Robinson.

Pita M. 2009: *Truth is the Soul of the Sun*. Kindle Edition.

Poe E. A. 1850: *Some Words with a Mummy*. Kindle Edition.

Pratchett T. 1989: *Pyramids*. London. Corgi.

Price C. & Humbert J-M. 2003: 'Introduction: An Architecture Between Dream and Meaning' in Humbert J-M. & Price C. (Eds) *Imhotep Today; Egyptianising Architecture*. London. UCL Press. pp. 1–24.

Pritchard J. (ed) 1958: *The Ancient Near East – Volume 1: An Anthology of Texts and Pictures*. New Jersey. Princeton University Press. pp. 227–230.

Ray J. 2001: *Reflections of Osiris*. London. Profile Books.

Ray J. 2007: *The Rosetta Stone; and the Rebirth of Ancient Egypt*. London. Profile Books.

Redding R. 2007: 'Main Street Faunal Remains' in Lehner M. & Wetterstrom W. (Ed) *Giza Reports: the Giza Plateau Mapping Project*. Volume1. Research Associates Inc. Boston pp. 171–8.

Redford D. 1984: *Akhenaten; the Heretic King*. Princeton. Princeton University Press.

Reeves N. 1995: *The Complete Tutankhamun*. London. Thames and Hudson.

Reeves N. 2001: *Egypt's False Prophet; Akhenaten*. London. Thames and Hudson.

Rice A. 1989: *The Mummy*. London. Penguin.

Rice M. 1997: *Egypt's Legacy*. London. Routledge.

Ricks D. 2004: 'Cavafy's Alexandrianism' in Hirst A. & Silk M. (Eds). 2004: *Alexandria: Real and Imagined*. London. Kings College. pp. 337–51.

Rider-Haggard H. 1912: *Smith and the Pharaohs and other Tales*. Wildside Press.

Robins G. 1991: The Mother of Tutankhamun in *Discussions in Egyptology* 20 pp. 71–3.

Robins G. 1993: *Women in Ancient Egypt*. London. British Museum Press.

Roessel D. 2004: A Passage through Alexandria: the city in the writing of Durrell and Dorster in Hirst A. & Silk M. (Eds). 2004: *Alexandria: Real and Imagined*. London. Kings College. pp. 323–35.

Rosati G. 2003: 'Neo-Egyptian Garden ornaments in Florence during the 19th century' in Humbert J-M. & Price C. (Eds) *Imhotep Today; Egyptianising Architecture*. London. UCL Press. pp. 221–230.

Ryan D. 1990: 'Who is Buried in KV60: Could it be Hatshepsut herself?' in *KMT 1990* Vol. 1 pp. 34–39, p. 58.

Said R. 1993: *The River Nile: geology, hydrology and utilization*. Oxford. Pergamon p. 273.

Sakovich A. P. 2002: 'Counting the stones; How many blocks comprise Khufu's pyramid?' in *KMT* Vol. 13 No. 3 pp. 53–7.

Samson J. 1985: *Nefertiti and Cleopatra*. London. Rubicon.

Schul B. & Pettot E. 1976.*The Psychic Power of Pyramids*. London. Coronet Books.

Science Daily 2007: 'Pharaoh DNA Analysis: Preliminary Results Support Positive Identification Of Egyptian Queen.' 7: http://wwwsciencedailycom/releases/2007/07/070716133119htm, accessed November 2010.

Sélincourt A. 1954: *Herodotus; the Histories*. London. Penguin.

Silk M. 2004: 'Alexandrian Poetry from Callimachus to Eliot' in Hirst A. & Silk M. (Eds). 2004: *Alexandria: Real and Imagined*. London. Kings College. pp. 353–71.

Speke J. H. 1864: *What Led to the Discovery of the Source of the Nile*. London. William Blackwood and Sons.

Strunsky S. 1928: *King Akhnaten: A Chronicle of Ancient Egypt*. London Longman, Green and Co.

Tafla B. 2000: 'The Father of Rivers: The Nile in Ethiopian Literature' in Erlich H. & Gershoni I. (Ed) *The Nile; Histories, Cultures, Myths*. London. Lynne Reinner Publishers. pp. 153–70.

Temple R. 1979: *The Sirius Mystery*. London. Arrow Books.

Tyldesley J. 1996: *Hatchepsut; the Female Pharaoh*. London. Penguin.

Vandenberg P. 1975: *The Curse of the Pharaohs*. London. Coronet Books.

Velma 1927: 'The Fatal Curse from the Tomb' in Frayling C. 1992: *The Face of Tutankhamun*. London. Faber & Faber. pp. 243–44.

Viegas J. 1999: 'Curse of the Mummies; Unearthing Ancient Corpses' www.toxicmold.org/documents/0407.pdf, accessed November 2010.

Vilela E. 2006: 'Imagining Egypt; a portfolio of recent artwork' in *KMT* 17(1) pp. 75–82.

Von Däniken E. 1968: *Chariots of the Gods*. London. Souvenir Press.

Vrettos T. 2001: *Alexandria; City of the Western Mind*. London. Freepress.

Walker S. & Ashton S-A. 2006: *Cleopatra*. Bristol. Bristol University Press.

Waltari M. 1949: *Sinuhe, The Egyptian*. London. Putnam and Co. Ltd.

Watterson B. 1984: *Gods of Ancient Egypt*. London. Sutton Publishing Ltd.

Watterson B. 1999: *Amarna; Ancient Egypt's Age of Revolution*. Stroud. Tempus.

Watts. E. 2010: *Riot in Alexandria*. London. University of California Press.

Weeks K. 2009 'Archaeology and Egyptology' in *Egyptology Today*. Wilkinson R. H. (Ed) Cambridge. Cambridge University Press. pp 7–22.

Weigall A. 1911: *Akhnaton Pharaoh of Egypt*. London. William Blackwood and Sons.

Weigall A. 1923: 'The Malevolence of Ancient Egyptian Spirits' in Frayling C. 1992: *The Face of Tutankhamun*. London. Faber & Faber.

Whitehouse H. 2003: 'Archaeology wedded to art; Egyptian architecture in 19th century painting' in Humbert J-M. & Price C. (Eds) *Imhotep Today; Egyptianising Architecture*. London. UCL Press. pp. 41–55.

Whitehouse H. 2003a: Egypt in the Snow in Humbert J-M. & Price C. (Eds) *Imhotep Today; Egyptianising Architecture*. London. UCL Press. pp. 57–73.

Whitman R. 1992: *Hatshepsut, Speak to Me*. Detroit. Wayne State University Press.

Wodzińska A. 2007: 'Main Street Ceramics' in Lehner M. & Wetterstrom W. (Ed) *Giza Reports: the Giza Plateau Mapping Project*. Volume 1. Research Associates Inc. Boston pp. 143–152.

Zivie-Coche C. 1997: *Sphinx; History of a Monument*. Ithaca. Cornell University Press.

Zuhdi O. 2003: 'Pharaoh's Daughter and her adopted Hebrew Son' in *KMT* Vol. 14 no. 4 pp. 42–51.

INDEX

Abydos 41, 189, 196
Actium 144
Afrocentrism 117, 119, 157
Air Shaft 42, 43
Alcott, Louisa May 164
Alexander Helios 143, 144
Alexander the Great 11, 26, 45, 67, 72
Alien 13, 54, 55, 58, 64, 65, 89, 201
Alma-Tadema, Lawrence 161, 200
Amarna 112, 115, 116, 118, 120, 121, 122, 123, 127,
    128, 129, 130, 132, 133, 135, 136, 166, 167, 168,
    175, 196, 201
Amduat 49
Amenhotep III 113, 120, 131, 190, 193
Amun 69, 97, 98, 100, 101, 105, 109, 110, 111, 120,
    121, 126, 129, 133, 167, 193
Antinous 191, 192
Aristotle 76
Asp 145, 147, 152, 153, 154, 200
Aspergillus 173, 174
Ass's milk 11, 150, 152
Aten 115, 116, 117, 120, 121, 122, 123, 124, 125,
    126, 127, 129, 130, 132, 133, 135, 136, 167
Atlantis 47, 49
Austin, Jane 164
Bananaman 182
Bandages 178, 179, 180, 181, 182, 184
Bara, Theda 149, 155
Benben 37, 43
Bible 33, 47, 48, 72, 95, 96, 124, 126, 127, 163,
    181
Bibliotheca Alexandrina 72, 81, 82, 88, 89, 92
Black Adder 201
British Museum 173, 176, 196
Burton, Richard 155
Buscot Park 192
Caesar, Augustus (see also Octavian) 69, 142
Caesar, Julius 29, 32, 69, 78, 137, 138, 139, 140,
    141, 148, 151, 155, 158
Carnarvon, Lord 164, 166, 167, 168, 170, 172, 177

Canopus 69, 87, 151
Carmichael, Leslie 202
Carreras Cigarette Factory 195, 196
Carter, Howard 106, 164, 167, 170, 171, 172, 173
Cataract 19, 21, 25, 26, 27, 36
Cavafy, Constantine 72, 83, 84, 85, 90, 91
Cayce, Edgar 49, 65
Caesarion 80, 140, 141
Cheiro 166, 177
Cholera 161
Christie, Agatha 28, 32, 136
Cinema 155, 180, 197, 198
Cleopatra Selene 143, 144
Cleopatra's Needle 185
Colbert, Claudette 149, 155
Co-regent 96, 99, 104, 117, 141
Cruise 14, 21, 27, 28, 29, 30, 31, 32, 36, 200
Curse 11, 13, 155, 163, 164, 167, 168, 169, 170,
    171, 172, 173, 174, 175, 176, 177, 178, 180, 183,
    185
Dahebeeya 28, 30, 36
Dahshur 38, 39, 48, 49
Darvi, Bella 136
Deir el Bahri 59, 97, 99, 102, 107
Diodorus 51, 79, 83
Djoser 38, 42, 123
DNA 99, 107, 115
Eady, Dorothy 45, 46, 189
Elder Culture 57, 58
Elizabeth I 94, 95, 98, 99, 101
Exodus 33, 95
Feminist 14, 84, 95, 111
Freemasons 11, 193, 194, 195
Frölich's Syndrome 114
Futurama 52, 65, 179
Gardiner, Alan 169, 170, 171
Giza 34, 37, 39, 40, 42, 43, 44, 45, 47, 48, 49, 50,
    51, 52, 53, 54, 57, 58, 62, 66, 67, 119, 120, 169,
    190, 200
Hall of Records 43, 49, 50, 58

Hapy 19, 20, 22, 23, 26, 34, 144
Harbour 72, 74, 76, 83, 88
Harrods 196, 197
Hebrew 33, 70, 76, 95, 96, 126, 127, 150
Herodotus 21, 26, 43, 51, 52, 53, 56, 59, 74, 181, 200
High Dam 17, 24, 25
Highgate Cemetery 188
Hitler 112, 130, 131
Hollywood 52, 107, 149, 155, 179
Homosexual 84, 116
Horemheb 116, 127, 136, 174
Hymn to the Aten 122, 123, 124, 125, 126
Hypatia 11, 78, 80, 84, 86
Ibn Tulun 74
Ice-house 192
Inundation 17, 19, 20, 22, 23, 24, 25, 26, 34, 53, 59
Isis 12, 23, 41, 43, 56, 80, 81, 96, 138, 194
Islam 22, 82, 119
Israel 33, 81, 82, 200
Jochebed 33, 95, 96
Karnak 29, 36, 61, 100, 102, 104, 110, 114, 116, 118, 133, 187, 190
Khnum 26, 53
Khufu 39, 40, 43, 44, 51, 52, 53, 65, 66
King's Chamber 42, 43, 45, 46, 47, 64
Kite 57
Kom el Dikka 70
KV20 95, 103
KV35 119
KV38 103
KV42 103
KV55 115, 119, 120, 135, 166
KV60 107
Leigh, Vivien 32, 149, 155
Levitation 57, 66
Lighthouse 11, 72, 74, 75, 83, 144
Lipodystrophy 114
Lost race 54
Love poetry 35
Louvre 130, 133
Lumley, Brian 178, 202
Maat 102, 104, 118, 123
Marc Antony 69, 137, 142, 145, 148, 151, 152, 155
Marfan's Syndrome 115
Mars 55, 65
Martyr 72, 80, 81, 130
Master plan 48
Mausoleum 146, 147, 156, 162, 188
Meidum 38, 42, 49, 52, 62
Memphis 20, 36, 69, 198
Military 74, 95, 101, 116, 128, 129, 136, 143, 150, 158, 162, 187

Miriam 33, 95, 96
Mob 79, 80, 81, 82, 84, 85, 86, 87, 140
Moses 32, 33, 34, 36, 95, 96, 112, 118, 126, 127, 136
Mouseion 70, 75, 76, 77, 78, 79, 80, 83, 88, 88, 89
Murder 11, 28, 79, 80, 86, 95, 99, 139, 141, 142, 154, 161, 168, 180, 201
NASA 55
Natron 160
Nazi 130, 136
Nefertiti 112, 114, 116, 117, 118, 119, 120, 123, 127, 130, 132, 133, 136, 168, 201, 202
Nightingale, Florence 31, 45
Obelisk 11, 57, 100, 102, 104, 185, 186, 187, 188, 191, 193, 195, 198, 199, 201
Octavian 137, 141, 142, 143, 144, 145, 146, 147, 149, 150
Omm Sety 45, 189
Orion 43, 48
Osiris 12, 23, 41, 43, 48, 50, 57, 65, 122, 175, 192, 193, 194
Oxen 20, 22, 59, 72, 189
Paser Stela 116
Pearls 44, 151
Petrie, W. M. F. 49, 57, 61, 161, 199
Pharos 67, 70, 72, 74, 82, 87, 88, 91, 144
Pilgrimage 34, 69, 70, 72
Plague 132, 154
Pliny 51, 188, 151
Poirot, Hercule 28
Pompey 77, 85, 138, 139
Pompey's Pillar 77
Pratchett, Terry 65, 66, 108
Prostitutes 69, 151
Ptolemy I 68, 69, 72, 76
Ptolemy II 68, 69, 70, 72
Ptolemy III 76
Ptolemy XII 79, 137, 142
Ptolemy XIII 29, 138, 139
Ptolemy XIV 140, 141
Ptolemy XV 140, 141
Punt 102, 107
Pyramid Texts 23, 38, 41, 48
Pyramidology 62
Pythagoras 57
Qait Bey 75
Queen's Chamber 40, 42, 43
Rabbis 70
Radiation 173, 174, 175
Ramp 52, 57, 59, 61, 62, 74
Ramses II 32, 65, 135, 158, 178, 197, 199, 202
Reanimated 158, 162, 177, 178, 179, 180, 181
Reanimation 55

Red Dwarf 52
Rhakotis 67
Rice, Anne 158, 161, 202
Ritual 22, 23, 24, 96, 102, 193, 194
Rome 69, 74, 83, 138, 140, 141, 142, 143, 144, 146, 147, 149, 154, 156, 189, 190, 192
Sarcophagus 46, 57, 68, 95, 103, 162, 174, 175, 176
Satire of the Trades 17, 34
School 77, 136, 181, 190, 191
Scooby Doo 65, 155, 178, 179, 184
Senenmut 97, 98, 99
Senusret I 41, 199
Septuagint 70
Serapeum 76, 78, 79, 80, 144
Sety 45, 46, 196, 199
Shu 117, 123
Simpsons, The 52, 183
Sinuhe 135, 136
Sirius 43, 201
Slaves 33, 52, 53, 61, 64, 65, 72, 95, 109, 118, 146, 200
Smenkhkare 116, 120, 132
Sneferu 38, 39, 42
Sokar 49
Sonic technology 13, 57, 58

Sphinx 12, 21, 47, 48, 49, 50, 55, 65, 87, 90, 120, 186, 187, 190, 191, 192, 193, 194, 195, 196, 198, 200, 202
St Mark 47, 72
St Sergius Church 34
Stalin 112, 131
Talmud 127
Taylor, Elizabeth 149, 155
Tefnut 117, 123
Thomas Cook 30
Thutmosis I 95, 96, 103, 107, 110
Thutmosis III 95, 96, 98, 99, 100, 101, 102, 103, 104, 105, 107, 110, 199, 202
Tibet 58
Titanic 175
Tiye 113, 118, 119, 120, 131, 135
Trade 30, 74, 82, 102
Tutankhamun 11, 32, 112, 115, 119, 120, 124, 163, 164–172, 173, 174, 177, 180, 183, 185, 186, 195, 197
Tutenstein 181
Unwrappings 162
Velma 166, 167
Vilela, Eduardo 201
Zoo Detroit 198
Zoo, Antwerp 198